PRINCE
EDDY

PRINCE EDDY

*The King Britain
Never Had*

ANDREW COOK

TEMPUS

First published 2006

Tempus Publishing Limited
The Mill, Brimscombe Port,
Stroud, Gloucestershire, GL5 2QG
www.tempus-publishing.com

British Library Cataloguing in Publication Data.
A catalogue record for this book is available from the British Library.

ISBN 0 7524 3410 1
Typesetting and origination by Tempus Publishing Limited
Printed in Great Britain

Contents

Acknowledgements 6

Preface 7

1 Scandal 1889 12

2 Great Expectations 1864–71 27

3 Britannia 1871–79 46

4 Bacchante 1879–82 70

5 Student Prince 1882–85 95

6 Privacy in Public Life 1885–88 121

7 Cleveland Street 1889 145

8 Under the Carpet 1889–90 187

9 Indisposed 1890 215

10 Resolution 1890–91 238

11 Devastation 1892 262

12 Aftershock 1892 to the present 277

Appendix I 297

Appendix II 299

Abbreviations Used in Notes and Bibliography 302

Notes 303

Bibliography 312

List of Illustrations 314

Index 316

Acknowledgements

I have many debts to acknowledge in the preparation of this book. My particular thanks go to the researchers who assisted me: Michel Ameuw (France); Jordan Auslander (USA); Ramesh Chandra (India); Terri McCormack (Australia); Stephen Parker (UK); and Graham Salt (UK).

Special gratitude is also owed for the assistance given by Dr Michael Attias, Major P.J.C Beresford (Regimental Curator, The King's Royal Hussars); Michael Foy (Queen's University, Belfast); Adam Green (Assistant Archivist, Trinity College, Cambridge); Robin Harcourt Williams (Librarian & Archivist to the Marquis of Salisbury); Penny Hatfield (College Archivist, Eton College); Lord Romsey; Reverend Sergio Pagno (Archivio Segreto Vaticano); Hannah Renier; Andrew Roberts; John Ross (Specialist Crime Directorate, New Scotland Yard); Mark Tami MP; Caroline Theakstone (Hulton Getty Archive); Hugo Vickers; and Dr C.M. Woolgar (Archivist, University of Southampton). Furthermore, I would like to thank Bill Locke at Lion Television (Executive Producer of the Channel 4 film *Prince Eddy*) whose support and enthusiasm enabled the project to go forward. I am also indebted to Ralph Lee at Channel 4 for commissioning the story and thus enabling the new evidence surrounding Prince Eddy's life to be presented to a wider audience. Thanks must also go to Producer/Director Garry Hughes and Associate Producer Melisa Akdogan for their part in making *Prince Eddy* such a groundbreaking film.

Finally, a special thank you to Caroline Beach, Monica Finch, Patrick Ooi, Bob Sheth and Chris Williamson, for all their hard work at various stages of this project.

Preface

O ne needs to go back to the Middle Ages, to Richard III and John, to find a significant royal figure whose reputation has been so besmirched by the retrospective historical record as Prince Albert Victor, Duke of Clarence and Avondale. Eddy, as he was known throughout his life, was the eldest son of Edward VII and heir presumptive to the throne for the twenty-eight brief years of his life.

Eddy was as popular and charismatic a figure in his own life-time as Princess Diana a century later. As in her case, his sudden and unexpected death in 1892 resulted in public demonstrations of grief on a scale rarely seen at the time. A century after his death, it was even rumoured (as in Diana's case) that he had been murdered to prevent him tainting the reputation of the monarchy. Had he lived, he would have been crowned King Edward VIII in 1911, ushering in a profoundly different style of monarchy from that of his younger brother, who ultimately succeeded as George V.

Eddy's life was virtually ignored by historians until the 1970s, when myths began to accumulate and his character somehow grew horns and a tale. As a result, he is primarily known today as a suspect in the Jack the Ripper murders of 1888 and for his alleged involvement in the Cleveland Street homosexual brothel scandal of 1889. Like Richard III and John, whose reputations have very much been determined in the contemporary mind by William Shakespeare, Eddy has certainly been shaped by popular films such as *Murder by Decree* (1976), *Jack the Ripper* (1988) and *From Hell* (2001).

For those who have seen these films and read Ripper books by Stephen Knight and Melvyn Fairclough, it may come as something of a surprise to learn that rumours of Eddy's involvement in the Ripper episode can be traced back no further than four decades. It is now acknowledged by most serious researchers of the Ripper killings that the creator of the Eddy Ripper myth was eighty-five-year-old Dr Thomas Stowell, whose article 'Jack the Ripper – A Solution?' appeared in the *Criminologist* (Vol. 5, No. 18) in November 1970. His article painted a picture of a crazed syphilitic murderer roaming the East End, vainly pursued by his doctor. The killer, referred throughout the article as 'S', was apparently a patient of the Royal Physician Sir William Withey Gull, who was convinced that S was the Ripper and strove to have him certified insane. The article also provided a potted biography of S, which quite clearly points the finger at Prince Eddy. Not unsurprisingly, the media seized on the story, which was very soon reported throughout the world as effectively naming Eddy as the murderer. Stowell, stunned by the degree of attention the article received, wrote to *The Times* in panic, lamely denying that S was Eddy. Before he could be subjected to further scrutiny, Stowell died on 8 November 1970, and his son tried to defuse the furore by destroying his papers. Although the article contained numerous factual errors and recycled several already established Ripper tales, the fuse had already been lit. Numerous others would follow in Stowell's footsteps, each embellishing and refining the story. The more extreme and fanciful of these stories are examined in more detail in chapter 12.

For those reluctant to accept that Stowell was the creator of the Eddy Ripper myth, the coming to light of a little-known 1962 French biography, *Edouard VII*, by Philippe Jullian, must have seemed like manna from heaven. On p. 171, the author boldly states that, 'on one occasion the police discovered the Duke in a maison de recontre… the rumour soon gained ground that he was Jack the Ripper'. Here, then, was a source that pre-dated

Stowell by some eight years and seemed to be based upon some much earlier source.

However, according to the writer Colin Wilson, in August 1960 he had lunched with Stowell, who had propounded his Eddy theory in some detail. Wilson, who was at the time writing *Encyclopaedia of Murder* (published the following year), was not wholly convinced by the theory. However, that same evening Wilson related the story that Stowell had told him to the biographer and politician Sir Harold Nicolson. Although the Jullian book contains no index or source notes, its acknowledgements page contains the following sentence: 'In England it is to Sir Harold Nicolson, for allowing me to delve into his works and for telling me a number of hitherto unpublished anecdotes, that I am most indebted.' So, after much twisting and turning, the trail finally returned to Stowell. From so little substance, so much has subsequently been made.

The eccentric theories possibly reached their nadir in 1991, when Melvyn Fairclough published *The Ripper and the Royals*. Reproducing extracts from a diary allegedly written by Ripper investigator Inspector Frederick Abberline of Scotland Yard, Fairclough not only tied Eddy into the Ripper murders, but implicated a host of others, including Lord Randolph Churchill. New Scotland Yard have subsequently expressed the view that the 'Abberline Diary' is a forgery.

The fact that on each and every occasion a Ripper murder took place Eddy was not only out of London, but was attending functions in front of large numbers of people, seems to have escaped the attention of many writers determined to place him in the Ripper frame. Fairclough also took the theory that the cause of Eddy's death had been murder rather than influenza to its illogical conclusion. In a tale that bore more than a passing resemblance to *The Man in the Iron Mask*, he claimed that Eddy had been kept a prisoner at Glamis Castle in Scotland to prevent him from ascending to the throne. He apparently died, still a prisoner, in 1933. Fairclough's book even offers proof of this theory by publishing a photograph of Eddy, aged forty-six, 'eighteen years after his official death.' In order to subject this claim to scientific analysis, his photograph and one of Eddy taken in 1890 were presented to the forensic imaging expert Ken Linge BA, MSc, FBIPP. Linge is one of the UK's leading experts on facial mapping and a veteran Old Bailey forensic witness. The results of computer analysis using morphological, anthropometric and biometric techniques found numerous and significant differences between the two photographs, leading Linge to conclude that they were, without doubt, of two entirely different people.

So much for the fabrications. This book presents an entirely new Eddy. It cuts through the tissue of myth and misinterpretation with which he has long been surrounded, and demonstrates that far from being a liability to the royal family and the nation he was destined to rule, he was, in reality, a figure of unfulfilled potential who could have made a significant difference to the lives of his subjects.

Earlier studies have tended to centre on the likes of the Cleveland Street Scandal and the Jack the Ripper murders, which have detracted from other episodes in his life and have inevitably clouded the water in terms of discovering the reality. The jigsaw pieces that collectively tell the story of Eddy's life have been concealed in a variety of haystacks around the world, and have now been brought together for the first time in this book. Many have not previously seen the light of day, and collectively combine to put Eddy into a new focus.

I have been fortunate in locating a number of Eddy's previously unknown and unpublished personal letters, which shed some light on his innermost thoughts and opinions. In fact, my objective throughout has been to get back to Eddy himself, who has been somewhat lost over the years in books focusing on the person he was not and the things he did not do, as opposed to the person he really was and the things he actually did and said.

The approach of this book is also thematic, in order to place Eddy in the context of those aspects of his life that mattered most to him and his contemporaries.

Although rightly placing emphasis on the realities of Eddy's life as opposed to the myths, we still have a duty to discover how and why past biographers and film writers have found it so easy to saddle Eddy with such an odorous legacy. In beginning our search for the real Eddy, we must now return to the defining moment in 1889 that, in effect, became the foundation on which all later distortions and fantasies were built.

I

Scandal
1889

The first thirty-eight years of Lord Arthur Somerset's life were perfectly delightful. The third son of the Duke of Beaufort, brought up at Badminton, educated at Eton, he had by 1889 survived military action in the Sudan to become a senior Guards officer, Superintendent of the Stables and Extra Equerry to the Prince of Wales. As a nobleman in the inner circle surrounding the future King of England and Emperor of India, no doors were closed to him. He dined at the best houses and belonged to the best clubs in the biggest and most powerful city in the world. The rich and beautiful of London society were delighted to call him a friend.

At the start of July 1889, all this would change. Some lives are like that; a paralysing accident, the sudden death of a beloved partner, a crash in the value of stock – an unexpected event turns them upside down. And so it was with Lord Arthur Somerset.

Worse still, his reaction to this personal disaster would resound for well over a century. It would result first in the shameful dismissal of Prince Albert Victor, the Prince of Wales's heir, from royal history, and eighty-five years later to the final calumny: that the young prince's outrageous misbehaviour was the dark secret behind Jack the Ripper.

Lord Arthur's nemesis arrived in the prosaic surroundings of Post Office headquarters in the City of London, on Thursday 4 July. Happily ignorant of the disaster that would soon overwhelm him, the distinguished soldier was busy a few miles away with the Shah of Persia's visit to Marlborough House in the Mall. The Shah had arrived in London at the start of the week with a retinue of forty, and was staying as the Queen's guest at Buckingham Palace. Persia was strategically important in the rumbling disagreement between Turkey (a British ally) and Russia, and the Queen supported her politicians by flattering the Shah with pomp and ceremony. At sixty years of age, his moustachios as black as ever and his reputation as savage, he cut a fine figure.[1] Cheering crowds lined the streets to welcome him, while the Crown had provided a splendid complement of gilded coaches and attendant cavalrymen, including Prince Albert Victor himself, to accompany the visitors to Windsor, the Guildhall and Covent Garden, as the exhausting week of formalities progressed.

Today, a party of Persian notables would bowl down the Mall to visit the Prince of Wales at Marlborough House. The sixty horses in the Royal Stables, which Wales inspected every morning, would await visitors in a state of gleaming perfection; Lord Arthur Somerset, of the Blues, was an efficient master and would make sure of that.

Meanwhile, three or four miles away in the City's main sorting office at St Martin's Le Grand, a telegraph boy called Charlie Swinscow had been hauled in front of Post Office Constable Luke Hanks to explain himself.[2]

In 1889, money was generally conveyed from person to person not by banks – whose branches were inconveniently located and whose clientele was a small, well-heeled minority – but by postal order or cash, through the mail. The system offered ample opportunity for theft. Post Office delivery boys and men must, therefore, be trustworthy and be seen to be trustworthy. They were prohibited from carrying cash or personal effects of any kind; their own items must be kept in lockers back at headquarters.

So when fifteen-year-old Swinscow was found to have eighteen shillings in his possession – one and a half times his weekly wage – PC Hanks interviewed him at once. The boy denied having stolen the money. He had done some 'private work away from the office', he said. Questioned further, he insisted that this work was nothing to do with his job.

The internal police of the Post Office were an astute body of men. Many had formerly served in the regular Metropolitan service. And PC Hanks, like his colleagues, was persistent. Finally, Charlie Swinscow admitted having earned the money from gentlemen who paid him a guinea for his sexual favours. But not, he insisted, on Post Office premises. These activities had taken place at an address in the seedy Bohemian district of Fitzrovia, two or three miles west. He would pass on his guinea to the landlord, a Mr Hammond, and receive four shillings to keep. He explained that he had originally been seduced (after a fumble in the basement toilets of the Post Office) by another boy at St Martin's Le Grand, appropriately called Newlove. Newlove had introduced him to the house in Fitzrovia, and he was not the only one. Other young employees had been earning four shillings a time at 19, Cleveland Street. It was a regular racket.

The Post Office employed hundreds of boys to deliver urgent messages throughout London. They were aged from thirteen upwards, and made a charming picture in their little blue jackets, smart trousers and caps. But the Post Office could not afford to gain a reputation as an employer to which mothers dare not send their sons, an employer which could not guarantee a reputable job, with prospects. PC Hanks informed his superior, John Phillips. John Phillips told the Postmaster General.

On the Friday, Hanks and Phillips interviewed telegraph boys Wright and Thickbroom (another name not easily forgotten). They confirmed that Newlove, who had since been promoted and was a clerk, had introduced them to Hammond. All four boys were suspended on full pay.

The Post Office was a vitally important department of state and must not be involved in a scandal; but as things stood, at least one of its employees might well be charged under the Labouchère Amendment to the Criminal Law Act. This controversial addition to the law was only four years old, and allowed for penalties of up to two years for committing, or procuring or attempting to procure others to commit, the sexual act with men. It made even consensual non-penetrative sex between men illegal, which is how it became known as the Blackmailers' Charter. A poorly drafted piece of law, it had inspired little Parliamentary scrutiny or objection, because the entire subject of homosexuality was judged too indecent to discuss even in the House of Commons. No decent person, at any level of life, mentioned such things.

The Postmaster General informed Commissioner Monro of Scotland Yard about the boys, the gentlemen clients, and the brothel.

Commissioner Monro agreed that his best men must be employed and the matter cleared up and swept away, immediately. Only one detective would do. Inspector Abberline stood out from the rest, which was why he had been working on the Jack the Ripper murders since they began about ten months ago, and no one was sure that the Ripper's activities had ceased. Nonetheless, Monro told Abberline to step down and direct all his attention to this Cleveland Street affair. It must be stopped before it attracted any publicity.

Abberline acted immediately. He arranged a special Saturday sitting at Marlborough Street Magistrates' Court. Newlove, or someone who had so far evaded contact with the investigators, must have got a message to Hammond, the proprietor of 19, Cleveland Street, that boys had been suspended from the Post Office and the wind was up. Hammond, an old hand at brothel-keeping now in his forties, didn't need to be told twice. On Saturday 6 July, when police forced an entry to the house, they found that he had made a hurried exit from his place of business, with its good furniture, antimacassars and tastefully placed mirrors, having lugged his personal items away in a large portmanteau and abandoned a pile of dirty laundry.

Warrants were issued for the arrest of Hammond and Newlove, on charges of conspiring to incite and procure the named boys to commit buggery.

Hammond may have vaporised, but Newlove was innocently staying with his mother at 38, Bayham Street, Camden Town, and PC Hanks collected him from that address without trouble on Sunday morning, 7 July. Hammond, who was wily and understood that a name dropped in the right place and time could cool the heat, had left a message for Newlove that he must deny everything; Hammond would take control. He knew that at least one of his clients would bring influence to bear, rather than face a potential scandal.

But Henry Newlove was just a boy, and did not understand. He complained bitterly to Hanks that his own seducer at the Post Office, a boy called Hewett, was not being charged. He pursued this grievance as they walked together to the police station. He didn't see why he should get into trouble while there were plenty of people in a high position who had visited Cleveland Street. Lord Euston went there, and Colonel Jervois, and Lord Arthur Somerset. PC Hanks wrote this up in a report when they got to the station.

The Sunday papers rounded up the news of the week. The Prince and Princess of Wales had announced the engagement of their eldest daughter, Louise, to the Duke of Fife; there would be a royal wedding at the end of the month. It was expected, reported *Le Courrier de Londres*, that the Waleses' elder son, Prince Albert Victor, would soon become betrothed to Princess Victoria, a sister of the young German Emperor.

On Monday 9 July, Newlove, now remanded in custody, repeated his allegations to Inspector Abberline. Lord Arthur Somerset, he said, called himself Mr Brown, but everyone knew who he was.

Hammond, who had until now been hiding at the home of a relation in Gravesend, took the boat for France.

On the Tuesday, PC Hanks got a surprise when he visited Newlove's mother. They were in the middle of a heart-to-heart when a caller arrived. Hanks, concealed in a corridor, saw and heard a man he recognised. His name was Veck; he liked to dress as a parson, and had been sacked from the Post Office at Gravesend years before for interfering with telegraph boys. 'Do you want any money just let me know,' he heard Veck say to Mrs Newlove. 'I'll instruct a solicitor to defend Henry in the morning.'

If Abberline were to make a sound case, deflecting blame from the Post Office and placing it firmly at Cleveland Street, he would need to prove that Hammond, probably with the connivance of Veck and others, had enticed boys to his infamous house; and if the telegraph boys were going to stand up in court and name names, there must be some evidence to corroborate what they said. He asked Monro for men to stand watch round the clock at the vacant house in Cleveland Street.

A PC Sladden, from Tottenham Court Road police station, was on surveillance duty that week and saw dozens of men arrive, and leave disappointed. Many were well dressed, or in military uniform. He followed several. One turned out to be a Member of Parliament and another a member of the National Liberal Club. But he lay in wait for even bigger fish. On Wednesday 10 July,

Hammond's sister-in-law Florence and another woman entered the house after lunch. At ten to five, Lord Arthur Somerset came in a hansom, and had a conversation at the door with someone inside. He must have heard some bad news then, but perhaps it was inconclusive. He waited in the street. Twenty minutes later, a corporal of the Second Battalion, the Life Guards, joined him, and the two walked together towards Oxford Street.

On the Thursday and Friday, Veck was at Cleveland Street packing up goods, which were removed by a furniture van; he then left. On the Saturday, at teatime, Lord Arthur Somerset and the corporal once again turned up for an assignation which could not take place. The house was shut.

Henry Newlove, a Post Office clerk third class, earning less than a pound a week, had made a preliminary appearance at Marlborough Street Court. Abberline now became aware that Newlove, and Hammond and Veck should they be caught, were all to be represented by Arthur Newton, at twenty-eight already making a name for himself as a criminal law solicitor. Abberline's suspicions were confirmed. Arthur Newton knew that clients in a case like this would pay anything to be cleared, and he would charge accordingly. His fees must be coming from somewhere; evidently a person of influence had a lot to lose if any of the accused spoke his name in open court.

Lord Arthur Somerset, as a younger son, would inherit no land. He lived on his army pay, in a style commensurate with his status in the royal fast set, and gambled. Newton's legal fees for at least three cases would have stretched his resources considerably. On the other hand, he was among the Upper Ten and so were all his friends. These were the 'upper ten thousand', those English families who at this time still owned eighty per cent of Great Britain's farmland, city streets, docks and mines. They lived largely on rents and income from shares. Somerset's father, the Duke of Beaufort, possessed land, castles, stately homes and Tintern Abbey, possessions judiciously accumulated by the family over 600 years of marriage and investment, and including 50,000 acres of Gloucestershire, Wiltshire, Monmouthshire, Brecon and Glamorgan.[3] Were Somerset's name to remain honourable, he had every chance of a rosy future.

The Post Office was determined to pursue this case to the limit of the law, regardless of who was implicated. In serious cases, then as now, the police hand over the file to the Director of Public Prosecutions, who conducts the prosecution. In 1889, the DPP was known as the Treasury Solicitor. On 19 July, Monro finally passed the Cleveland Street dossier to Sir Augustus Stephenson at the Treasury. If Lord Arthur Somerset did not yet know he was in serious trouble (and the likelihood is that he had been approached already by Arthur Newton), then he may well have heard now. Stephenson's brother was an equerry to the Prince of Wales.

Lord Arthur Somerset's greatest dread was that his employer, the Prince of Wales, should learn of his involvement in this. Wales stood in relation to him almost as a father figure. He was the leader of fashionable society; the arbiter of male taste; the person who knew most about racehorses and cards. And women. His mistresses were important to the Prince of Wales. In a flamboyantly heterosexual culture, his command of the affections of a string of beauties rendered Wales's virility, real or imagined, the envy of every red-blooded Englishman. Including, the world might think, Arthur Somerset.

Stephenson did not want anything to do with this male brothel dossier. A hotter potato he had never seen. He returned it to Monro, saying that it was 'public policy' not to give undue publicity to such cases and he really felt the police should deal with it. Perhaps Monro should consult the Home Secretary, who was responsible for the Metropolitan force.

Accordingly, Monro forwarded the dossier to Home Secretary Matthews, along with a request for Hammond's extradition; for by now he knew that Hammond, and a boy companion who read and wrote for him, called Bertie Ames, were staying close to the Place de la Pigalle in Paris, where John Phillips, the Post Office investigator, was watching their every move.

Home Secretary Matthews, himself an eminent QC, repeated that he really thought the Treasury Solicitor should handle such a case. However, in his capacity as head of the Metropolitan Police, he wrote to the Foreign Office asking for a warrant for Hammond's extradition. Lord Salisbury, who was at the time both Foreign Secretary and Prime Minister, wrote back on 24 July saying that extradition was not called for. This was a clear hint that the whole affair must be played down.

Inspector Abberline must have felt extremely frustrated. Lord Arthur Somerset went about his business. So did Lord Euston, Colonel Jervois, the MP and the member of the National Liberal Club. Hammond wrote regularly to his wife, complaining that he was being watched. As for the telegraph boys, they were still suspended on full pay. Swinscow and Thickbroom were taken to Knightsbridge barracks where they identified Lord Arthur Somerset, a tall fair man with a high-bridged Wellington nose and piggy eyes, as a regular client known to them as Mr Brown.

Stephenson, the Treasury Solicitor, realised that he must handle this case, but his own superior in these matters, the Attorney General, had a large and lucrative titled clientele and was not keen to get involved. Finally, on 25 July, Stephenson took decisive action anyway. All four boys and Veck were re-interviewed. Just a week later, Counsel advised that the Foreign Office had been wrong; Hammond must indeed be extradited. However, there was as yet 'no evidence against Lord Arthur Somerset'.

Nor would there be, as long as Hammond could be kept out of the English courts. The Post Office and Scotland Yard agreed that a warrant for his extradition must be obtained somehow, regardless of Foreign Office opposition. Lord Arthur, mounted on a fine charger, appeared in public on 7 August as part of the state ceremonies in honour of Kaiser Wilhelm II's visit; two police constables came to Knightsbridge Barracks that same day, and interviewed him (the record is lost).[4] Behind the scenes, letters were flying between the offices of the Attorney General, the Treasury Solicitor, and the Home Secretary. None was anxious to assert authority in this case; they had scented trouble, and feared that bold action would give offence and their careers slide gently into oblivion as a result. At this high point of the British Empire, just two years after Victoria's Golden Jubilee, top civil servants, the law, the Church, the aristocracy, the army and many bankers shared a tightly knit social web of nepotism, freemasonry, intermarriage and general social interdependence. At times of crisis, the web tightened in self-defence.

Abberline, in Paris, could not induce the French police to act without diplomatic intervention, but he seems to have recognised Hammond. He returned to London and immediately interviewed John Saul at 150, Old Compton Street. Saul was a gossipy transvestite approaching middle age, whose homosexual exploits had been ghostwritten in lurid detail and published seven years before as *Sins of the Cities of the Plain*. He was an Irishman, long resident in London, who had been peripherally involved in the Dublin Castle homosexual vice ring exposed in the early 1880s, and who was also familiar with Boulton and Parke, a couple of transvestite prostitutes prosecuted in London in the 1870s. Saul said he had known Hammond for ten years and lived with him in Soho before Hammond's marriage to Madame Caroline, when the acquaintance seems to have cooled.[5]

On 12 August, the Prime Minister was consulted by the Home Secretary. There was a long silence.

On 17 August, the Attorney General, having consulted the Home Secretary and the Lord Chancellor, wrote to the Treasury Solicitor saying there would be no proceedings against Lord Arthur Somerset.

On 20 August, the police arrested Veck at Waterloo station, with documents in his possession relating to a Mr Brown and an Algernon Allies, of 16, Gregory Street, Sudbury, Suffolk.

Lord Arthur Somerset, now well aware that disgrace was thundering relentlessly in his direction, wrote to his friend Reggie Brett (Lord Esher) that this case would cost him a thousand pounds he hadn't got.[6] He then departed for Homburg, the Prince of Wales's favourite German spa, where he sat next to one of Wales's sisters at dinner with the royal party and was his normal charming self.

The dogged PC Hanks travelled to Sudbury, where he found that Algernon Allies was a good-looking curly-haired youth of nineteen, employed until two years ago as a pageboy at the Marlborough Club. This was a smart gentlemen's club in Pall Mall opposite Marlborough House, which had been founded over twenty years ago by the Prince of Wales and some of his friends. Wales and his sons Prince Albert Victor and Prince George were frequent visitors, as of course was Lord Arthur Somerset.

In 1887 Allies, like Swinscow two years later, had been found in possession of more money than a good boy ought to have: £16, in fact (a working man's wage was around £1 a week.) He had been dismissed without a character and had been for some weeks afterwards a guest at the Hill Street home of Lord Arthur Somerset. He had then been introduced to Mr Hammond, and had continued to meet Lord Arthur at 19, Cleveland Street until earlier this year, when he had retired to his parents' humble home in Sudbury. A fifteen-shilling postal order was sent to him every week from London, and sometimes an affectionate letter from 'Mr Brown'. Only yesterday, in fact – on 22 August, just two days after Veck's arrest and one day after Arthur Somerset departed for Homburg – an anonymous letter had arrived telling him to burn anything that Mr Brown had ever written to him. He had complied at once. He still had three £1 postal orders, though, issued at the Post Office nearest to Knightsbridge Barracks. And one last note from Mr Brown, explaining that he might be away for some time.

Allies was taken back to London and kept under police supervision in rooms above the Rose Coffee House at Houndsditch. The day after he left, his mother answered the door in Sudbury to a citified fellow called Augustus de Gallo, whose card announced that he worked for a London solicitor, Mr Arthur Newton. He seemed anxious to obtain any letters from a Mr Brown that young Algernon might have left behind. The Treasury Solicitor was working from home because of illness in his family, but his Assistant, the Hon. Hamilton Cuffe, sent a report about Allies and Somerset to the Home Secretary and the Attorney General. The Home Secretary insisted that there was insufficient evidence against Lord Arthur.[7] The word of this boy was not enough to prove any indecency had taken place.

It was now near the end of August, and committal proceedings against Veck, Newlove and the absent Hammond were about to start. Committal, in the English court system, is the prosecution's opportunity to set out its case and convince a magistrate that this case is serious enough to be tried at a higher court – in this case, the Old Bailey. There would be publicity, and Lord Arthur might well be named.

Reggie Brett, Lord Arthur's friend, had been approached by Arthur Newton and was trying to raise money to pay the costs of the defence. The Prince of Wales was unaware of any scandal; he left Homburg to stay with his daughter and new son-in-law at Mar Lodge, their home in Scotland. Hamilton Cuffe, the fair-minded deputy to the Treasury Solicitor, pointed out in a memo to his superiors that if Veck was culpable, then the evidence so far indicated that Lord Arthur Somerset was even more so: it was morally indefensible not to act.[8]

But everyone knew that the political significance of a scandal like this, should it erupt so close to the Prince of Wales, could not be underestimated. The lives of royalty and their intimates and political advisors in the tiny ruling class had almost nothing in common with those of most English people. The royal family and a few thousand wealthy families, such as that of Lord Arthur Somerset, held the title deeds to most of Great Britain, spent lavishly on their social lives and were attended by the best-respected members of that servant class to which one in seven of the working population belonged. A deferential attitude towards the 'upper class' was all-important to the maintenance of social order. Fortunately, deference was habitual among the bourgeoisie and that emergent class of clerks who would some day have the vote; but, as education spread throughout society, dangerous pockets of derision were appearing. Journalists and politicians of independent spirit were not afraid to offend the landed aristocracy; tabloid journalism was accessible to a large class of industrial workers with little to be grateful for; and the Prince of Wales, a self-indulgent hedonist known as Tum-Tum, had been embroiled in one scandal after another. Any association between the 'Marlborough House set' and boys at a sordid brothel could dent the royal reputation permanently.

On 2 September, committal proceedings began at the court opposite Arthur Newton's office in Great Marlborough Street. Lord Arthur Somerset, Cuffe reported, seemed to be abroad. Abberline had men watching the Knightsbridge Barracks. The Treasury Solicitor feared that one of the accused might refer to Somerset in court. And Mr Hannay, the magistrate, was fretting; it seemed that other members of London society, a Captain Barber and a Mr Ripley, might be named. He was aghast at the very thought. Already, he had heard of activities and people the like of whom he had never suspected. 'What *is* a Mary Anne?' he had had to ask at one point. Strangled silence in court. 'It is a man who earns his living by bad practices, Sir,' murmured a policeman at last.[9]

On 12 September, committal proceedings having succeeded, *The Times* and the *Pall Mall Gazette* reported that Newlove and Veck would be tried at the Old Bailey. A few days later, in *Man of the World* magazine, the name of Lord Arthur Somerset was juxtaposed with a report of a 'gross scandal' in the offing.[10] Stephenson, the prosecutor, was by now furious that nothing was being done to bring Somerset to book. On Sunday 15 September, he wrote a strong letter which he instructed Cuffe to send to the Home Secretary: children must be protected from the likes of this man, regardless of his position.[11] Cuffe, however, had heard something.

'I am told,' he wrote delicately, 'that Newton has boasted that if we go on a very distinguished person will be involved (PAV)...'[12]

This was a bombshell. The name of the Prince of Wales's elder son, and heir, had never been mentioned in association with homosexuality. And as for small boys... A rather dozy, likeable young man, an officer in the 10th Hussars, he had inspired no speculation beyond which of the royal princesses of Europe he might some day marry.

Others in the Prince of Wales's circle had been disgraced: Captain Valentine Baker, accused of indecently assaulting a young woman on a train, had even been imprisoned. He had found employment abroad, thanks to Wales's intervention.[13] But this was nothing to do with girls. That was the difference. Wales would be appalled. Lord Arthur Clinton, poor boy, had killed himself rather than have his name publicly linked with Boulton and Parke.

And now Wales's own son... Somerset, the one person against whom these boys were certain to testify, was a member of the Prince of Wales's household. Prince Albert Victor must be acquainted with him. Of course, Somerset was nearly forty, a completely different type... But even if the young prince hardly knew Arthur Somerset, a jury would see both of them as part of the Prince of Wales's set. The slightest mention of Prince Albert Victor would condemn him by association.

Every day, Lord Arthur Somerset woke up in dread. Suicide? He had seen enough of the world to know that it was a big place, and memories were short; no disgrace was worth that. But if he fled the country, how would he live? He would have to resign his commission. Would he spend the rest of his days in obscurity, teaching English in Vienna, or training soldiers in Africa, shunned by every traveller of his own class?

He must have cursed his own recklessness. A love affair with a bootboy – and letters to prove it. On the other hand, if the letters had been destroyed, and if Hammond got away, then maybe his good name could be saved; things had not gone so far that the prosecution might not be induced to leave him alone. But he had no bargaining power. He would not be so dishonourable as to betray other homosexuals. His friends would never speak to him again. Yet it really was unfair. It wasn't as if he was the only one…

A common reaction to humiliation is a sense of victimisation, born of self-pity. Henry Newlove, the Post Office clerk, had not seen why he, a mere minnow in the pond, should be the one who got into trouble. Other people, more important and noteworthy than he, should be prosecuted before he was, and he was quick to name them.

But there *was* no one more important and noteworthy than Lord Arthur Somerset.

Unless – it seemed so unlikely. But was it possible? Had the young prince really been to Cleveland Street? The more Arthur Somerset thought about what he had heard, the more aggrieved he felt on his own behalf. Since of course he would never break his code of honour by repeating what he had heard in court, he also felt somehow rather noble.

And frankly, Prince Albert Victor had always been rather a mystery to everyone.

2

Great Expectations
1864–71

C andlelight illuminated the vestments of the churchmen, the magnificent tapestry above the communion table and the furs and velvets of fashionable women. The Archbishop of Canterbury peered down at the fretting baby in its Honiton lace robe, and enquired what its name was to be.

The question was answered not by the baby's father, but by a small woman in widow's cap and diamonds. Queen Victoria[1] said firmly: 'Albert Victor Christian Edward.'

The barest intake of breath signalled surprise among the crowd, before the ceremony moved majestically forward. Prayers followed the address; the Archbishop changed his purple stole and cope for white and processed towards the silver-gilt font, attended by his chaplains and his clerks of the mitre, book and hand-candle, a crossbearer and two acolytes with candles, reciting the Creed; the Prince and Princess of

Wales and the three distinguished godparents followed; the
throng gathered around the font and the baby whimpered his
small protest.

The water had been gently warmed, for the private chapel
at Buckingham Palace was chilly at this time of year. At last,
the baptismal act was performed. The Archbishop, murmuring
'Albert Victor Christian Edward, I baptise thee in the name of
the Father', poured water in the form of a cross upon the baby's
head, '…and of the Son', as he poured a second time, '…and
of the Holy Ghost', and a third time. 'Albert Victor Christian
Edward, enter thou into the Temple of God, that thou mayest
have part with Christ unto everlasting life. Amen.'

So it came about that before Leopold, King of the Belgians,
Lord Palmerston, and every state official who mattered, the
grandmother named her first grandson. Victoria, Queen of
England, was forty-five years old, squat, heavy, and perpetually
clad in black like an old woman. She had been a widow for
only three years, and consulted the shade of Albert, her dead
Consort, on every matter. Their own first son had been named
Albert Edward. His son was to be Albert Victor because Victoria
had so decreed: all royal sons, until the end of time or as long
as the monarchy endured (which amounted to the same thing),
would have Albert among their names, and all royal daughters
would have Victoria.[2]

This had come as a surprise to the child's parents. The Princess
of Wales had first heard what her baby's name was to be from
her lady-in-waiting, Lady Macclesfield, who had been told
by Princess Beatrice, the Queen's youngest daughter. Princess
Beatrice was six. The Prince of Wales had written in restrained
annoyance to his mother to ask whether his little sister's report
was true, and had received confirmation, and explanation.[3]

Bertie, as the twenty-three-year-old Prince was known to his
friends, and his twenty-year-old Danish wife, could not defy his
mother. The Archbishop conducted the christening ceremony

without hindrance. But their beloved little boy was called Eddy from the first, by everyone other than his grandmother.

The baby was strong and healthy, although he had weighed less than four pounds when he was born, two months early, in the evening of 8 January 1864. That afternoon, Princess Alexandra, who was beautiful and charming and had been married for less than a year, had been taken to watch her adored Bertie playing ice hockey on a frozen pond at Virginia Water, near Windsor. Afterwards, what larks! she was whirled – in her pregnant state – across the ice on a sledge. So, although her desperate anxiety about the Schleswig-Holstein question was later said to have induced Alix to give birth so soon, perhaps one should rather blame the sledge.

Fortunately, it was an uncomplicated and swift birth, even though it did not take place where and when it was supposed to. The official residence of the Prince and Princess was Marlborough House, a fine mansion opposite St James's Palace in London, and their country home was Sandringham House in Norfolk; but early in January they were staying at Frogmore, where the Queen accommodated guests in the grounds of Windsor Castle.

Lady Macclesfield, lady-in-waiting to the Princess, was well qualified to take command of the situation, since she had given birth thirteen times herself. She sent for Dr Brown from Windsor and – since no layette had been prepared here – despatched a footman to Caley's, the local drapers, for two yards of coarse flannel, six yards of superfine flannel, a sheet of wadding and a basket to put the baby in.[4] Protocol insists that the Home Secretary must be present in an adjoining room during royal births, to attest to the legitimacy of the infant heir, but the Home Secretary was out of reach. It was Victoria's policy to sit with and encourage her daughters and daughters-in-law in labour, but she had been at Osborne, in the Isle of Wight, since Christmas. Accordingly, Lord Greville, a guest at the house, stood in for the Home Secretary and Alix, two doctors and Lady Macclesfield managed without the Queen's advice, which was probably a good thing. Victoria's contented observations about the proximity of Frogmore to Albert's mausoleum might not have been well received.

The following day, England woke up to find that the Prince and Princess of Wales had produced a son and heir presumptive to the throne. 'A *n-ice* child', some wit called him, with that peculiarly Victorian fondness for the groaning play on words.

This happy event, at the start of 1864, was an astonishing culmination to the last twelve months for Alix. Last January, she had been a modest Danish princess in a cheerfully middle-class Danish family. Her father, Prince Christian, a former army officer, the declared heir to King Frederick VII of Denmark, brought up his large family on an extremely modest income by royal standards. Her mother, Princess Louise, had been born a Hesse-Cassel and was closer to the succession, in genealogical terms, than her husband. They had six children, of whom Alix was the eldest girl.[5]

Queen Victoria would much have preferred a German bride for Bertie. No Danes of her acquaintance appeared to possess that serious-minded rigour of which she so approved. However, a suitable German candidate was nowhere to be found. And Alix (who had been discovered by Bertie's sister, *Almanac de Gotha* in hand) was charming; Victoria was personally won over, despite her misgivings, and Bertie was certainly smitten with Alix, who was outstandingly pretty.

They had married in March of 1863. Prince Christian and Princess Louise, Alix's two sisters and three brothers and a couple of uncles had arrived to represent the Danes. Queen Victoria, who paraded the German loyalties of her deceased consort as a badge of honour, dreaded that her Prussian relations would interpret a showy wedding as approval of Denmark's rule over Schleswig and Holstein. The Germans and Danes were at loggerheads over possession of these two duchies and she sympathised with Germany's need for a land passage to the North Sea. Prince and Princess Christian were offended that neither the Queen nor the Prince of Wales had bothered to organise the formality of a request for his daughter's hand in marriage.[6] The wedding ceremony was kept as quiet as possible, taking place not in St Paul's or the Abbey but in St George's Chapel, Windsor, with the Queen in her sombre clothes observing from Catherine of Aragon's Closet, in that lowering, joyless way she had ('these ceremonies and events are painful in the extreme to me, as you know').[7] The guests were nonetheless enchanted by the wedding's pageantry; Tennyson wrote a poem in the young couple's honour and Mr Frith painted a fine picture. The train home was so crowded with dignitaries that Disraeli, giggling, had to sit on his wife's knee.[8]

Queen Victoria liked Alix very much, and thought she would be a good influence on Bertie, but in matters political she was firmly on Germany's side. Her own eldest daughter was a Crown Princess of Germany, while of the Danish royal family she knew nothing favourable. But Bertie had learned to go his own way. He proved to be a supportive husband, quite prepared to listen to the Danish view, and when, after their honeymoon, the young couple moved into Marlborough House and started to entertain, they made an effortless conquest of London society and reinforced opinion on the Danish side.

The next astonishing event took place within weeks of their marriage, when Alix's seventeen-year-old brother William was staying in London. At this time, powerful people decided that a King of Greece must be installed in Athens. Alfred – Bertie's brother Affie, who, like Alix, was just twenty – positively refused to be chosen. In fact, there were no takers for this job, with its ramshackle palace and distant, hot location. Rather as one stops the nearest passer-by to discover the *vox populi*, a senior official in a quandary chanced upon William. Would *he* be willing to become King of Greece? Well, he had nothing better to do. By the end of May, and thanks perhaps to the subtlest of manoeuvring by his mother, preparations for his coronation were under way.[9]

In November, their father inherited the Danish crown. Alix's parents were now King Christian IX and Queen Louise. When the family looked back on 1863, they must have felt that some kind of magic had been at work. From having been the poor relations at every regal gathering, they now included the Kings of Greece and Denmark, besides the future Queen of England and mother-to-be to the next monarch but one.

Tensions at the christening were more serious than mere concern over Eddy's name. Within a week of the baby's birth, Prussia and Austria had invaded the twin duchies of Schleswig and Holstein and claimed possession of both. Or rather, repossession: the duchies had been ceded to the Danes in 1851 in a move that Bismarck, the Prussian Chancellor, never admitted was legal. Of the long-running dispute that came to a head in January 1864, it was notoriously said that nobody understood its convolutions except Albert, the Prince Consort, who was dead, a German professor who had gone mad and Lord Melbourne, who had forgotten.

Among the British royal family, battle lines were firmly drawn (although, of course, no overt confrontation took place). Alix was desperately sorry for her father, who had neither resources nor allies to drive the Germans out. Bertie, the British government and the British press were on the side of 'poor little Denmark'. It was Queen Victoria and her eldest daughter who would not countenance any resistance to Prussia, and in 1864, Queen Victoria's opinion held sway. British assistance was not forthcoming. By May of 1864, Denmark was forced to concede the territory.

Alix remained bitter for a long time; and when in 1865 it became clear that Helena, Bertie's younger sister, would marry the new – German – Prince Christian of Schleswig-Holstein, salt was rubbed into the wound. Alix was fond of her autocratic middle-aged mother-in-law, but not of German royalty, and could not bring herself even to speak to Bertie's twenty-four-year-old elder sister, Crown Princess Frederick of Prussia. Everything German she found self-righteous and overbearing.

Queen Victoria, much as she loved Alix, could not abide Alix's mother. Queen Louise had been born into a family considered frivolous and fashionable, two qualities that Victoria abhorred, and she thought Louise, who was deaf, was a knowing, scheming woman. As for Alix's father, King Christian, she had deeply disapproved of the louche old King Frederick and had no particular respect for his successor. Altogether, she found her Danish counterparts as grandparents most unsatisfactory. Had they only been German, everything about her daughter-in-law would have been perfect.

In this family, a frigid silence over the breakfast egg might be caused by one's brother invading one's husband's sister's country. As baby Eddy cooed in his crib in those first few months, as the multitude of nurses and servants and courtiers and young uncles and aunts peered at him and disappeared again, his little world must have seemed a kaleidoscope of incomprehensible tensions and languages and enthusiasms.

One is struck by the sheer number of people who were either part of the family or dependent upon them. Back and forth between Marlborough House, Sandringham and other grand houses, along with the Prince, Princess and baby Eddy travelled the peripatetic household of coachmen and grooms, chefs and sous-chefs, and those courtiers and servants who danced attendance upon each royal personage: the Prince with his equerries and valets, the Princess with her lady-in-waiting and ladies' maids, a secretary each for Alix and Bertie and, of course, a nanny for the baby and a 'nursery footman', Charles Fuller, hired when Eddy was just two weeks old. At each house there were gardeners, laundresses, scullerymaids, upholsterers, seamstresses, carpenters, footmen, butlers and under-butlers, housekeepers and cooks and maids – and, at Sandringham, dairymen and dairymaids. At Marlborough House alone there were sixty horses in the stables, with grooms and coachmen.

The Wales household of under 100 was not uniquely large; many great ducal families were better off, and owned better-appointed houses, and the Wales retinue was modest by comparison with the Queen's. Victoria had nine children, aged between six and twenty-four, when Eddy was born. All but the eldest daughters were still very much part of the domestic circle and each of the royal princes and princesses merited his or her own attendants. Wherever Eddy's grandmother happened to be – at Balmoral in Scotland in the summer, at Windsor, or at Osborne (she rarely visited London) – she would be surrounded by an inner circle of courtiers including 'two Ladies in Waiting and two Maids of Honour, each of whom had a ladies' maid; a Minister in Attendance, the Keeper of the Privy Purse, the Master of the Household, a Lord in Waiting, a Groom in Waiting, two Equerries and a Gentleman Usher each with a manservant, plus family, friends, and a huge domestic and outdoor staff.'[10] On weekdays, she would consult her private secretary, deal with papers and express her views without restraint to the Prime Minister, in person or by letter; on Sundays, she attended church. She moved between her draughty palaces in a private train with several sitting rooms and a dedicated *fourgon*, or luggage van.

In due course, the new grandchild was presented to everyone who mattered. Mrs Clarke, Eddy's first nurse, was eventually replaced by Mrs Mary Blackburn.[11] The Queen expressed her opinion that the Wales baby was a frail little thing. Wiseacres, hearing this, doubted that he would ever inherit. They had said the same of Bertie. The Queen had a view on everything. Mrs Blackburn, who spent every day with Eddy, did not agree with her in this matter. He was her favourite above all the Wales children who came after, and when he lost his first tooth she asked for it and 'had it set into a ring with turquoises'.[12] Thirty years passed before anyone interviewed Mrs Blackburn about her recollections of Eddy, and she still had that ring, and was most emphatic that he had never been a delicate baby at all.

Alix adored him, and would put on a flannel pinafore and bathe him herself and put him to bed. She was a good-natured, maternal girl from a close and happy family, and insisted that she and Bertie should spend some time with her parents in Denmark to show Eddy off. In any case, although Schleswig and Holstein had been lost, there was soon something to celebrate; Alix's younger sister Dagmar became engaged to marry Nicholas, heir to the Tsar of Russia.

Gatherings of the Danish royal family now became a regular institution, as the children took up their responsibilities all over Europe. They would gather at Bernstorff, a country house on the outskirts of Copenhagen, or at Fredensborg, which was much grander and set in a park further out of the city. In these early years of the Wales marriage, there is no indication that the unstoppable activity, childish japes and merry fun and games in which Alix and her siblings so delighted seemed anything other than charming to Bertie. But one or two visits were enough. Were a person to prefer their own company and a book, they would be hunted down, chided, pounced upon and teased until forced to participate in the general jollity. Wales confided to his friends that there was only one thing more boring than being at Fredensborg, and that was staying at Bernstorff.

His mother disapproved, too. She felt that the baby heir presumptive was out of her control – almost that he had fallen into enemy hands – when Alix took him to Denmark for weeks on end. Accounts of Victoria laughing are rare, but one is in this respect significant. Mary Blackburn told her interviewer that she had once been holding the baby on the rough sea in the royal yacht on the return journey from Denmark, when he was

thrown sharply against her and she got a black eye. She went
from England to Balmoral, and had to face the Queen: who 'on
seeing the state of things, and hearing the cause, laughed heartily.'[13] Given the views she had about long absences in Denmark,
she probably thought it served them right for leaving England
in the first place.

When Eddy was one and a half, his brother George was born,
a month early, on 3 June 1865. Victoria wrote to King Leopold:
'the child is said to be much larger than little Albert Victor,
and nice and plump. Bertie seems very much pleased with
this second son.'[14] The Wales marriage seemed stable and the
Queen must have rejoiced at that, although she was concerned
by Alix's having, for a second time, given birth prematurely.
Queen Victoria had never thought much of her son Bertie, suspecting that moral turpitude seethed not far below his surface,
and an early marriage had been her solution to keeping him
out of trouble. From his earliest youth, she had demanded that
he behave with both the gravitas and the boundless energy of
his father Albert, the Prince Consort. As he grew up, she and
Albert constantly reproached him for laziness and expressed
disappointment in his character and achievements. And then
there had been the affair, too shocking to speak of, with Nellie
Clifden, the young 'actress' into whose clutches Bertie had
briefly fallen during a stay in Dublin. Both Victoria and Albert
had been devastated to hear that Bertie had been seduced
– that he had been 'weak' when confronted by 'temptation';
and when Albert fell ill and died, shortly after a long, cold
journey to see Bertie and speak to him on the matter, all
Victoria's misery and anger were directed at her son. It had
been his fault; he had killed his father with his behaviour. And
now, if his wife gave birth early, they had no one to blame but
themselves, in the Queen's view. He and Alix stayed up too late
and kept company with 'fast' smart friends who were tolerant
of immorality.[15]

It has often been observed that parents tend to repeat their own parents' emotional stance towards their children, and this seems to have been the case with the Prince of Wales, despite his most heartfelt efforts to the contrary. It is certain that he tried hard not to repeat, with Eddy, any of the mistakes he felt had been made with him. Albert and Victoria had been distant, humourless parents. He was determined to treat his own off-spring with kindness (he would write to his mother that too much severity makes children 'fear those whom they ought to love')[16] and he and Alix agreed that mothering is best done by the mother.

Yet very few parents, in any age, are able to feel relaxed about the upbringing of an eldest child. It is notoriously the eldest who challenges authority, whose independence first creates anxiety, and whose skirmishes with parents elicit the most extreme response. Eddy, as a baby, was of course subject to all the anxious, loving fluttering around his health and behaviour that a first child usually provokes, but he was no ordinary first child. Eddy was destined for the most important job in the nineteenth-century world. As king, he would be revered by peoples of every colour and creed throughout the quarter of the earth's land surface that was the British Empire. Bertie had personally suffered dreadfully from the expectations inherent in being such a person. Frankly, he had found it impossible to be good enough, and this had made him rebellious. Accordingly, he and Alix did their best never to make exacting demands while their children were young.

In Alix, as it happened, Bertie had found the perfect abettor in this approach. Had she been a German or an English princess, it might have been different. E.F. Benson, who was of a slightly later generation than Eddy but knew in later life many of the same people, wrote about the upbringing of girls, as laid down by Prince Albert: a life of backboards, scales on the piano, French exercises, globes, the seaside for its tonic air, rugs for the knees,

'prohibition to read anything amusing, particularly novels', charity trips to the village, 'restricted pocket money and cloistered
ignorance of all that was likely to be met with in later life'.[17]

But Alix had been brought up in quite a different style. There
had been lessons by their mother for the girls, assisted by masters
in deportment, music and dancing; there had been tutors for
the boys – but little self-discipline in the matter of study. There
was no 'cloistered ignorance', but no novels, either. One picked
up what one needed – languages, and so on; heaven forbid
that one should be dull, or indeed solitary. So for her own
children, although 'a German and a French lady in the nursery
were present in order that they might be familiar with foreign
languages from their earliest youth'[18] – 'familiar with' is what
Eddy and George remained. There was no organised teaching
in their early years.

As small children, Eddy and George were usually under the
same roof as their parents. They spent the London season from
spring until midsummer at Marlborough House, two weeks at
Cowes in the Isle of Wight for the regatta, the shooting season
in August and September at Abergeldie in Scotland, and the
winter mainly at Sandringham. There were occasional weeks at
Osborne, and long stays at Bernstorff, Rumpenheim (Queen
Louise's family home near Frankfurt), Balmoral and elsewhere.
Always new faces… it was not the most settled existence.

In 1867, Alix fell ill with rheumatic fever. She was at the time
expecting her third child, and night after night Bertie stayed out
playing cards. They had never been inseparable, but his absence
now was painful. He did not appear to understand quite how
ill she was. He lacked sticking power in his amorous relationships and, oddly for one so successful in love, real empathy
with women, and the marriage may already have been coming
adrift. If so, his self-indulgence now did little to assist its repair.
The Princess was ill for many weeks, and took a long time to
recover from Louise's birth. Visiting her bedside, Bertie tactlessly

informed her that her grandmother had died. She had adored her grandmother and was distraught. He had no idea. 'He really is a child about such things,' wrote Lady Macclesfield in exasperation.[19] He was, at the time, twenty-six.

The rheumatic fever left Alix with a permanent slight limp. It was also severe enough to provoke that otosclerosis, or congenital deafness, from which Queen Louise suffered, and which had been largely dormant in Alix until now. It is a condition that tends to worsen during pregnancy or following a trauma, and so it proved for Alix. She became noticeably deaf. Bertie may well have been too selfish and impatient to make the extra effort that would have helped them to regain the intimacy of the early years. As it was, the Marlborough House set remained as glamorous as ever, but Alix was now somewhat isolated by her disability.

There is an early picture of the princes at Abergeldie riding in baskets slung on either side of a beautiful palomino pony. Alix is wearing a fetching tippet and a crinoline; little Eddy is not yet three, and well muffled against the Scottish cold.[20] For the boys, as the decade drew to a close and baby Louise was followed by Victoria and then Maud, life was still delightful. The emphasis, as always, was on having fun: on being taken to visit wealthy neighbours in Norfolk, or the jolly family in Denmark, or enjoying treats at home. A tour of the grounds, a visit to the dairy, chasing games in the endless corridors of great houses: these were the amusements available to them.

The young Annie de Rothschild wrote to her mother about a visit to Holkham in Norfolk in 1869. She and her sister Constance were staying there, and the Prince and Princess were guests one afternoon.

> The two little boys toddled in first with great self-possession, followed by the Princess, who looked very duckish and his Royal Highness in apparently a very good temper... [Alix] is decidedly deafish and always answers *à tort et à travers*.[21]

Two days later, the Waleses were back, and Annie's sister Constance wrote a letter:

> The Royal Highnesses like nothing so much as a romp…The Royal babies came in to be looked at yesterday afternoon; they are very nice little boys, rather wild, but not showing signs of becoming too much spoiled; they make very ludicrous attempts at being dignified. The princess generally brings her dog among her numerous retinue. Imagine that they bring twelve menservants; is it not dreadful!

The next day, while the Princess was playing the piano with Annie (Alix played well):

> …Meanwhile I had a fearful romp with the little princes. We taught them blind man's buff and ran races with them. The eldest is a beautiful child, the image of the Princess, the second has a jolly little face and looks the cleverest. The Princess said to me: 'they are dreadfully wild, but I was just as bad'.[22]

Later historians have written of Alix as a lightweight, a scatter-brain. Yet Reggie Brett, Lord Esher, who was a perspicacious and well-informed acquaintance of the family, wrote, 'Her cleverness has always been under-rated — partly because of her deafness. In point of fact she says more original things, and has more unexpected ideas than any other member of the family.'[23]

The de Rothschild accounts differ also from later assessments of Eddy. The boy of whom many historians write is a sickly child, but few contemporaries noticed any frailty. On the contrary, he throve, dosed regularly with 'cod-liver oil and steel — unless Sir William Jenner directed otherwise',[24] and allowed plenty of boisterous exercise and regular abundant nourishment. We may trace the misconception about his health to the aesthetic of the period as expressed by Queen Victoria. Eddy would turn out to be tall and slim with a long neck, like his mother, while the Victorian ideal was rather more mesomorphic. The Queen objected when her daughter-in-law looked 'too thin'. Stoutness was well tolerated in a man, *embonpoint* admired in a woman, and the ideal baby was as fat as butter.

Nor is there any suggestion, in these cheerful letters from gossipy young women, that the boy was deaf. It was General Sir Henry Ponsonby, the Queen's private secretary, who, when Eddy was nearly twenty, found him unforthcoming and suggested that he might have inherited a hearing impairment from his mother. But nobody else remarked on any deafness, and surely it would have been drawn to medical attention.

Six months after the birth of their fourth daughter, early in 1869, a six-month visit to Turkey and Egypt had been arranged for the Prince and Princess. Before this, they were to spend some days at grand public events in Paris, and six weeks in Denmark with the children. Queen Victoria was extremely cross about her grandsons' prolonged stay over Christmas with the Danish grandparents, but Bertie persuaded her to allow it. The Queen was further incensed when the boys and Louise were sent home from Hamburg in January, in the royal yacht, unsupervised by anyone more senior than Mrs Blackburn. In her view, the children required someone to exercise discipline. She had deplored forcing them to learn when they were toddlers – 'It weakens their brains', she had opined in a letter to her eldest daughter in 1867[25] – but now they were boys of school age, and it was high time they applied themselves. Bertie wrote back expressing reservations about too severe a regime, for 'we should naturally wish them to be very fond of you, as they were in Denmark of dear Alix's parents. I quite agree with you that the question of a governess being appointed must be considered on our return.'[26]

When the boys were reunited with Alix and Bertie in the autumn of 1869, Eddy was nearly six, and a Miss Brown was at last appointed to school them. Quite how effective she was is unknown. Alix is believed to have written a little rhyme for Eddy to recite to her father on his birthday on 9 November, and if this is the case he could probably read its eight lines aloud to Papa.[27]

The boys' education was not uppermost in their parents' mind at this time. There was a perceptible anti–royalist sentiment abroad. 'The Queen is invisible and the Prince of Wales is not respected' Gladstone wrote in a letter to Granville at the Foreign Office.[28] Queen Victoria had been absent from public life for too long. She was rarely seen by anyone other than courtiers or related royal families, and the hundreds of rooms in Buckingham Palace were kept empty, the furniture under dust covers for years on end. 'There is only one great capital in Europe where the Sovereign is unrepresented and that capital is London' one of her own equerries confided to Gladstone.[29] Exhorting his mother to spend even a little time in London, Bertie pointed out: 'We live in radical times, and the more the people see the sovereign, the better it is for the sovereign and the country.'[30]

Alix, when in London, delighted in being seen with her little boys. She would sit squeezed between the two comfortable corner seats in the barouche as it bowled through the Park; once, when this was remarked upon, she had answered wryly that she was there as a buffer state between two warring elements – for Eddy and George constantly squabbled and made up. But now the public seemed to have tired even of the Prince and Princess. In October, Bertie felt aggrieved that the firm hand of government was wanting, and wrote to his mother:

> I heard that there was a tremendous crowd in the Park, and I have no doubt much treason was talked….The more the Government allow the lower classes to get the upper hand, the more the dem-ocratic feeling of the present day will increase… I hear some speakers openly spoke of a Republic![31]

While all the Queen had to do, it seemed, was to be seen, the Waleses had a tougher job if they wanted the public to admire them. Bertie, for one, would have to change his entire cast of mind and style of life. As it was, people grumbled that the Waleses were gadabouts who preferred to spend their time on the continent. It is true that in 1869, not long back from the Middle Eastern tour, Alix took the children to Denmark in July and went to Germany for treatment to her knee; Bertie spent the autumn in Germany and shooting in Scotland. Both were back in London for the birth of Princess Maud in November, but the new royal baby did little to weaken public cynicism.

That Christmas was spent at Cromer, since Sandringham was being extended and the builders were in. But in the few months after Maud's birth, for a brief moment there was a threat to the Wales marriage. The least sensitive child is generally aware of unhappiness between his parents, and Eddy must have known that there were difficulties, all the more frightening for being left unsaid. Children are sensitive to a look, a refusal to answer, to any hostility which is not explained; and these were children who had always, as a matter of family policy, spent a good deal of time with their parents. They knew what to expect and would have noticed when anything went wrong, little realising that even more than their parents' relationship was at stake. Thanks partly to their father's first major 'scrape', the Crown really was in an ignominious and perilous position.

The cause of the trouble (and of course Eddy and his brother cannot have known this) was the Mordaunt divorce. At the end of January 1870, Sir Charles Mordaunt, a Member of Parliament, filed for divorce from his wife. She was a young woman who, when her little son went blind, announced that this tragedy was Heaven's punishment for her many affairs. Among her lovers had been two men of the Marlborough House set and 'several others', as the newspapers delicately put it. Her father, appalled at the prospect of divorce, alleged in a counter-suit that his daughter was insane.[32] Sir Charles's lawyers, determined to bring evidence of his wife's infidelities, found letters that

Lady Mordaunt had received from several men, including one
or two from the Prince. It was not the detail that mattered (he
had written nothing of an amorous nature), but the humiliation of her husband's having to go into the witness box in such
tawdry circumstances must have annoyed Alix. What he could
have been thinking of, to write to this woman – and now, what
people would think!

> Dear Lady Mordaunt,
> I am sorry that you are unwell and cannot see me today. I am
> hunting tomorrow and Saturday, but may I come and see you on
> Sunday at five? Hoping you are quite well, believe me to be
> Sincerely yours
> Albert Edward.[33]

In court, Bertie was asked why he had always visited Lady
Mordaunt alone… why he had arrived always in a cab, rather
than in his carriage? He dismissed any imputation of misbehaviour, but the public did not scrutinise details; in 1870,
divorce was extremely rare, a luxury only the upper classes could
afford, and mere association with such a case was enough to
confirm suspicion that these people were no better than they
should be, and their indulgence a waste of public money to
boot. 'Never since the reign of George IV had royalty been so
unpopular.'[34]

Queen Victoria, of course, was appalled – and vindicated. She
had never approved of the fast set in which the Waleses moved,
and now look what had come of it!

Worse was to come. The alterations at Sandringham were
finished, and the family had taken up occupation, when Alix
announced in the autumn of 1870 that she was expecting another
baby. In the April of 1871, she produced a little boy – the first
after three girls – but the poor baby died within twenty-four
hours. The Queen had always said that Alix dashed around too

much and now... Eddy and George wore kilts at the funeral, and walked behind the little coffin with their father. The Prince and Princess of Wales were devastated.

Queen Victoria approved of a quiet, homey existence. She dreaded everyone whose behaviour proclaimed them to be smart, amusing, and rich. In fact, she expressed a compensatory love of all that was cosy and middle-class. Family life, and propriety carried to almost stifling lengths, she justified as the preference of her people. In her view, royalty should actively avoid seeming 'too grand' and sophisticated; the people disliked that. She saw nothing dreary in things 'simple', 'wholesome' and 'manly'.

Faced with the sordid story of Bertie and the Mordaunt couple, followed by an unsuccessful outcome to Alix's pregnancy, she decided that the Wales children, at least, would benefit from association with someone who exemplified all the virtues. The very person was close at hand.

3

Britannia
1871–79

My father was the son of a country clergyman. He was born
in 1839, went to school at Blackheath and thence to Clare
College, Cambridge, as a scholar. He took a Third in Classics
and a First in Theology, and rowed in the Clare Second Boat.
He entered the Church and, while a curate at Whippingham in
the Isle of Wight, at the age of 31, he caught the eye of Queen
Victoria, who in 1871 appointed him tutor to the two 'young
princes'.[1]

Hugh Dalton, Chancellor of the Exchequer in the
Labour government of 1945, wrote with great affec-
tion of his father, the Reverend John Neale Dalton.
Whippingham was the parish church at Osborne attended by
Queen Victoria and her courtiers every Sunday. Canon Prothero's
young curate was possessed of a magnificent, booming voice.

Everyone noticed it and indeed he seems to have been rather an actor *manqué*, his sermons being

> … more often interesting for their vigorous delivery than for their content. Every hearer was impressed by the wonderful voice, ranging from a high falsetto to a thunderous bass… And as a reader he had no living equal.[2]

Dalton was a kind, opinionated, strong-minded man: an all-round good sort. The Queen could not have proposed a more suitable candidate as tutor to the young princes. He was diligent in carrying out his duties, was not such a prig as to exasperate Bertie, and, above all, he had that resonant voice, so Alix could hear what he said. He was not of a paedophile bent, which was a great relief and rarer among Victorian schoolmasters than might be supposed, and he was never a fawning sycophant.

> No one I have ever known was less of a snob and less like the traditional picture of a courtier. He made friends, on equal terms, with all sorts and conditions of men. He had no use for lords, or for rich men, as such.[3]

Decades later, his duties at Windsor Castle would involve visits to the lodgekeepers on the estate. After Canon Dalton (for such he became) died, the daughter of one of these royal retainers wrote to Hugh Dalton about his father's visits to her own 'dear old dad' at Christmas:

> …'"there you are my old shipmate' in his deep booming voice – banging down a bottle of whisky on the kitchen table – They loved spinning sea yarns together… He always called her mother his 'old sweetheart'.[4]

By all accounts, the boys liked him from the start, and yet they
must have been difficult pupils. Royal children were brought
up to treat servants politely, but Mr Dalton was not a servant,
and it does not seem that anyone until now had taken them in
hand. They would have done everything they could to test him
– which was quite a lot. They 'made hay in my room besides
ringing every bell they could catch hold of', wrote an exasperated Lord de Ros to Sir Henry Ponsonby at the end of 1871.[5]
'They are such ill-bred, ill-trained children', the Queen complained, about a year after Dalton had taken charge.'I can't fancy
them at all.'They were 'as wild as hawks'.[6] Eddy was less trouble-
some than his brother. As he grew up, Dalton would describe
his 'infinite sweetness of nature'. George could be quite vicious,
unless put sharply in his place. A gentleman of the Household
who had been kicked in the shins smacked the boy instantly
and was rewarded with friendly respect.[7]

Dalton had a magnificent solution to problems of indiscipline:
fatigue. By the age of eight or nine, the boys were pursuing
a regimen that would have worn out a degree student.[8] On
weekdays, they rose at seven and prepared their geography and
English before breakfast. At eight, they had Bible reading or a
history lesson, and at nine, algebra or Euclid. At ten, an hour was
devoted to games; then they studied French or Latin for three
hours until the main meal at two. In the afternoon, there was
riding or cricket. Then tea, and after it English, music (in which
Alix took a keen interest) and preparation for the following day.
They went to bed at eight.

And so, year after year, the boys were drilled in the accom-
plishments expected of a royal personage. There were less
demanding interludes. When Eddy was twelve or thirteen, drawing was taught by a Mr Weigall, and they seem to have enjoyed
it. 'We have just had a drawing lesson, and I drew an elephant
for Papa and Eddy drew a tiger', George would write to his
grandmother.[9] (Eddy, who chose the tiger, later developed a

passion for shooting them.) At around this time a Henry Weigall, according to the memoirs of Lillie Langtry, was the protégé of Lord Houghton, a distinguished Liberal peer whose patronage helped many talented people in their careers. Weigall frequented that artistic bohemian household in Salisbury Street, off the Strand, where Frank Miles, the artist, occupied the top floor and the young Oscar Wilde lived in rooms on the floor below. Miles met Langtry as early as 1876, and made pencil sketches of her which were reproduced and sold in their thousands. From the beginning of her affair with the Prince of Wales, Langtry introduced him to her interesting friends at 13, Salisbury Street; the Prince bought a drawing from Miles.[10] One glimpses the web of connections that led to the hiring of a drawing master. Bertie was a networker of genius; he could do something for everyone. At some time, of course, those favours might be called in.

Dalton was a physically fit young man, and when it came to 'games' was much better suited to the role of elder brother than their father (who according to the historian Harold Nicolson insisted that he be regarded in that light). George retained fond memories of sport in the grounds at Sandringham into much later life: 'It was here that Dalton used to teach us to shoot with bow and arrow, and down there that he ran when he allowed us to shoot at him as the running deer.'[11] And of course there was riding; everyone rode, and the princes had ponies of their own on which they went out at least three mornings every week. As apprentice public figures, they must possess every accomplishment. At Marlborough House:

> ...a drill sergeant used to attend regularly and there were also gymnastic and fencing instructors. In the mornings, the young princes were subjected to the severe training of the riding school at Knightsbridge Barracks. In addition they took dancing lessons with their sisters and were coached in tennis, croquet and football.[12]

At the age of twelve, they learned to handle guns at Sandringham, where the dairy and piggery, ornamental gardens and kitchen gardens and farmland of the estate were surrounded by wild woods and game. It was unthinkable that Eddy would not have cause to employ all these skills as king one day. And yet the unthinkable was being thought quite often now, and in 1871 a respected Member of Parliament publicly opined that, like the French, the British should move towards republican government.

In the autumn of 1871, there appeared a pamphlet: *What does she do with It?* Said to have been written (anonymously) by a future Chief Secretary for Ireland, G.O. Trevelyan, it asked a question typical of the hard-headed, no-nonsense, philistine age. What value for money were the British public getting from their reigning monarch? The Queen never toured the countries of her Empire. She was never seen in London. Her most intimate friend appeared to be John Brown, the Scottish ghillie. Should she receive distinguished visitors or otherwise undertake duties of state (and such occasions were rare), it was as likely as not that Parliament would receive the bill. The public appeared to be supporting an old lady who travelled between three vast palaces simply in order to enjoy the scenery, entertain descendants from all over the continent of Europe and marry them off to each other, thus perpetuating an entire class of parasites.

It was protested in the Queen's defence that she had been ill that summer, and hence incapable of carrying out official duties. Sir William Jenner loyally confirmed this, but to no avail; it seemed that Trevelyan had made a point that 'oft was felt, but ne'er so well expressed'. In France, the disastrous Franco-Prussian War had been followed by the deposition of Napoléon III and the declaration of a republic. Now, early in November, Sir Charles Dilke called on Parliament to depose the Queen and do the same. *The Times* was horrified, and apoplectic royalists called for Dilke to be shot, but he had the support of sections of the press.

It was fate, and the clever manipulation of public sympathy, that intervened to save the royal family, if not from a constitutional crisis, at least from further humiliation.

Bertie caught typhoid. He had spent the autumn at Oberammergau and at Homburg, taking the waters; and late in October he had gone to stay at Londesborough Lodge, Scarborough, where he is believed to have been infected. Lord Chesterfield had fallen victim to the disease at the same place, and died. There was nothing unusual in this. Typhoid is spread by ingesting polluted water. Insanitary conditions prevailed throughout the housing stock (the first Public Health Acts were only five years old) and stately homes were as likely to have leaking, stinking drains as anywhere. George (later Lord) Curzon, who was pretty much a contemporary of Eddy's, lost his mother to typhoid not long afterwards; 'infectious fevers' were a frequent complaint among staff at the War Office and 10, Downing Street.[13] Bazalgette's supremely effective sewage system for London was not yet entirely in place, and the rest of the country was far less advanced. Sir William Jenner, whose work in distinguishing typhus (which is spread by lice) from typhoid had gained him a knighthood and a lucrative practice among the aristocracy, had been the Prince of Wales's Physician in Ordinary since 1863, and was in the opinion of Lady Macclesfield 'reckoned first rate for fevers, though a mean time-server and a dismal croaker',[14] but even he could not cure the disease. Supportive and symptomatic care was the best the nineteenth century could offer. It had not been enough in Prince Albert's case. He had died, the disease resisting Dr Jenner's best efforts, almost ten years ago.

Late in November, Bertie's condition was giving cause for concern. Typhoid fever takes two or three weeks to reach its height and, in its latter stages, may damage the internal organs permanently. The Queen particularly dreaded 14 December, the anniversary of her Consort's death. Early in the month, the Prince seemed to be getting better, but optimism was premature. As the fever grew worse and 14 December approached, 'during the last week almost all private and public hope had been abandoned.'[15]

At Sandringham, the Prince of Wales lay on what would almost inevitably be his deathbed, raving in delirium. 'That was once but is no more; you have broken your vows!' observers heard him cry.[16]

Should the Prince die, Eddy at seven years old would become heir apparent. If Queen Victoria were to die before Eddy's majority, Prince Alfred, who was at present twenty-seven years old and unmarried, would probably be Regent. Regencies have no great record of success. But if, as seemed likely, the Queen went on for another decade or two, Eddy was destined to become king as a young man. The one advantage nobody, least of all the politicians, could deny the present Queen was respect due to age and experience. A young monarch would be a different matter.

The world held its breath for the outcome of the Prince of Wales's serious illness. He survived. In February 1872, the Queen, the Wales family and the great and good of the nation attended a service of thanksgiving in St Paul's Cathedral. Tennyson wrote an ode. Public support was vehement. There was no more talk of a republic.

Everyone agreed that Eddy was good-looking, sweet-natured and charming. Mr Dalton seems to have been the first to complain that the boy was apathetic. In one of many famously gloomy phrases, he referred to 'the abnormally dormant condition of his mind'.[17] Eddy sounds like the kind of boy who in a public school of the time would have found the chalk-rubber flying at his ear – 'You, boy! Dozing there at the back.' Yet in accounts of play with children of his own age, he seems as lively as his brother. He had learned to speak Danish, so there was nothing wrong with his intellect. Perhaps Eddy's lack of animation during lessons was a reaction to Dalton's booming voice ('No one ever went to sleep during one of his sermons',

Queen Victoria said grimly)[18] and the relentless task-driven programme. Facts were what Dalton was determined to force-feed into those two royal skulls, and many children, royal or otherwise, learn more willingly on a less rigidly prescribed path. There was a good deal of rote learning in Victorian education – incurious absorption and retention of information for later retrieval at the time of some test. And history has demonstrated that royal children are never motivated by tests. Their exam results are usually undistinguished. Why would they be otherwise? There is no incentive for royal children to learn anything they are not particularly interested in. Their role is laid down for them at birth, and whether or not they pass exams is immaterial.

Dalton grumbled that the constant disruption – the moves from house to house and country to country – did little to help. George seemed quicker on the uptake than his brother, but he was not particularly well motivated either. Dalton was undeniably right that there was disruption, but he had known when he joined it that this was a peripatetic household. There were other parental influences that he was in no position to confront. Children do not learn to learn in a vacuum, and neither Alix nor Bertie had any experience of study or intellectual enthusiasm to pass on to their sons. Alix loved music, but she would have been mystified had either son seemed bookish; she was, if not suspicious of learning, indifferent to it. Bertie read French and English daily papers and the racing press, but had never learned to apply himself and was actively discouraged from doing so in adulthood. There was no reason for him to spend time at a desk. He was not allowed even to see key state papers. The Queen had instructed her ministers to keep them from him, as he was notoriously indiscreet.

Now that he was well again, he and Alix seemed determined to celebrate by having a jolly good time. They exploited their position and social genius, for such it was, to the full. It was all very public. Balls during the season at Marlborough House grew more dazzling than ever in the 1870s.

> I can recall no evening that could vie in sheer happiness with that of a Marlborough House Ball. The Prince would have his army friends... There would be the racing folk, represented by the big owners, and the financiers, the Sassoons, the Rothschilds, Baron Hirsch, and the rest. The Princess would be seen with her great friend, Lady de Grey, and the music lovers. Under the Marlborough House roof, and in the gardens, all these diverse types mixed quite happily and informally.[19]

The London house was a small palace, originally designed by Wren although altered since; its entrance hall was two storeys high and huge frescoes of Marlborough's battles occupied entire walls, below painted ceilings. In 1873, Eddy and George, as small boys, appeared at a fancy-dress ball as pages to their mother. Bertie, in a curly wig, made a rather stocky Charles I.

The Grand Duke Alexander and his wife, Alix's sister Dagmar, heirs to the Russian Empire, visited that year with their retinue (Dagmar had married Alexander after the death of his brother Nicholas, her fiancé), as did the Shah of Persia. At last, for the first time in fifty years, there was a sophisticated court: a series of circles – political and aristocratic, sporting and fashionable – centred upon Marlborough House, forming opinion and reporting it, from all parts of Europe and beyond.

Within these circles was an inner, somewhat bohemian côterie of witty women and sporting men. Often, at Sandringham, the Waleses stayed up late playing cards; there was no reason to rise early and they would not come down to breakfast until after eleven. In these years, Wales began to accumulate gambling debts that would eventually reach colossal proportions. He had begun, also, to accumulate that adiposity that eventually made him reach colossal proportions of his own. Food was one of his great passions. He employed a huge kitchen staff, working under a chef whose job was to titillate the Prince's greed.

Indulgences such as balls, deerstalking parties, dinner parties, race meetings, Saturday-to-Monday visits to great houses and preparation for travel would be the talk of the household. From the boys' point of view, the only person to whom Caesar's Gallic Wars or the Diet of Worms could possibly have seemed relevant was Mr Dalton. Classics were for professional men – clerics or doctors or lawyers – and from an early age Eddy must have known that this was not the class to which he belonged. History related as a matter of victories and dates, and geography as land mass and population, were tedious. Doggedly, Dalton ploughed his unrewarding furrow in the classroom, while everyday conversation revolved around horses or yachts or travel or weddings: people to meet, wonderful things to buy, new clothes. For immediate interest, there was really no contest. It is doubtful whether the real significance of their family's political rôle was ever brought to the boys' attention: for example, the fact that one entertained the Shah of Persia or the Sultan of Turkey for a reason – to protect India – or the fact that one's grandmother must be persuaded to remain at Windsor, rather than depart for Balmoral, so that she might greet the Tsar of all the Russias and thus, in Disraeli's words, avoid a war in Afghanistan.

Modern languages were the most obvious subjects in which their education failed. It seems unlikely that Dalton was fluent in French or German himself. He had been born in 1840 and had received that classical education in which, until the 1860s, science and modern languages barely figured. He was a good Hebrew scholar and, according to his son, he had an intelligent layman's interest in the natural sciences. But if he was typical of his age and class, he had probably never crossed the Channel. A Monsieur Mariette was brought in to assist when the boys were young, but no amount of French instruction reduced their self-consciousness about trying out the language in one another's

company. Maybe that was part of the trouble: sibling rivalry. They
were always together and always squabbling. Dalton noted in
George's album of progress on 23 September 1876 that he 'shows
too much disposition to find fault with his brother'. As for Eddy,
who was less rough and noisy, 'there was in him an apathy which
his father tried – perhaps rather roughly – to combat'.[20]

When, in 1877, they had at last to work for an exam, their
mother wrote to Mr Dalton (she was in Athens at the time) telling him that they must be made to work and above all, to stop
quarrelling: 'they always break into everybody's conversation and
it becomes impossible to speak to anyone before them'.[21] She
pleaded, in her letters to George, that he must stop picking
fights with Eddy.[22]

The Waleses no doubt expected that their sons would just
pick languages up. After all, they had. Queen Victoria complained that Bertie had been fluent in German, French and
English by the age of six (English was not his first language,
and he retained a German accent throughout his life); why
were Eddy and George so slow? The present crop of German
cousins spoke good English. While her Wales grandsons were
not monolingual (they had Danish, albeit a language of limited
currency), they seemed never to talk more than two of the
seven languages that their cousins in Denmark used between
them. King George of the Hellenes (Alix's little brother Willie)
and his wife Olga, in Athens, had begun to produce children who would grow up much better educated than Eddy
and George. Alix's sister Dagmar, whose engagement to the
Tsarevich Nicholas was sadly concluded when he died before
the wedding, had married his younger brother Alexander; they,
too, brought cousins to Bernstorff and Fredenborg who spoke
French as well as Russian and English at an early age. Another
brother married a Swedish princess and had seven or eight
children. In this polyglot company, with every opportunity to
become multilingual, one must presume that the Waleses simply

got by in English most of the time. They were three years older than Constantine of Greece and Nicholas of Russia, the boys closest in age to them, so they could expect the others to fall into line behind them. Yet their younger sisters were never able to communicate in any other language either. Years later, the Duke of Windsor would say that his aunts 'could just read and write, period. That was all.'[23]

In London, in Osborne and at Sandringham, they saw many children, but above all the Tecks. The Duke and Duchess of Teck – the Duke rather ineffectual, the Duchess an extravagant cousin of Queen Victoria, known as Princess Mary Adelaide, who was sadly fat – were friends, whose daughter, little Victoria Mary, known as May, best matched Eddy and George in age (her own brothers were still babies). Princess Mary was always happy to be invited, although preferably when Bertie was not around to tease her about her weight. John Gore records how the three children, at Osborne, were once led out by Queen Victoria and ceremoniously planted a tree in the grounds. Eddy was six at the time. This was the future: a little light tree-planting, cutting a fine figure in uniform, and hunting. Not Euclidean geometry.

In 1875, there was another upset between the boys' parents. The Prince of Wales was to spend some time away from home, and this time Alix would not accompany him. Alix was deeply hurt. She had adored her visit to the Middle East, and now Bertie was going to India without her. India was the country she had always longed to visit. Everyone was curious about it; the sinuous Mogul motifs and Arthur Liberty's orange and pink silks glowing under the sun were the most advanced of tastes, and London was fascinated by handsome maharajahs. India at this time appeared to be the most romantic place on earth. And Bertie had arranged the whole thing behind her back.

One report indicates that he didn't want to go. He wept when he set off, in company with a number of cronies, and was particularly affected at parting with the boys.

One does not know what he told Alix, but she can hardly have
been convinced that he was to tour the subcontinent alone as the
best emissary of his mother, for Alix herself was the royal family's
greatest asset. She was charming, curious and sympathetic. Bertie
was charming too, but inclined to be petulant. He liked things
his own way. He seems to have decided to travel halfway round
the world to solve what is now called an image problem, and
succeeded only in making matters worse. The Marlborough
House set had never seemed more seedy and the Mordaunt
divorce case was still, in its minor aspects, before the courts when
the visit was announced. And as if that were not enough, another
friend of Bertie's, Colonel Valentine Baker of the Tenth Hussars,
would be sent to prison in the summer for indecently assaulting
a 'winsome young lady of distinctly prepossessing appearance' on
a train. He had put his arm around her waist and tried to kiss
her; but that was enough to get him a year in jail and a £500
fine. October 1875 was a good time to get out of town. Bertie
invited a party of friends – Lord Charles Beresford, 'Sporting
Joe' Aylesford, Prince Louis of Battenberg, Lord Alfred Paget,
Harry Chaplin and others – to join him on a long voyage east
with some tiger-hunting at the end of it.

Off he went, and Alix took the children to Denmark, and
stayed there. As autumn turned to winter, and her daughter-
in-law showed no sign of returning, the Queen grew annoyed.
She felt a loss of control. Her English grandchildren were out of
reach, and under Danish influence; she wanted them back, and
wrote to Alix that as Bertie was away and always accompanied
her to the state opening of Parliament, she, Alix, must return at
once to stand in for him. The Queen insisted. Her own conven-
ience must take precedence. Alix could not argue.

In India, the Prince of Wales was enjoying hospitality on
an almost unimaginable scale. One Mr William Potter, sev-
enty-two years old, an enthusiastic traveller and royal-watcher
who had toured the continent before and was sure to arrive

everywhere before the Prince and even occasionally – oh joy!
– to talk to him, wrote home to his sister describing maharajahs
whose costumes and turbans literally dazzled with diamonds and
emeralds, and hundreds of elephants caparisoned in scarlet and
gold, bearing magnificent notabilities perched within jewelled
howdahs. Each procession – one was two miles long – was more
extraordinary than the last, until Mr Potter could hardly contain
his excitement ('I will just add that one chief had the housings
and front piece of his elephant entirely composed of rupees
strung together, like scale armour, and his elephant painted a
deep blue').[24] He marvelled at the wealth displayed at balls, often
held within the illuminated gardens and marble halls of some
palace. Once, he toured the accommodation prepared for the
Prince before his arrival. The rooms were all ready, the ceilings
sixteen feet high, a solid silver bath in the vast room adjoining
the bedroom and every detail considered, including a bottle of
Truefitt's Hair Shampoo.

In February, the spell was broken. A letter arrived. Lord
Aylesford's wife had taken advantage of his absence to conduct
an affair, and wrote to inform him that she wanted a divorce; she
would henceforth be the partner of the Marquess of Blandford,
heir to the Duke of Marlborough. In his haste, Lord Aylesford
is said to have started for England upon an elephant; since he
arrived in London in the normal manner he must have thought
better of it.

The misunderstandings and reversals that arose from the
Aylesford affair are too convoluted to relate in detail. In London,
Lady Aylesford produced letters from the Prince, who had
enjoyed a liaison with her some years before; Lord Randolph
Churchill, Blandford's younger brother, was virtually accused
of blackmail; Wales's seconds challenged Churchill to a duel.
All this caused a furore in society and must have been painful
to Alix. The entire brouhaha was resolved on Bertie's return in
May 1876, when he and Alix spent an hour together before he

disembarked from the ship. That night, he and she, Eddy and
George, appeared before the *haut ton* of London in a box at
Covent Garden: a happy Victorian family, reunited.[25]

In 1877, Eddy would reach the age of thirteen, when most
English boys of his age and class would start to board at a public
school. Academically, there was not much to choose between
the few top schools, of which Eton was the most prestigious.
Wellington, founded only five years before Eddy was born, was
the one best known to the royal family, since the Prince Consort
had been involved in every detail of its conception – even
the uniform, which 'remarkably resembled that of the porters
and ticket-collectors of the South Eastern Railway on which
Wellington College was situated'.[26] But there were doubts, and
not just about school uniform.

For one, public schools were out of favour. In 1872, there had
been a scandal at Eton where adolescent homosexual passions,
sometimes reciprocated, had become notorious. The headmaster
was now alert to signs of 'unnatural' intimacy, and in 1874 an
amiably eccentric master called Oscar Browning had been despatched to outer darkness, after accusations about his friendship
with the young George Curzon. Frank Harris would later write:

> If the mothers of England knew what goes on in the dormitories
> of these boarding-schools throughout England, they would all be
> closed from Eton and Harrow upwards, or downwards, in a day.[27]

No one of any sophistication was left unaware of the possibility
that their sons might be seduced or bullied into compliance
by a predatory schoolteacher or an older boy, and Wales, who
had never attended school but had always had tutors, was no
exception.

Queen Victoria had further reservations about public schools.
Certainly, she did not want Eddy and George to meet with 'bad
influences' of a sexual kind, but she also feared they might pick

up aristocratic snobberies. She was determined that they should continue to feel safest in the bosom of Home (she used the capital letter) and remain respectably middle-class in outlook.

Then again, neither Bertie nor Dalton wanted to separate the boys. If Eddy were to go to Wellington School, and George to join him later or to join the navy as a cadet, preparatory to the career he was later expected to pursue, an unhappy history could repeat itself, for Bertie never forgot how much he had hated enforced separation from his younger brother Affie. Anyway, Dalton was adamant that separation would be a bad thing. George was an unprincipled big-head, inclined to feel he had nothing to prove. Dalton wrote on 30 December 1876:

> Prince George wants application, steady application... his sense of self-approbation is almost the only motive power in him. He has not nearly so high a sense of right and wrong for its own sake as his elder brother...[28]

Were George to be separated from Eddy, he would be easy prey for every kind of flatterer. Eddy kept him grounded. On the other hand, Eddy appeared to have no 'motive power' in him:

> Prince Albert Victor requires the stimulus of Prince George's company to induce him to work at all... the mutual influence of their characters on one another (totally different as they are in many ways) is very beneficial. Difficult as the education of Prince Albert Victor is now, it would be doubly or trebly so if Prince George were to leave him.[29]

If these arguments were insufficient to deter attempts to send Eddy to school, there was a minimum standard, set by the Public Entrance examination, that a new public schoolboy of the 1870s could be expected to reach, and Eddy – who would by the time he went off to school have been in Dalton's care for seven years – came nowhere near it. Had his level of achievement been anything but abysmal, he might perhaps have started at Wellington a year late, with George; but George was no further advanced. As the royal children they would be conspicuous, and their ignorance would make them a laughing stock.

Dalton began to coach them for the naval cadetship examinations to be held in the summer of 1877. Their grandmother had no greater fondness for the navy than for public schools, for she feared that it might make them insular, or even rough in their language and outlook; but she offered no alternative plans.

Whether or not Eddy actually passed the exam is not clear, and no papers remain. It seems that George did. In any case, if either prince had failed they would not have been alone among the forty-eight cadets who got aboard the training ship *Britannia* at Dartmouth that autumn, thanks to a little bending of the rules. Rosslyn 'Rosy' Wemyss had defective eyesight; but

> ...by a lucky chance, the doctor who was making the examination happened to have been shipmates with his father, Hay Wemyss, and realising who he was, put him through an easy test.[30]

It was the start of a career in which Rosy would become Lord Wester Wemyss, GCB CMG MVO Admiral of the Fleet.

That summer, Eddy caught typhoid. He was attended by Dr Gull, who had often assisted Sir William Jenner. There was of course no cure, but it is a testimony to his strong constitution that he fought off the infection and recovered well. Because of this illness, he and George began life on the *Britannia* two months late.

When, in September, the boys were entrusted to Captain Fairfax of the *Britannia*, they left Alix and Bertie in a subtly altered relationship. The boys would not have known it, but when their mother returned from a holiday in Greece in the spring of 1877 she had found that her husband was smitten. Lillie Langtry had become his mistress. She was a charming and intelligent young woman, and it seems that Alix now resigned herself to the conclusion that was to sustain her throughout the rest of the marriage. 'Jealousy is the bottom of all mischief and misfortune in this world.'[31] In the next eighteen months, he would have every excuse to spend time in Paris, in his capacity as organiser of the British section of the Paris Exhibition; traditionally, it was the city in which to conduct discreet liaisons. In the spring of 1878, when 'everybody knew', Langtry was presented at court, wearing the Prince of Wales's feathers on her head. Alix may have consoled herself that she was, and well into middle age remained, more attractive than any of his mistresses.

For the first time, Eddy and George were alone amid 200 boys of their own age and older. They had Mr Dalton, of course, acting as chaplain to the ship for the duration of his stay, but he had his own acquaintances to make and his position to fortify. The *Britannia* was moored permanently at Dartmouth. At the Admiralty's request, the princes were accommodated apart from the others, their hammocks slung in what had been the captain's cabin, which was 'a space about twelve feet square behind a separate bulkhead'.[32] They were otherwise treated like any other cadets. Their clothes were stowed in sea-chests and they took their lessons and did their drill and messed with the other boys.

The other new cadets were reasonably well born. There was no question of the Wales boys mixing with the hoi polloi. Rosy Wemyss, who became a special friend of Prince Eddy and Prince George,[33] was a great-grandson of a Duke of Clarence; his great-grandmother (a Fitzclarence) had been born illegitimately to an actress, Dolly Jordan, by whom Clarence had ten children. That Duke of Clarence had become Lord High Admiral of Great Britain. The family seat was Wemyss Castle, in Scotland,

and the Wemysses could trace their Scottish lineage for over 700 years. Francis Osborne would inherit the dukedom of Leeds, and among others who became friends were Charles Cust, Charles Dormer, George Hardinge, Heathcote Grant and George Hillyard, all of whom were the sons of distinguished families and most of whom would make the navy their career.

Hillyard, unlike several others, never rose beyond the rank of commander, but he seems to have preferred tennis anyway. In later life, he wrote about tennis and played tennis; his wife played tennis; and he haunted the courts of Europe, lawn and covered, for many years. He would come to know King Edward as a frequent spectator of matches in the south of France. Pleading for greater encouragement of the game at public schools, he wrote, in middle age: 'I firmly believe a great percentage of these lukewarm cricketers... would readily take to lawn tennis given the opportunity. This at all events was found to be the case in HMS *Britannia*, the training ship for officers of the Royal Navy.'[34] As an old man, he made a broadcast in bluff sea-dog style to schools which, as it is perhaps the only account we have by a contemporary of the princes aboard the *Britannia*, is worth reproducing.

> I wish I could describe the picture of that old wooden ship the *Britannia* lying in the river Dart, below a hill covered with beech-woods. She was an old warship of one hundred years ago, broad in the beam, and painted black and white, like the ships of Nelson's day – for she was one of them.
>
> ...In due course the princes arrived, Prince Eddy rather tall for his age (he was nearly fourteen), slight and good-looking, Prince George, who was some eighteen months younger, very fair and small, but also nice-looking. They seemed a bit shy and quiet at first, which was not surprising when you come to think of it. Two youngsters like that being suddenly pitchforked into a den of about two hundred ravening wolves such as we were! For those

were no soft days. The *Britannia* was a hard school, though, mark you, a splendid one. It made little difference whether you were a prince or a commoner – you had to take what was coming to you, and believe me, it came pretty often during the first two terms on board! The princes were treated exactly the same as all the rest of us. Their sole privilege, as far as I remember, was a sleeping cabin to themselves under the poop, which as you all know is the after part of the ship.

However, they soon settled down, and after a time, I believe they thoroughly enjoyed the life. And what healthy-minded youngster wouldn't? It was hard certainly, we were worked hard, and we played hard, for games were by no means neglected. We had an excellent cricket ground, and a very good cricket coach – dear old Bentley, the Yorkshire professional. A racquet court, a pack of foot Beagles, boats to sail, and boats to row, what could the heart of a boy ask more? It was a good and healthy life, and on the whole, most enjoyable…I remember one incident in those two years very clearly. A boat-race among the cadets, pulled in either twelve or ten-oared cutters, I forget which. I was starboard bow oar, and Prince George, on the same thwart from me, pulled the port bow oar. Prince Eddy was our cox. Well, somehow or other, we managed to win that race, and to our great delight, Her Majesty Queen Victoria sent each of us a very handsome memento of the occasion.[35]

Both boys were popular, and George was nicknamed 'Sprat'. His own recollections of that time, recounted years later, were less sentimental.

It was a pretty tough place, and so far from making any allowances for our disadvantages, the other boys made a point of taking it out on us on the grounds that they would never be able to do it later on. There was a lot of fighting among the cadets and the rule was that if challenged you had to accept. So they used to make me go

up and challenge the bigger boys – I was awfully small then – and
I'd get a hiding time and again.[36]

They had a shilling a week each to spend, and the bigger boys
made little George spend some of that on illicit 'tuck', which he
would have to smuggle aboard for them (he was often caught,
and suffered the penalty). According to John Gore, who knew
Prince George well in later life, they and Dalton invited special
friends to tea in the 'quarters specially built for the princes', that
is to say, the twelve-foot-square cabin behind the bulkhead. Alix
can never have imagined anything quite so cosy.

Mr Dalton took a friendly interest in one of the midshipmen, Hugh Evans-Thomas. This young man had an older sister,
Kitty, who corresponded with him. Mr Dalton may have seen
a photograph; he certainly liked what he heard of the girl. He
needed a wife, and he started to dream.

Meanwhile, he had his royal charges to consider. Their classes
included mathematics and seamanship, and they took French lessons with a 'worldly, witty Frenchman'[37] named Monsieur Hua.
Nothing in the academic line seemed to work, much. From the
Britannia, Dalton wrote to the Queen, who had expressed anxiety for Eddy's welfare after his illness, on 14 November, 1877:

> Mr Dalton… has the honour to inform her Majesty that Prince
> Albert Victor and Prince George of Wales are both in thorough
> health. The elder… has increased two pounds in weight since
> his arrival here. It is impossible that two lads could be in more
> robust health or happier than the two princes are. Their studies
> also progress favourably. Mr Dalton thinks there is no fear of the
> elder Prince working too hard, or overtaxing his powers, as your
> Majesty seems to fear; in fact he might work harder than he does
> without any risk of detriment. They both sleep well and have
> good appetites.[38]

Dalton's position aboard was difficult. As chaplain and part-time tutor, he did not really have a lot to do, and it is easy to see how some of the officers may have regarded him as 'supernumary', as Gore puts it. He busied himself writing friendly homilies for delivery on Sundays. Reading his sermons, one hears a vivid speaker, straightforward, and not at all pompous – a good storyteller, who draws effectively upon the Old Testament and explains what he means, without being too abstract for adolescents to understand. 'Heaven is not a place, but a state of mind,' he would tell his son later. His brother, the prolific writer Sir Corrie Dalton, was agnostic, but Dalton seems to have favoured that muscular Christianity typical of his day. On Advent Sunday, 2 December 1877, he spoke on strength of body, of mind, and of character.

> Loiter not listlessly away your hours of recreation; be careful that neither by idleness nor sloth, neither by vice nor folly, you waste or impair your God-given strength of body…Who more wretched than the listless waverer? Who sooner sinks to his level than the boy weak of purpose, the boy easily led by others, unstable, foolish, irresolute?[39]

It was stirring stuff, bristling with references to manliness, honour and courage, but that was just the start. By March, he had come face to face with some of the realities, and Obedience was the theme.

> When… on leaving the ship you go and either in the boats or ashore break some or other of the regulations you know you ought to keep, or go out of bounds, then in that act of disobedience… you are dishonourable.

Regulations were made for the boys' own good and they must not go out of harbour because of dangerous currents; some boys had been 'carried ashore by the Mewstone the other day, and lost their boat'. Also, some had been copying older boys, and smoking.

> You are undermining your vigour, you are taking so much deadly
> poison into your body and on to your brain, the effects of which
> you will only fully know in years to come.

He had already spoken to one or two boys privately about this. If one of them was Prince George, the talking-to had little effect, for he smoked heavily for the rest of his life, and in later years Dalton provided cigarettes whenever he was asked.

A year later, he frowned upon a group who spent most of their free time scoffing tuck and gossiping.

> When after your appetite is satisfied, you still go on merely for the
> pleasure of the thing, then your lower nature is getting the mastery
> of you... And certainly some of your number fall very far short
> of self-mastery in this matter, when they pass the most part of
> their time ashore in simply walking up to the field and indulging
> themselves in this way, and then walk down again without ever
> joining their comrades in healthy games at all.

As for the cadets' library:

> ...that has lately been augmented and rearranged... when... you
> find that you have taken out in succession more than two or three
> novels, and are reading no other sort of books in your spare time
> either on wet days or Sundays, then it is time for you to think of
> exercising a little self-control on your fancy...

He recommended instead 'stirring tales' of adventure and travel, natural history, and naval history. And some boys were so selfish!

> Will wasted opportunities, will abused privileges, will stolen pleas-
> ures taken in secret, make up to anyone for the loss of virtue, the
> loss of manliness, the loss of self-respect?

Unfortunately, the kind of child to whom this kind of thing is
addressed generally gives not a fig for the loss of virtue; they are
both too knowing and too ignorant for well-meaning exhorta-
tions to have the slightest effect. Two months later, there had
been no improvement. One imagines not the well-scrubbed
lads who had come aboard in '77, but a bunch of surly youths
barely fit to be let off the ship.

> Are there not even now some dark stains that lie upon some of
> your lives already?... more than once within the last two or three
> weeks the sin of lying has been noticed amongst some of your
> number... the most terrible of all sins a boy can commit.

He named the seven sins: Pride, Covetousness, Lust, Envy,
Gluttony, Sloth and Anger; and proceeded to warn against them,
one by one. 'Lust', when it came down to detail, was renamed
'impurity'. Which was part of the problem, really, as it would
have been impossible for the canon to call a spade a spade in
this regard. The Church taught that sex was sinful, unless for the
procreation of children. Boys and girls were kept in ignorance
of what it was, while being told not to do it. It was all very
confusing. What was a 'virgin'? What was 'adultery'? Many boys
of the upper and middle classes were expected to retain their
childlike innocence until their late teens, at some point beyond
which they would be initiated into a male culture of shameless
lasciviousness.

Eddy and George were of this type. However, in July 1879, it
was time to leave the *Britannia*.

4

Bacchante
1879–82

In the summer of 1879, Prince Eddy was fifteen and a half and Prince George just fourteen, and nobody was quite sure what to do with them.

Early that year, it had been proposed (presumably by the Admiralty, where Mr W.H. Smith, the First Sea Lord, was susceptible to Bertie's prompting) that the princes should spend the next three years at sea. They would sail the world, continuing their education, visiting every accessible part of the Empire, broadening their outlook and learning naval discipline.

It is impossible to write a pithier summary of the controversy that followed than that contributed to history by the Queen's private secretary, General Sir Henry Ponsonby:

Plan proposed to the Queen who did not at all like it.

Dalton sent by the Prince of Wales to urge it. Queen's objections not pressed.

Unanimous condemnation by the Cabinet of the plan.

Indignation of the Queen and Prince at their interference.

Cabinet said they didn't. Plan adopted.

Controversies on the selection of the officers. The Queen supporting what she believed to be the Prince of Wales' choice. Sometimes it appeared he wished for others. Final agreement on the officers.

The *Bacchante* announced to be the ship. Who chose her, when and where I don't know.

Chorus of approbation.

Strong whispers against her. No stability. The Queen doubtful. The Prince of Wales doubtful. Dalton very doubtful – prefers *Newcastle*.

Smith furious, outwardly calm. Offers to turn over crew to *Newcastle* – an old ship full of bilge water. Sends report in favour of *Bacchante*.

Scott ordered to cruise in search of a storm so as to see if she will capsize.

Scott returns, says she didn't. Dalton not satisfied. Wants to separate princes.

Queen says this is what she first thought of but Dalton said it was impossible. Let him consult Prince and Princess of Wales.

Queen mentions doubts to Lord Beaconsfield.

B. observes he has been already snubbed – but if his advice is wanted, he will give it.

Knollys says Dalton is wrong.[1]

Knollys was Francis Knollys, Bertie's private secretary; Scott was Lord Charles Scott, Captain of the *Bacchante*; Beaconsfield was Benjamin Disraeli, then Prime Minister. By midsummer, everyone was heartily sick of the whole issue and Dalton (who had in a three-day courtship met, proposed to and been accepted by Hugh Evans-Thomas's sister) had resigned. No better plan having prevailed, it was settled: the boys would go to sea together. To attend to their private needs, they would take Fuller, the faithful 'nursery footman'.

Naval cadets who would accompany them included boys from the *Britannia* such as Arthur Limpus, Hugh Evans-Thomas, Rosy Wemyss, Lord Francis Osborne, the Hon. George Hardinge (who would one day be Viceroy of India) and Hillyard, the future tennis obsessive. To achieve appointment to the *Bacchante*, these boys had creditably 'passed out' – that is, done well in their final examinations on the training ship. 'Rosy' Wemyss, for instance:

> ...having done very well and obtained a second class in Mathematics and firsts in Extra Subjects and in Seamanship...He also gained ten months' promotion out of a possible twelve, by which he became a Midshipman two months after leaving the *Britannia*...[2]

The princes would for the moment join the *Bacchante* as cadets, and be promoted to midshipmen in due course. This was the beginning of George's formal training as a naval officer. Again, we do not know whether or not Eddy passed his exams. He would spend more time aboard on academic study with Mr Dalton, who was persuaded at the last minute to resume his post. In Neath, Miss Kitty Evans-Thomas would await his return.

During the regatta of 1879 at Cowes, the two princes stayed with the Prince and Princess of Wales and their three sisters, aboard the royal yacht *Osborne*. The marriage of Bertie and Alix had evolved into a pattern which seems to have suited them. Together, they entertained: at Sandringham in midwinter, in London in the spring, at Cowes in late July, and in Scotland for a few weeks in August or September. In the meantime, Alix spent a few weeks in spring with her brother in Athens and part of the summer in Copenhagen. Bertie vanished to the south of France in spring, and to a spa, usually Homburg, late in the summer. He also snatched weeks and weekends away, mostly in

Paris. He visited Lillie Langtry at the tactfully vacated homes of friends.

Langtry's stage career had not yet begun. She was merely a married 'beauty', among those women whose faces were popularised on a million Victorian postcards. She was neither titled nor an actress. She was simply the first 'official mistress'. She and Wales appeared together in the royal box at Ascot and were seen almost daily, riding in the park. Society hostesses knew that it was pointless to invite one without the other, and equally pointless to invite Alix, who preferred to remain with her court at Marlborough House. Oliver Montagu was a particularly devoted courtier, but no one ever seriously suspected an affair. So Alix, excluded by her deafness from the witty repartee and subtle flirtation of the London dinner party circuit, withdrew from it gracefully, but was always kind.

At Cowes, she invited the Langtrys aboard the *Osborne* for intimate Sunday dinner parties with the family, including her parents and sister, Princess Thyra. Langtry and her *mari complaisant* were put up on the *Helen*, Sir Allen Young's vessel, for, as her autobiography wryly points out: 'At the period to which my memory has taken me, Mr Langtry had sold his last remaining yacht…'.[3] They were both, as she admitted, fond of a little 'quiet squandering'. Another summer, Wales lent the couple the *Hildegarde*. Lillie Langtry was among the party that saw Eddy and George leave the *Osborne* for the *Bacchante* in the first week in August, and one might suspect that, like his father, Eddy had rather a crush.

> …There was a jeweller's shop in the High Street called Benson's, where we used to buy each other inexpensive presents. Being in Cowes when the two princes set off in the *Bacchante* for a voyage round the world, I gave a small trinket as a souvenir to the Duke of Clarence [his title was awarded much later]. The next day he showed it to me on his watch-chain, saying 'I had to take off my grandmother's [Queen Victoria's] locket to make room for it.'[4]

HMSS *Bacchante*, the warship in which they were to spend the next three years, was a 4,000-ton corvette, fully rigged as a sailing ship but with back-up engines. Not until the following year would they set off on their 'voyage round the world', for the first cruise was to be to the West Indies, via Madeira.

The *Bacchante* had to undergo further trial voyages in the English Channel, and the boys went with her. In London, at about this time, their father had met with yet another embarrassment, more serious than ever. A small magazine called *Town Talk* began to run stories about 'the Langtry divorce', in which, it alleged, Mr Edward Langtry was citing Lord Londesborough, Lord Lonsdale and the Prince of Wales. *Town Talk's* circulation rose like a rocket and the Prince could do nothing to stop it. He dared not appear in court. Alix's patience was not infinite; it was conditional upon her husband retaining his dignity in public. After a few fraught weeks, in which Bertie's temper was presumably at its most volatile, Alix took her sons away from the *Bacchante* to Denmark, for a quick visit to their grandparents before their first eight-month journey. When she returned with them to London, the *Town Talk* question remained unresolved.

Perhaps noticing a certain *froideur* at Marlborough House, the boys rejoined the ship on 18 September 1879. They were escorted by their father on the train to Portsmouth. 'I hear that the Prince of Wales snubbed Prince Eddy uncommonly', noted Sir Henry Ponsonby.[5] Bertie was going through a difficult time, but it was significant that Eddy should be the victim of his ill humour.

There had always been 'chaff', that kind of public ribbing which is aggression disguised as 'only joking'. What was it about his eldest son, whom he undoubtedly loved deeply, that so irritated Bertie? Eddy, by now much taller and slimmer than his brother, was always said to look like Alix, yet he had that round, soft 'hopeless chin', as James Pope-Hennessy unforgettably calls it, that can be seen in photographs of Bertie before he grew a beard. Was it the resemblance to Alix, or the resemblance to himself? Nothing about

Alix, excepting her chronic, incurable unpunctuality, ever angered their father. But there was something about the boy that Bertie recognised only too well. Eddy, like him, had slightly protuberant, heavy-lidded eyes and an oddly languorous quality. Bertie's physical and mental laziness had been a trial to his own parents, and as the Queen's admonitory tone towards him was a continual reminder of those deficiencies, he was perhaps over-anxious that his son should compensate for his own failings. If so, he was demanding too much and probably undermining the boy's self-esteem. One can see in his brusque dismissal of Eddy the attitude that underlay George's sniping at his brother, as well as Eddy's withdrawal. As a boy between the ages of about eight and sixteen, Eddy was diffident. He never said much when adults were around.

This diffidence could make a favourable impression. When the *Bacchante* finally set sail from Spithead, her first port of call was Gibraltar, in the second week of November. Lord Napier of Magdala, the island's governor, spent a few days' fox-hunting in Spain with the princes and wrote:

> The youngest is the most lively and popular, but I think the eldest
> is better suited to his situation – he is shy and not demonstrative,
> but he does the right things as a young gentleman in a quiet way.
> It is well that he should be more reticent and reflective than the
> younger boy.[6]

Whether for good or ill, Eddy was always being judged. The whole world seemed to be anxious about him; he bore, from birth, the almost impossible burden of becoming a figurehead for the nation.

The *Bacchante* proceeded on a short voyage across the Mediterranean to Sicily, where both boys were drawn about Messina in a carriage and Eddy climbed Monte Pellegrino alone with Lord Charles Scott, the captain. The ship returned to Gibraltar before setting out for Madeira and the Canary Islands.

Aboard ship, they messed with the other cadets and midship-men. The midshipmen, only a few years older in some cases than they were themselves, had of course been hand-picked, but no screening system is perfect, and by the time they reached Gibraltar for the second time one of them had proved unsuitable. Mr Dalton, Acting Chaplain, knew how to exercise influence when he must. Harold Nicolson writes in a footnote:

> The Senior Midshipman, Mr E L Munro, was not regarded by Mr Dalton as a fitting companion for the two princes. 'His almost feminine ways,' wrote Mr Dalton 'and silly over-deference to them induced them to take liberties with him which they should not.'[7]

Young Munro was 'invalided home' on 15 November.

Back in England, the editor of *Town Talk* had gone too far as well. Realising that the circulation-building, but entirely ficti-tious, Langtry divorce story had nowhere to go, he wrote that it had been dropped, Edward Langtry having been bought off with a diplomatic post abroad. This fabrication, at least (that Langtry had been bought off), was a criminal libel which could be proved without any court appearance by the Prince of Wales; and so it was. The editor was sent to prison for eighteen months and once again Bertie was saved from a serious 'scrape'.

On HMSS *Bacchante*, the princes shared quarters as before. Harold Nicolson describes 'a cabin on the port side under the poop; it communicated with that of Mr Dalton and con-tained two swinging cots and two sea chests'. Inevitably, over three years they would make friends, although Nicolson says that Mr Dalton was wary of influences other than his own, and 'discouraged any close familiarity, any partial preferences, any selective fraternisation'. The meals must have given them something to talk about. Sixty years later, Hillyard remembered the lack of fresh vegetables and the horrid food – mostly salt pork and ship's biscuit. George retained into later life, as an affectation, his old habit of tapping biscuits on the table to make the weevils fall out.

With the other cadets, they took classes in navigation and mathematics from Mr Lawless. The Assistant Paymaster was a Mr Sceales, who had been brought up in France and would assist them with their reading in that language. Physically, their training was tough and character-building. The entire crew were working as a team, and on their obedience and correct action men's lives might depend. They must learn to be sure-footed aloft on the rigging, to perform gun drill correctly and to excel at general seamanship. Idlers were not tolerated, and if Eddy had once seemed, as Alix put it, 'slow and dawdly', he had little opportunity for slacking now; when they were crossing the Atlantic, every minute of the day between half-past six in the morning and half-past eight at night was accounted for. In their few moments of private recreation, they had Kingsley's *Heroes* and *Westward Ho!*, among other books, to read.

They also kept diaries. George, at any rate, kept a diary from May of the following year (1880) until the day he died. Eddy is supposed to have done so, but almost all his records were included among the many royal papers later destroyed by Princess Beatrice and others. The impressions Eddy committed to paper on that voyage have been lost. Sarah Toohey, an early (1902) biographer of Alix, says he was 'at times a little homesick'.[8] We shall never know. Mr Dalton's job, once the princes had left the *Bacchante*, was to write an account of how they had spent their time abroad between 1879 and 1882, assembling and editing together everything his young charges had written. The resulting account of the *Bacchante*'s voyages took four years to produce and was, by common consent even at the time, ludicrously unlike any diary kept by teenage boys and certainly unlike anything produced by those two. It is voluminous, erudite, sometimes opinionated, and packed with meticulously researched facts. Its moral tone is elevated. However, it lets us know where the princes were on any given day, for which the biographer must be thankful. It is neither gossipy nor entertainingly aggrieved, but it does at least give the reader a sense of place, and is more readable than the 'got up – had porridge – still raining' catalogue of his entire life kept by George, of which Kenneth Rose wrote wearily 'it is idle… to sigh for the richer fare of a Pepys or a Creevey…'.[9]

Early in December, they were in Teneriffe, where they landed several times and toured the island in the carriage of a hospitable American resident. On 6 December, they left for the West Indies. By Christmas time, they had anchored in Carlisle Bay, off Bridgetown, Barbados, and were for the first time enjoying sights and sounds entirely new: palm-fringed beaches and beaming black ladies wearing startling colours, who were rowed out to the ship to sell fruit and trinkets. Wealthy families on every island vied with each other to offer dinners and dancing and excursions for the officers and especially, of course, the princes. Sometimes they went ashore and simply played cricket. Their royal parents were horrified to read in the newspapers that both boys had been tattooed on the nose. 'How could you have your impudent snout tattooed?' wrote Alix to George. The Prince of Wales was furious with Dalton, who wrote patiently back:

> The princes' noses are without any fleck, mark, scratch or spot of any kind whatever. The skin is as white as the day they left home.

A journalist had seen them emerging from the Botanical Gardens in Barbados with lily pollen on their noses.

One of the highlights of the season took place after a dinner at the governor's mansion in Trinidad, when the boys attended a ball given by Mr Leon Agostini.

> The ball began… amidst a fine display of festooned lights and parterres surrounded by negroes and mulattoes bearing coloured

lamps... But supper was not served until midnight was past, and then, in that supper-room in the cool garden where four hundred guests could be seated simultaneously, it came suddenly to mind that it was Prince Albert Victor's birthday and the customary toasts were drunk.[10]

On the next day, the birthday proper, the boys put on a show as 'Christy Minstrels' aboard the *Bacchante* and Eddy and George were rated midshipmen. They would wear patches, to distinguish them from cadets, on their mess jackets; their ordinary working dress was a short monkey jacket. Here, in the tropics, they wore white trousers.

Eddy was now sixteen. Aboard ship, and socially, he was expected to behave as a sober young man. His later letters show that he was sensitive to criticism, in most respects empathetic, and certainly emotional. This was a frightening time for him. During the boys' last year on the *Britannia*, they had lost an aunt and a cousin to diphtheria. Three people they knew on the *Bacchante* now died within two months: a sailor in a fall from the rigging at Barbados, Mr Sims, a schoolmaster, also at Barbados, and a stoker at Grenada. And then HMSS *Atlanta*, a warship with which they had been in port, left the West Indies within days of their own departure and was never seen again. The crew included midshipmen and cadets of their own age, whom they had met. Eddy was supposed to shake his head sadly and get on with life, like everyone else.

As far as his parents were concerned, he was still a child. Lady Waterford described a visit on 26 August 1880, before their third voyage on the *Bacchante*, to Highcliffe Castle on Christchurch Bay; one somehow imagines she is describing much younger boys.

I had a great surprise in the unexpected visit of the Prince and Princess of Wales with their two sons and the two little Princesses landing on the beach, coming up to tea, and drawing nets on the shore till evening – the young princes swimming about in flannels, and finally the Prince and his two sons swimming away to join the steam tug.[11]

Just a month before, his father had written to Queen Victoria that he and Alix were sure the boys would for a long time remain 'simple pure and childlike' and 'innocent'.[12] He undoubtedly meant it. How he imagined any boy of sixteen who had been in the navy since he was thirteen – and there were thousands like that – could remain entirely 'childlike', one does wonder. Eddy and George had been growing up away from home for the past two years and Bertie and Alix probably underestimated their children's maturity. Besides, there was a Victorian cult of childhood, a sentimental myth of innocence and purity – a pallid, saintly, ideal child like Little Nell or a defenceless little chimney sweep from *The Water Babies*. If the Waleses saw this myth challenged almost daily by streetwise ragamuffins in the Strand, they were perfectly capable of shutting out contradictions. Like the White Queen, and most of us, they could believe six impossible things before breakfast. Eddy, at sixteen, was expected to react like an obedient boy of twelve.

His later correspondence, and friendships, show that if he was never hard-headed, he was not a fool either. Yet, as far as we know, he did not do as well as his brother in the exams at the end of the cruise. According to the exasperated Dalton, he:

> ...sits listless and vacant... and wastes as much time in doing nothing, as he ever wasted... This weakness of brain, this feebleness and lack of power to grasp almost anything put before him, is manifested... also in his hours of recreation and social intercourse. It is a fault of nature...[13]

When they sailed back to Spithead in May, and the Prince and Princess, the three Wales girls and Prince Edward of Saxe-Weimar came aboard to lunch, Eddy's parents and Queen Victoria were still baffled by his lack of ambition or staying power. At least one writer has speculated that Eddy's vacancies were that kind of mild epileptic attack called *petit mal*.[14] With the benefit of hindsight, one may also surmise that his inertia could have originated in an anxiety state, which can result in

> ...feelings of being unreal or far away; paralysing weakness of the
> limbs; and a sensation of faintness and falling. If fear or anxiety goes
> on for a long time, even healthy people become tired, depressed,
> slowed down, restless, and lose their desire to eat.[15]

On the other hand, given the evidence of his letters as an adult, which show him to be as intelligent as most people, it is not outrageous to interpret his blockheadedness as a kind of mute rebellion. He was, after all, living an extraordinarily powerless life in which the only decision open to him was whether or not to comply with adult demands. If he chose not to, perhaps that is not surprising.

Did Eddy hear gossip about his father's peccadilloes? Maybe Dalton managed to isolate the boys while they were in his care. In any case, when they returned to England, Wales's affair with Lillie Langtry was ending. That spring the pair had been seen in Paris, indiscreetly kissing on the dance floor, shopping in the Rue de Rivoli for diamonds and buying frocks at Worth. But it seems that Lillie Langtry's affections had already been engaged elsewhere, by a man Eddy would come to know well.

Prince Louis of Battenberg was thirteen years younger than Bertie, and ten years older than Eddy. Bertie had always liked him. He was a polished young man who had been brought up all over Europe before joining the British navy at fourteen, having made up his mind to become a naturalised British subject; he had accompanied Bertie on the 1875 trip to India. Until last year, he had been an officer on the royal yacht *Osborne*, and was now awaiting a posting.

Queen Victoria insisted he be posted overseas because she wanted him out of the way, for she was suspicious of his attentions to her youngest daughter, Beatrice. This was not only because she disliked the idea that Beatrice would leave her, but because she considered Prince Louis a dangerous reprobate. He and his two brothers were good-looking men and as the eldest, the most cosmopolitan and the most notorious charmer, Prince Louis would have been a good catch but not at all an ideal husband.

Inevitably, Prince Louis met Lillie Langtry. Perhaps Bertie suspected an affair. In the summer of 1880, the relationship with his mistress grew difficult and at a private party Lillie Langtry went too far. She pushed ice cubes down Bertie's back. He would not be made a laughing stock. He left. It was over. For a few months, until a cooler friendship was restored, Langtry was dropped. News raced through society like a forest fire. Within days, the tradesmen knew, and began to chase unpaid Langtry bills.

Langtry's husband ('an uninteresting fat man')[16] was already a hopeless alcoholic. Her affair with Prince Louis either began in earnest, or continued.

While Eddy's father suffered the sad end of a love affair, in the summer of 1880 his sons sailed on the refitted *Bacchante* for a short training cruise to Bantry Bay and Vigo, with the combined Channel and Reserve Squadrons.

In September, the princes re-embarked, this time on a round the world voyage. The *Bacchante* was now part of the Detached Squadron, of which HMSS *Inconstant* was the flagship. Aboard the *Inconstant*, one of the officers was a member of their family: Prince Louis of Battenberg had at last received his long-awaited overseas posting.

As the squadron sailed down the Channel (the *Inconstant* would not return for two years), Lillie Langtry fell ill during a small dinner party at Marlborough House. She describes in her autobiography how kindly the Waleses treated her. Sir Francis

Laking, now the Physician in Ordinary, visited her at home the next day. Later, the Princess arrived alone, and could not have been nicer. Lillie was pregnant, and the baby would be Prince Louis's child. Bertie made out a cheque for £10,000 payable to her through his discreet friend, Sir Allen Young. She left for Jersey; she had the baby, Jeanne, in March or April of 1881; she would then return to London, and live alone in a small apartment in Ely Place.[17] Ely Place was where George Lewis, her solicitor, had his office, at numbers 10 and 11. He was the intimate friend and legal advisor to the Prince of Wales, indispensable to high society for his discretion in handling the consequences of their indiscretions.

Prince Louis of Battenberg was safely at sea. HMSS *Inconstant* accompanied HMSS *Bacchante*, *Tourmaline*, *Carysfort* and *Cleopatra* through terrible weather to Madeira and the Cape Verde Islands.[18] At the end of November, they 'crossed the line' for the first time, attended by the raucous ceremonial humiliations of King Neptune's Court, on their way to Montevideo. They were in Argentina for Christmas, and once again were invited everywhere, learning to play polo and throw the *bolas*, or lasso. At the Estancia Negretti, the estate of a British settler called David Shehan, Prince Louis, Eddy and George and Rosy Wemyss were playing polo when Rosy Wemyss was badly thrown and concussed, although he quickly recovered.

On Eddy's birthday in January, with the squadron due to leave for the Falkland Islands the following day, a grand ball was given by the British Ambassador at Montevideo. Everyone was on top form, especially the Ambassador, who had just become engaged to the Consul's beautiful daughter. The following day, the squadron left; they would sail south and, after a day or two in the Falklands, would round the Horn and travel north towards the Galapagos Islands.

The day after their departure, the Minister found in a jacket pocket a telegram, handed to him as he went onto the dance

floor with his bride-to-be on his arm, which in the heat of the
moment he had forgotten. It contained orders to the Admiral,
aboard the *Inconstant*, to head at once for South Africa.

The Boers of the Transvaal had declared a republic a few
weeks before Christmas and Sir George Colley, the High
Commissioner, had retaliated by descending upon them with
a force of 1,400 men. This was not enough. Unable to prevent
the settlers from invading and occupying Laing's Nek, on the
spectacular coast of Natal, Colley now required naval support.

But the squadron had gone; it was hundreds of miles away,
ploughing steadily through the South Atlantic. The only solution
was to send a fast gunboat in pursuit. HMS *Swallow* caught up
with the *Bacchante*, the *Inconstant* and the rest in the Falklands.
They set off within six hours for Cape Town, and arrived in
Simon's Bay on 16 February.

In London, the Queen was alarmed. She had instructed the
Admiralty that her two grandsons were not to be involved in
fighting. (Their father thought it might do them good. He lacked
experience of battle.) In the event, Eddy and George were non-
combatants, and were as usual invited to take excursions ashore.
They visited an ostrich farm and went to meet King Cetawayo
of the Zulus, nephew of the great Chaka. Photographs were
exchanged. Prince George wrote home to his parents:

> He himself is eighteen stone and his wives sixteen and sev-
> enteen stone; there are four of them. They are all very fine
> women, all over six feet.[19]

The naval reinforcements had arrived too late. The British were
defeated at Laing's Nek, and Sir George Colley died at Majuba Hill.
Still more ominous news arrived by telegraph: thousands of miles
away, the Russian Emperor, Alexander II, had been assassinated.

The squadron set out for Australia in April and the boys
resumed their disciplined lives as midshipmen, with rifle and

cutlass drill, climbing the rigging, the responsibilities of the watch and the tedium of Mr Dalton's instruction. Their waking hours were planned for them from six in the morning until eight or nine at night.

Dalton was not universally popular. As a chaplain and a royal tutor, he was treated with respect, lodged in comfort, invited to mess with the captain. The officers of the wardroom, however, did not care to have this opinionated parson thrust upon them. They thought him too zealous in supervising the leisure of his charges: a prig, a killjoy, a sneak – even a man who would not scruple to listen at keyholes. Dalton must have sensed such resentment and suffered accordingly.[20]

He had always had doubts about setting sail in the *Bacchante*. One hopes that he kept quiet and out of the way when disaster struck, which it did. A month out of Simon's Bay, a fierce storm blew up. In the *Inconstant* (a safer, more elegant ship altogether), Prince Louis on the middle watch could see by a full moon that:

> …the seas were parallel hills and vales, stretching to right and left as far as the eye could reach. They were so far apart that this long ship could run down one side and up the other, just keeping ahead of the seas which were continuously breaking astern of us.[21]

Separated from the rest of the squadron, over 300 miles from their destination, with a horrible 'sensation of grinding beneath the screw-well and counter and by the rudder chains',[22] the *Bacchante* ran out of control. Her rudder head had snapped in two in heavy seas. For the next three days, gales drove her south, towards the remote Antarctic. The next vast wave might swamp her, and the crew were alone. Lord Charles Scott and his senior officers must improvise a solution, and none presented itself.

> It was the Commander who stepped in to save the day, by making the men climb the rigging, spread out and effectively pull the ship

hard round. Thanks to this long and perilous manoeuvre she came before the wind.

The other four ships had arrived safe in harbour at King George's Sound near Albany in Western Australia, but nothing, publicly, had been said about the non-arrival of the princes. A fire was lit on a hilltop and the horizon was scanned with increasing anxiety. At last, the *Bacchante* was seen, far out, making the nautical equivalent of a trudge across open sea. Once they were safely on shore, Dalton led the prayer of thanksgiving.

Before them was a wild and beautiful landscape, and a small party, including Eddy and George, set off almost at once to shoot quail near a rarely used quarantine station. It was set amid resin-smelling woods, full of parrakeets amid trailing creepers, wild orchids and unnameable brightly coloured flowers. The next day, they arrived to stay at a farmhouse; the settlers must have been taken very much aback by their unscheduled arrival, but were wonderfully hospitable. Mr Dalton's voice booms out of the account published four years later as the original work of Eddy and George:

> Mr and Mrs Young, their two sons and two daughters, gave us a hearty welcome, and after taking a draught of warm fresh milk (of which there seems an inexhaustible supply all over the place), we walk up to the small shanty in which we are to stay. This consists of two rooms completely empty and with bare floors. Each, however, has a large open fireplace and plenty of jarrah wood stacked for use during the night. Two grand wood fires are already burning, bright and dry, such a contrast to what we have had for the last few weeks on board ship. A small two-wheeled cart that has brought our mattresses and rugs, and what few things we wanted for the night, has arrived before us, and we proceed at once to make our toilet in the open air, for there is plenty of fresh water in the tank outside and a small wooden trough does duty by turns for each

of the party. Bevis, a large kangaroo dog, a sort of huge, brown, Scotch greyhound, looks on as we make ourselves ready for Mrs Young's tea-supper, for which we return to the farmhouse, and there every one was very hearty and jolly, and did ample justice to the fowls, minced kangaroo, the jam, cream, scones, and no end of beautiful fresh milk and butter, such as we have not tasted since we left England...After tea found our way up across the paddock to our night-quarters, and there we slept as soundly as possible (nine in the two rooms), with the windows open and the fires burning. There are two pails of fresh milk, which some drink neat and others prefer to take mixed with a little whisky before turning in. Some fall asleep at once, others not so soon, the American doctor's cheery ringing laugh sounding long on the quiet night air, as he and the commander tell alternately the most astounding yarns, each with a *dénouement* more startling than the last. [23]

The *Bacchante* had to be repaired, so within a few weeks the boys had travelled along the coast so that a passenger mail boat could take them on to Adelaide. In Southern Australia, the boys and Mr Dalton were the guests of Sir William Jervois, the governor. Their aide-de-camp was Lt Jervois, one of his two sons, who took a small boat out to meet the royal party off the mail boat *Cathay*. The *South Australian Advertiser* noted:

Prince Albert Victor, the elder, stands nearly four inches higher than his brother, and is a fair-haired intelligent-looking youth, bearing a striking resemblance to his uncle Prince Alfred. His height, as far as could be judged, is about five feet seven inches, and his physique slender but well-proportioned... [The princes] were dressed alike, both wearing loose grey ulsters and small black hats...As the tug left the bigger vessel's side the passengers on board the latter gave 'three cheers for the royal princes' in a very hearty manner. [24]

There was more cheering when they got to the jetty, 'and the
two brothers, who seemed surprised to see so many people
awaiting their arrival, lifted their hats in response'.[25] The summer
of 1881 in South Australia, Victoria and New South Wales was to
be their first extended period of public prominence.

One suspects that interludes like the one at the Youngs' farmhouse would have been more fun than the many formal occasions
the boys were called upon to attend in the weeks that followed.
They had not been scheduled to visit Southern Australia, but
wherever they went the locals (immigrants of mainly British
origin) turned out in force. (The indigenous population were
either not present, or invisible to journalists; they are never mentioned). Busy, prosperous little towns and straggly collections of
shacks alike would put up bunting and greenery, arrange a dais,
line the streets, wave flags, present an address, hear the reply – and
then the visitors had gone. It was usually Eddy who replied to
the mayor's loyal address. Early newspaper accounts suggest that
his voice was painfully quiet; he could barely be heard. But as
these genuinely delighted people welcomed the royal visitors
so warmly, and as town followed town – and in some of them
the ten-minute stay lengthened to a couple of hours, including
a descent into a copper mine or a visit to a local school – he
seems to have gained in confidence. There were no complaints.
As to what he actually said, his few short sentences of thanks
were probably written by Mr Dalton.

Socially, there were balls and tennis parties and fireworks,
and introductions to young ladies. Eddy opened the National
Art Gallery in Adelaide. They attended the Theatre Royal, and
the Cathedral; there was a corroboree and a kangaroo drive, a
football match and a performance by a military band. And so
they moved on to Melbourne by train and carriage, with many
stops. They cut ribbons, planted trees, laid foundation stones.
They listened to school choirs and were greeted by Oddfellows
and jostled by crowds and ate umpteen luncheons in Railway

Hotels. They admired newly installed gas lighting in small towns, and typically:

> The whole of the local constabulary (six in number) under
> Superintendent Chambers, guarded the strip of carpet laid across
> the footpath, as at this season of the year the streets of Hamilton
> are a little muddy.

In the weeks to come, they moved east for hundreds of miles by carriage and yet more hundreds by rail. Mr Dalton was within feet of them at all times, and was only too delighted to talk to the press.

In Melbourne, a court martial opened on board HMSS *Tourmaline*. It should have taken place aboard the *Bacchante*, but could not in view of the repairs. According to *The Argus* of 24 June 1881:

> The prisoner, Robert Baker, is a first-class petty officer on board
> the *Inconstant*, and the charge first investigated was that he inde-
> cently assaulted Charles Edward Ralph, a first-class boy, on two
> separate occasions. Captain C P Fitzgerald, of the *Inconstant*, pre-
> ferred the charges against the prisoner.

Whether or not the case was proven, it offers a glimpse of a life beyond Dalton's worthy and mundane version of shipboard existence. There were passions, and unchecked emotions; there was bullying, theft, unhappiness. The *Bacchante* must have been relatively untouched by this, as only one sailor deserted in Australia. The squadron lost over 100 men altogether from the other four ships, seventy of them in Melbourne.

When the princes reached the Ballarat mines, their party was joined by most of the captains and chaplains of the other ships, as well as Prince Louis of Battenberg, whose light-hearted presence must have been a relief. Eddy was first into the cage

which would carry them down the mineshaft. Four hundred and
twenty feet below ground, having been instructed in the correct
handling of a pickaxe, he drank a loyal toast and listened to the
miners singing the National Anthem.

The local people and dignitaries of Melbourne went out of
their way to entertain the princes; there were more dinners,
balls, and crowds, a tour of a billiard table manufactory and
a gold mine, a day at the Caulfield Races and an afternoon
at Melbourne Cricket Ground, where Eddy laid a foundation
stone: this visit being

> ...made on short notice, otherwise the committee (who were
> not aware that the visit would take place yesterday until they read
> the announcement on the subject in the morning papers) would
> have provided for a full attendance of the members of the club.
> It was intended to have held a spectacular football match for
> the entertainment of their Royal Highnesses, and the four lead-
> ing clubs had undertaken amongst them to provide the requisite
> players for a match on Wednesday or Thursday. Owing to the
> detached squadron having to leave this week, and to there being
> very little time left at the disposal of the princes, the ceremony
> could not be delayed.[26]

The squadron had been in Melbourne for seven weeks and it
would now sail on to Sydney, with Eddy and George aboard
the *Inconstant*, while the *Bacchante* followed later.

There is rarely a note of derision in these local accounts; the
rulers were British, sent out from London, and most Australians
were proud of their British heritage. They wanted the future
King of England to understand their country and to appreciate
its true worth, culturally as well as financially. They were also
aware that they could not in practice forever be governed from
a country 14,000 miles away, and there was vague talk of a future
federation of the 'various branches of the scattered but united

British family'.[27] Five years before, Queen Victoria had declared herself Empress of India. The Australians had no intention of being the subjects of an Empress. At this time in the nineteenth century, many wanted to remain nominally British, without ever going 'home'.

Whenever, on their world tour, they reached land, the princes were transformed from midshipmen, with all the cold and poor food and instant obedience that implied, to creatures regally fêted and treated with deference. It is no wonder that every civilian who met them exclaimed at their humility.

As they approached Sydney, they had to prepare for their annual examinations. Sail drill was part of their training, and there was a gale blowing. They had been aboard the *Inconstant* for just two days when a sailor fell from the rigging and was killed. To midshipmen who had to climb this same rigging, which soared hundreds of feet into the sky, in every kind of weather, this must have been particularly horrifying.

A minor epidemic of smallpox was at its height in Sydney, but despite fears, their visit went ahead. Late in July, while Eddy and George were playing tennis at Government House, their Admiral suffered a stroke while on deck of the *Inconstant* waiting to have his picture taken. His convalescence meant that plans were changed yet again, and the squadron's departure for Brisbane was delayed. The princes were kept busy laying foundation stones and planting trees and visiting hospitals, amid crowds and processions and bands. They were shown around a railway carriage factory and the multilingual Prince Louis was entertained by Sydney's *Deutscher Verein*. Every day, Eddy and George were taken, usually with a party that included Prince Louis, to some beautiful mainland location, or race meeting, or farm; on most evenings there was a grand dinner or a ball, and on one occasion *son et lumière*, with a German choir. Electric light was still a novelty, and much appreciated by the crowds.

In the middle of August, the Admiral was well enough to travel to Brisbane, where the governor of Queensland was a relative; the entire squadron, this time including the *Bacchante*, to which the brothers returned, moved on. There they were received with acclaim, and the *Brisbane Courier* said Eddy looked like his mother 'as she appeared when first brought, a young girl, in state through the swarming streets of London':

> They are two pleasant-looking, gentlemanly lads, and… sit their horses in a manner that might advantageously be copied by many a young colonial who may be very good after scrubbers, but who has not paid attention to the elegancies of horsemanship.[28]

In Brisbane were more balls, trips into the countryside, speeches and a generally good time, usually accompanied by Prince Louis, who flirted with Miss Kennedy, the governor's daughter. Before leaving Australia, the princes took a day trip to Captain Cook's Landing Place in Botany Bay, where they sampled that quintessentially Australian institution, the barbie on the beach. A turkey, plucked and ready for the fire, was seized by a marauding dog, and Eddy seized a stick and led the chase to retrieve it. He succeeded, and the dog fled howling. It is a flaw in his character – a flaw, at least, to twenty-first-century urban eyes – that he never missed an opportunity of chasing and beating or killing dumb animals. All the men in his family and social circle were the same. They had been brought up to hunt. Like some Master of Foxhounds doting upon a tame fox (and there have been a few of those), Prince George cheerfully kept birds, a wallaby and a kangaroo at various times on board – yet sharks were shot out of the water and an albatross shot and skinned with glee.

Their journey home from Australia, which took almost a year, was vastly more exotic. It took them from Fiji, where they met another huge king, to Yokohama, slowly under sail, and thence to

Tokyo in October. There, they inspected troops – Prince Louis was amused to see that the Japanese soldiers carried bows and arrows as well as guns – and met the Mikado. In Tokyo, they really did get themselves tattooed; Eddy would forever have blue and red dragons writhing down his arms. The Mikado paid a return visit to the *Bacchante* with great ceremony, after which the squadron spent some days at Kobe. They sailed up the Yangtse, lived in a houseboat at Shanghai, shot and hunted, as they did everywhere, and were treated to an extravagant firework display in Hong Kong.

Prince Louis and the *Inconstant* were left behind in the Far East around Christmas time. The *Bacchante* sailed around the southeast of Asia, stopping briefly at Singapore, and in Ceylon Eddy missed seeing elephants being driven into a *kraal* because he was ill. The subcontinent was barely glimpsed before the princes were on their way from Aden to Ismailia, via the Red Sea; there, the Khedive of Egypt welcomed them as his guest, and placed his yacht the *Farouz* at their disposition for the journey up the Nile to Luxor. Everyone was anxious that the princes be impressed, and the Khedive certainly succeeded. They were also instructed *in situ* in the wonders of ancient Egypt. Rosy Wemyss accompanied the princes on the Khedive's yacht, and in later years

> ...used often to relate how one evening after dinner, when play-
> ing whist, news came to Brugsch Bey (the archaeologist aboard)
> that a tomb was being excavated which was hoped might be that
> of the Pharaoh Rameses, which he was keen the princes should
> discover. Throwing down their cards, they jumped upon donkeys
> and raced in the moonlight over the desert, only to realize, after
> digging hard, that the find was an uninteresting one – but the fun
> had been the same.[29]

Arthur Sullivan, an occasional visitor to Sandringham, was at Sir Edward Malet's embassy in Cairo when they arrived there in March, and met them.

We played riotous games and separated at midnight. The Princes enjoyed themselves very much, were in riotously high spirits, and knocked me about a good deal. I was in good spirits myself.[30]

On went the princes: to the Holy Land, as it was then called, and to Athens, where they visited Uncle George and Aunt Olga and their cousins, and on across the Mediterranean. When the *Bacchante* drew close to the English coast, Eddy had 'seen the world' and, just as importantly, smelt it, and experienced it as he never could have done had he spent his time in any other way. The impromptu donkey race across the Egyptian desert could not have happened had he and his brother been so fussed over by their tutor as they were when they set off. Perhaps they had learned to escape Dalton's dominance in the few months they had been able to spend with Prince Louis.

In the summer of 1882, Eddy was eighteen and a half, and still enjoying Mediterranean sunshine, when the British government intervened to wrest control of Egypt – and the Suez Canal – from a military dictatorship. HMS *Inconstant*, fresh from India, bombarded Alexandria. The newly promoted Lieutenant Prince Louis landed in command of a battery of Gatling guns and helped to occupy the city.

The *Bacchante* sailed on towards England, where the Prince of Wales was pleading to be sent to Egypt in command of a military force. Bertie, fat and volatile and without military experience, was rejected out of hand, although many of his army friends were despatched to lead troops; Oliver Montagu went, and Lord Charles Bereford was particularly heroic. The British finally seized victory at the battle of Tel el Kebir.

5

Student Prince
1882–85

The Wales boys were never at a loose end. They had been back in England for only three days when their grandmother whisked them into Whippingham Church for confirmation by Dr Tait, the Archbishop of Canterbury. Eddy would, after all, one day be head of the Church of England. Besides, this Archbishop was in poor health (he would pass away before the end of the year).

And then what? The boys were to be separated, but not yet. Their parents were delighted to see them, but the voyage had not given Eddy, who would eventually follow his father as heir apparent, that cosmopolitan polish that one looked for in a European prince. Once again, he and his brother were packed off to improve themselves. This time, they would spend six months in Lausanne with Mr Dalton (who does not seem to have objected, as his long engagement became even longer),

Mr Lawless from the *Bacchante*, and Monsieur Hua, their French teacher from the *Britannia*. Mr Lawless taught mathematics and navigation. Perhaps George required extra tuition before rejoining the navy in the spring.

They stayed at the Hôtel Beau Rivage at Ouchy, near Lausanne. From this glorious lakeside hotel, they went for walks, visited the theatre and played bezique. As for their classes, at first Eddy made progress, and Monsieur Hua was a good teacher (he would be at Eton later, and would twenty years later teach George's children), but by the time they departed in June 1883 Dalton had returned to his familiar refrain about Eddy's lassitude.

They were eighteen and nineteen years old. One imagines that they made some kind of life for themselves beyond bezique with middle-aged tutors; but over the nature of that life, history – or at any rate George's diary – draws a veil.

Their father, during their absence in the *Bacchante*, had broadened his own outlook. Lillie Langtry had a baby daughter to bring up, and was now concentrating on her stage career, which would soon take her to America. Her rejected swain devoted more time and thought to political matters.

The early 1880s was a time of increasing strain between Ireland and the government. English absentee landlords expected steadily increasing rents, but, encouraged by Charles Parnell, a charismatic MP, many Irish tenants banded together and withheld the money, in an effort to renegotiate terms. In retaliation, troops and police evicted hundreds of poor families from farms. They literally turned people out into the country lanes and pulled their houses down. Radical Dublin papers reported that frail grandparents and small children had been left destitute and protestors jailed. As living symbols of the ruling class, the royal family were even less popular in Ireland than they had been in England in the early seventies. There had been a bungled attempt on the Queen's life, not a Fenian attempt[1] but none the less threatening for that, in March of 1882, while Eddy and George were enjoying spring sunshine in the Middle East.

The Prince of Wales discounted Irish discontent. The Irish
Question annoyed and puzzled him, and as Disraeli had died in
1881, he feared that Gladstone's Home Rule sympathies might
prevail. Parnell had been jailed and was now free. Bertie had no
solution beyond increased use of force, no empathy with the
peasantry of Ireland. His great strength lay not in his intellect or
understanding, but in his social adroitness. He managed to remain
on cordial terms with both Henry Labouchère, the wealthy
republican editor of *Truth*, and with Charles Dilke, who in 1873
had demanded that the House declare a republic forthwith. He
liked them, and made use of them. Labouchère's wife, Henrietta,
coached Lillie Langtry before her first stage appearances. Bertie
met the radical Dilke, who was now an under-secretary at the
Foreign Office, for the first time in 1880, and got on with him
well. They were both men of the world – that is, they were capable of keeping certain areas of their lives separate, and clandestine
– and, besides, Dilke was a more forthcoming source of diplomatic intelligence than Granville, with whom Bertie had never
felt at ease since he discovered that Granville routinely withheld
documents from him on the Queen's instructions.

Dilke liked the Prince well enough and was always ready to do
his bidding, within limits discreetly made clear to him by his superiors. The government was much exercised, around 1882 when the
princes returned from their world tour, by suspicions that Russia
was plotting to invade Afghanistan, which was strategically pivotal
to British interests in India, Persia and, ultimately, Suez; one day
Dilke was asked to travel down to Dover with the Prince of Wales
– the only spare time he had, on his way to make a royal inspection
of the Channel Tunnel works – so that Dilke could show him a
map of Central Asia and explain what was going on.[2]

In the view of Dilke, who liked him, Bertie late in 1882 was

...readily agreeing in the Queen's politics, and wanting to take
everything everywhere in the world, and to keep everything if

possible; but a good deal under the influence of the last person
who talks to him, so that he would sometimes reflect the Queen
and sometimes reflect me, or Chamberlain, or some other Liberal
who had been shaking his head at him. He has more sense and
more usage of the modern world than the Queen, but less real
brain power. He is very sharp in a way...[3]

In exasperation, the following year, he wrote 'he seems not to
listen and to talk incessantly except when he is digesting'.[4] They
remained friends, however. In the first few months of their
acquaintance, Dilke, the keen republican, had almost despaired of
Bertie's French royalist sympathies, noting that the Prince seemed
to believe everything he read in *Le Figaro*. It was Dilke who introduced him to more radical French viewpoints, even arranging a
breakfast meeting between Bertie and Gambetta at the Moulin
Rouge one morning in 1881. It went off most cordially. With
precious little encouragement from his mother, Bertie was doing
his best to understand what was going on.

Eddy and George returned from Lausanne in June 1883, not
much changed, George to begin a naval career in earnest and
Eddy to enter Trinity College, Cambridge, in October as a 'pen-
sioner'. Eddy must first travel to Balmoral, where the Queen
would invest him with the Order of the Garter; surely he must
have wondered what he had done to deserve it? And yet the
honours heaped upon royal personages for no better reason
than an accident of birth were taken for granted everywhere.
Very few people questioned the fundamentals of the aristocratic system. As an illustration of this, one may cite Henry
Broadhurst's account of his visit to Sandringham in December
of the following year.[5]

Bertie had (thanks to Dilke) been made chairman of a Royal
Commission on Housing of the Working Classes. He took a
genuine interest in this subject, which had been dear to Prince
Albert's heart, and as usual learned not by reading, but by listening

and talking to as wide a section of articulate opinion as possible. Broadhurst, a 'radical' Member of Parliament on the Commission, was a former stonemason. In the 1840s and 1850s, he had travelled from town to town in possession of a mason's card and in search of work. He had helped build the Houses of Parliament, St Thomas's Hospital and the Albert Hall. He understood, from experience, the problem confronting working people in search of decent accommodation, and it had not much changed when he wrote about it at the turn of the century:

> A man who earns 30 shillings a week has to pay about a fifth in rent. His travelling expenses to and from his work will usually amount to another shilling, so there he is with seven shillings a week the first and inexorable charges on his income, leaving only 23 shillings to meet all the requirements of his family – food, clothes, medicine, coal, club, amusements, charity and contributions to his place of worship. Add to this the period of non-employment during which rent must be paid just the same and it will be admitted that the question of rent in the large urban centres is one of the gravest and most difficult problems the social reformer has to face.[6]

This sort of thing, not to mention the starving tenants he was taken to see in London slums, must have come as a blast of icy water to the Prince of Wales, whose debts at times exceeded a million pounds. He invited the entire Commission to Sandringham for further discussion, but Broadhurst had to decline. MPs received no remuneration and he survived frugally on the £150 a year he was paid as a union official, which left nothing to spare for the demands of a house party.

What happened next illustrates not only Bertie's charm, but the hand-wringing obsequiousness of a late-Victorian working-class radical. When such deference was accorded them by such people, how could the royal family ever seriously have worried about being overthrown?

Hearing that I made it a rule not to dine out, and that I did not possess a dress-coat, the Prince of Wales renewed his invitation... (assuring) me that arrangements would be made during my stay at Sandringham to meet my wishes and insisted upon booking dates there and then... I spent three days at Sandringham with the Prince and Princess and I can honestly say that I was never entertained more to my liking and never felt more at home when paying a visit than I did on this occasion... On my arrival HRH personally conducted me to my rooms, made a careful inspection to see that all was right, stoked the fires... In order to meet the difficulties in the matter of dress, dinner was served to me in my own rooms each night.

We walked and talked, and inspected nearly every feature of the estate, including the stables, the kennels, and the dairy farm... The Princess herself, with characteristic graciousness, showed me over her beautiful dairy... The Prince took an evident pride in the beauty and comfort of the homes of his people, and I was particularly struck by the scrupulous courtesy of His Royal Highness in obtaining permission from the housewife before crossing the threshold.[7]

He explains that plenty of country landowners would just walk in. Wales took him into the village 'club' (a pub in all but name, with a limit on what you could drink), where they drank their half-pints of ale alongside farm labourers.

I must add that during my stay I had several conversations with the late Duke of Clarence and the present Duke of York, and found in both a total absence of affectation or haughtiness.[8]

Dilke would note in 1883: 'Completed my Royal Commission with fewer fools on it than is usual on Royal Commissions'.[9] Broadhurst was not a fool. Despite the Queen's and Alix's efforts to set an ordinary, cosy, homely example, the life of the royal family was so vertiginously elevated from the average that it could dazzle almost anyone.

At Balmoral for his investiture in the summer of 1883, Eddy endured a pre-university lecture from his grandmother. It was at this time that her private secretary, Sir Henry Ponsonby, speculated that Eddy might be somewhat deaf. (Yet again, one suspects that Eddy had taught himself to switch off anything he felt might be dull: literally not to hear it.) Otherwise, Ponsonby said: 'he is pleasing, talks well, and will be popular when he gets more at his ease'.[10] Alix received an equally favourable report from the Queen after the pep talk, which must have been a relief after Dalton's constant complaints about Eddy's 'indolence and inattention'. She wrote to Victoria that she was 'glad you didn't allude to the other things you were going to mention such as races, clubs etc. as he really has no inclination that way and it might only have put them into his head besides placing his father in rather an awkward position'.[11] How true.

Every effort was made to ease the transition between the navy, life in Lausanne, and Trinity. Once again, Eddy's associates were carefully selected from the top drawer. They included fewer aristocrats than before, and more high-achieving, academic sportsmen. Eddy would spend the summer being 'crammed' with information, so that he could at least understand what was going on when he got to Cambridge. There was a house called Bachelor's Cottage overlooking the lake at Sandringham; it offered quite ordinary accommodation for half a dozen young men intent upon study, and Eddy and his companions moved in. With Dalton, of course – and perhaps Fuller. And J.K. Stephen as his tutor. Stephen was one of the family which would produce Virginia Woolf, *née* Stephen. Still in his twenties, he was a good-looking homosexual of great charisma, but failed to keep every member of the company enthralled at Sandringham. Dalton wrote to George, at sea on HMS *Canada*, on 7 July 1883:

> I never felt so dull in my life. I shall be glad when our time is up. We miss your voice so at meals: they all sit round the table and eat and never say a syllable. I never knew such a lot...[12]

What an old woman he sounds. The others were a naval lieutenant (apparently Henderson from the *Bacchante*, who was injured
'and therefore here', according to a letter from Stephen), 'the son
of the Earl of Strathmore' (Patrick Bowes-Lyon), and 'a lively
little Frenchman', probably Monsieur Hua.[13] J.K. Stephen wrote
to a friend that Prince Albert Victor was

> ...a good-natured, unaffected youth, and disposed to exert himself
> to learn some history... We lead a quiet and happy reading-party
> sort of life with all the ordinary rustic pursuits. I have a fat and
> speedy nag all to myself, and I give him plenty to do.[14]

According to J.E.Vincent, his first biographer, Eddy had always
been interested in history and genealogy and 'had a singularly
retentive memory'. Allowing that this may be an exaggeration,
it is usual that members of the royal family take an interest in
history and genealogy; these are, after all, the keys to their existence. The silence at mealtimes could have had something to do
with one man's lowering presence. Dalton, wrote Stephen, has
a tendency to 'depreciate himself and others'.[15] The poor man
probably felt inadequate. He had spent fourteen years teaching
Eddy and, by common consensus, should have achieved more.
He was now edged out of his pedagogic role by a younger, less
pompous man, and left to write up the *Cruise of HMS Bacchante*
('the end bedroom I use for a writing room for the book').

Stephen invited his friends H.C. Goodhart and H.L. (Harry)
Wilson to join them. All three were in their early twenties, fit
and academically bright. Stephen himself was keen on amateur
dramatics. At least one slight account remains of a performance
he gave just weeks before he came to Sandringham.

That summer a marriageable, self-possessed American girl,
Maud du Puy, who eventually became Gwen Raverat's mother,
had arrived from West Philadelphia, Pennsylvania, to visit academic relations at Cambridge. In May or June, the relations took

Maud to London, to see a play at Lady Freke's. Lady Freke had a vast house in the Cromwell Road, where she held *tableaux vivants* and amateur plays; Lillie Langtry had appeared in productions here before her first professional engagement. Here, in the middle of Raverat's delighted quotation from her mother's letter, one meets J.K. Stephen in a social setting:

> Gladstone, Sir Isaac Newton [*sic*], Sir Frederick Leighton and some other great codger sat immediately in front of us. [*Query: who can Sir Isaac Newton have been?*] Gladstone looks exactly like caricatures of him... Sir F. Leighton had charge of the scenic effects and succeeded very well, only all the rouge and powder and Greek dresses could not make perfect beauties of the English girls. The play was called *The Tale of Troy*, and this night was spoken entirely in Greek. [*Of which, of course, she knew not a word.*] Mr Stephen [*J K Stephen*] was Hector and acted remarkably well. Lionel Tennyson as Ulysses would have been better had he known his part... [Italicised notes in square brackets are Raverat's][16]

Stephen was an extraordinary man, but it seems Dalton did not bring out the best in him. However, he came to share Dalton's opinion about one matter at least. As the start of term drew closer, he was not quite as sanguine about Eddy's potential as he had been at the start, and wrote to Dalton:

> I do not think he can possibly derive much benefit from attending lectures at Cambridge... He hardly knows the meaning of the words *to read*.[17]

That may have been the problem. Dalton's method of teaching had been catechistic: that is, he had asked questions and expected 'correct' answers, previously taught. Learning to read – really read, that is, to spend hours alone lost in a book – requires example and solitude, and is best picked up in childhood. Bertie and Alix did not read, so set no example. And solitude there had never been. From their earliest years, Eddy and George had been encouraged literally to fraternise: to spend time together as brothers. When they were not together, some relation or courtier or superior officer, lesson or journey or spectacle had claimed their attention. They may have had a few hours to spare on board ship, in which to read adventure stories. This was insufficient preparation for Trinity College, Cambridge.

Anyhow, Eddy went up to the University on 17 October, escorted once again by his father, as though he might otherwise escape. He had rooms 'on the top floor of the last staircase at the left-hand side of Nevile's Court as one faces the Library'.[18] On the ground floor 'at first was Mr Henderson, a naval friend of the Prince, and later Mr P. Bowes-Lyon. Halfway up the staircase were the rooms of Professor Stuart.' Mr Dalton occupied himself in writing about the *Bacchante*, because he had rooms in Nevile's Court too; nicer ones apparently than Eddy's, because they were cluttered with souvenirs of the voyage.

All this we know from the account of Mr J.E.Vincent, written in 1893. Vincent goes on to tell us that Eddy enjoyed occasional lectures in history and English literature; that he was 'quite properly' excused exams; that he had a tutor, Mr Prior; and that J.K. Stephen assisted in directing his reading. He was a member of the Amateur Dramatic Club 'and patronised its performances', although there is no mention of his having acted. He joined the Rifle Volunteers (he was a keen shot) and went to concerts. A 'fellowship of kindred spirits' – all men – is shown in a photograph. There is Eddy, and central is J.K. Stephen in his white floppy hat, with a pipe. He and his younger friends apparently enjoyed 'picking out airs upon the pianoforte'.[19]

Professor Stuart was a Fellow of Trinity who occupied rooms below Eddy's in Nevile's Court, and now he gained a seat in Parliament on a radical ticket. He was nonetheless impressed by his royal neighbour.

Though somewhat stiff and slow in his manner, he had yet a keen perception of what was necessary to put people at their ease. When I stood for the undivided Borough of Hackney in 1884, I pledged myself to vote against any further increase of grant to the Royal Family, and in particular against the grant which was then mooted to the Prince himself on coming of age. When I returned to Cambridge after my election, the Prince came into my room – exactly as before – and I noticed how, with a little awkwardness, and yet with such evident good feeling, he strived to let me see that my pledge, to which he somewhat slyly eluded, made no difference to his friendliness.[20]

Another, much younger man was to become Eddy's good friend in difficult circumstances later. This was a godson of Dalton's, who happened to visit Cambridge on the last Saturday of the winter term. Alfred Fripp, a medical student, was visiting his sister Jeanie at Girton, and took the opportunity to call upon his godfather at Trinity, noting in his diary:

> …introduced to Prince Edward before lunch with Mr Image and John Dalton – excellent champagne lunch.[21]

Mr Image was probably the Reverend William Thomas Image, who had graduated from Trinity thirty years before and had connections with both Norfolk and Windsor. He almost certainly would have been Dalton's guest rather than Eddy's. Alfred Fripp was a year younger than Eddy, and had been ploughed in his scholarship exam for Guy's – but was able to take the time to cram, thanks to a cheque from his indulgent cousin Sarah. Evidently they found plenty to talk about.

There were, of course, no women. No women anywhere, not even servants. Women of one's own class were part of another, less monastic life; the women of Girton were 'bluestockings' –

hardly female at all. Relations between the sexes, for a young man brought up as Eddy had been, were probably less excruciatingly painful than they would have been had he spent his adolescence at a public school. All the same, he was given little opportunity to make friends among girls of his own age and social class.

Most middle-class girls would have made impossibly embarrassing companions. Thanks to Gwen Raverat, we know what the young ladies of Cambridge, at least, were like. In the summer of 1883, Miss Maud du Puy wrote home:

> The English girls are so awfully susceptible; if a man speaks to them almost, they instantly think he is desperately in love with them.[22]

Addressed by a good-looking prince, they would have fainted dead away.

Eddy's studies at Trinity, such as they were, were interrupted by the demands attendant upon his position. Poor, sickly Prince Leopold, Bertie's youngest brother, died at Cannes in the spring of 1884, and Eddy was among the mourners. Dressed in the uniform of a naval sub-lieutenant, he was among the band of European royalty who accompanied the body from Portsmouth to its final resting place in St George's Chapel.

Notwithstanding – or perhaps because of – many interruptions and distractions, Eddy seems to have been happy at Trinity. For the first time, he went to dinner parties, played whist and made friends without Dalton or his brother. Dalton was present quite often; but not always. Perhaps it was Dalton who tried to protect Eddy from the pervasive agnosticism of academe, by introducing him to Oscar Browning's Sunday evening 'at homes'. Browning, the schoolmaster who had left Eton under a cloud many years before, was at least prepared, as he put it, 'to fwighten the agnoggers'.[23]

That this attitude was rare in Cambridge is shown in another entertaining letter to America from Maud:

The English service is so long; they repeat always two creeds and the Lord's Prayer three and often four times, and they never combine the Royal Family in one prayer, but always there is one for Victoria and then another for the Prince of Wales... I think I shall go to the chapel hereafter. They have a short service, no sermon and good music. The college people never go to any of the churches. Aunt C made GD [George Darwin, academic, son of Charles and later husband of Maud] go to chapel for the first time for a dozen years on Sunday. She says he is what they call an argonaist [sic]. I think that is the word. [*Agnostic?*] But it means an infidel who does not try to make other people infidels. So many of the people here are that kind. They, or at least a few, go to chapel, but only for the music.[24]

Browning gave cheerful, noisy, harmless Sunday evening musical parties, although as E.F. Benson noted, he did tend to make pets of those undergraduates who were handsome and attractive. He was also hilariously snobbish.

The really outstanding figure of that time, not among the dons of King's only, but of the whole of Cambridge, was Oscar Browning: he would have been notorious and absurd and remarkable any-where, and if he had ever succeeded in getting into Parliament he must have made a mark of some unusual kind there, as surely as he had made it everywhere else... He was a genius flawed by abysmal fatuity. No one had finer gifts than he: he could think on big lines, he could strike out great ideas, he had wit, he had the power of planning largely and constructively, he had courage and a high scorn of ridicule, it was impossible to come into contact with him without being conscious of great intellectual force. But it was impossible not to be aware that he was a buffoon... His snobbishness was of a really remarkable order: it was impossible not to respect a quality of such fire and purity, for, although already waddling with obesity, he took to playing hockey simply for the pleasure of being swiped over the shins by HRH Prince Edward of Wales when he was an undergraduate at Trinity… Came the end of [the summer] term, he went up to London for a month, taking lodgings as nearly as possible opposite Marlborough House.[25]

In June, Alfred Fripp, the medical student, visited his godfather again, this time for five days. On 9 June, his diaries tell us, he breakfasted with Eddy, Lord Charles Beresford and Mr Dalton, and went with them to a large ball that evening. They danced until half-past four. Next morning, Eddy had breakfast with him and Dalton, and Fripp recorded in his diary 'dined and spent evening in HRH's room – *tête à tête* for two hours with him, very good sort of fellow'. The following day, they again had breakfast and went to the Trinity College dance that evening, the last of his visit. By now Eddy's circle of acquaintance had grown, and he knew some girls; he was a regular attendee at Mrs Jebb's lawn tennis parties and would spend happy summer evenings lazing with friends in punts on the Backs. The Jebbs were Gwen Raverat's Uncle Dick and Aunt Cara. Mrs Jebb was a remarkable woman, an American who was always alive to the matchmaking possibilities of any social situation, so there would certainly have been plenty of nice young women, albeit painfully shy and awkward English ones, and 'she could always draw confidences from a heart of stone. Or, at least, from a man's heart of stone.'[26]

Eddy was being allowed to grow up, and he had time at last to reflect on his own feelings. Sir Lionel Cust, art expert and courtier, was of the same family as Harry Cust (later editor of the *Pall Mall Gazette*, and heir to Lord Brownlow), who was among Eddy's circle; another Cust was Charles, who was at that very moment on board ship with George. Lionel remembered in his autobiography half a century later:

…one summer day in 1884, when, while I was on a visit to Trinity College, Cambridge, circumstances made me spend a few hours

alone with the young Prince. During that period the Duke [ret-
rospectively, Eddy is referred to as the Duke of Clarence and his
mother as Queen] and I became quite confidential in discussing
various members of our respective families, and the Duke told me
of his devotion to his mother… from whom he inherited much
which, had he lived, would have perhaps gone to a nation's heart
and won it as Queen Alexandra had done herself. He confessed,
however, to being rather afraid of his father, and aware that he was
not quite up to what his father expected of him.[27]

Queen Victoria astutely remarked that some people (and she felt
Bertie was one of them) work hard only under pressure. She was
right about Bertie; when, at last, he succeeded, he was not the
sporting wastrel so frequently discounted by the government,
but a diplomatic asset. He could put his mind to something if
he chose. That was the key to Eddy, too. He who so notoriously
reacted with 'indolence and inattention' could spend long evenings concentrating on the complexities of whist, and furiously
energetic afternoons playing hockey or lacrosse, because these
things mattered to him.

If nothing other than games, hunting and cards seemed particularly important, perhaps nothing much was. Eddy's father
still stood between him and the throne. His time would be
organised for him, whatever preferences he might express; and
he expressed none. Maybe he got slapped down if he did. When
Lionel Cust met Eddy at Trinity he was twenty years old, the
age at which a bride had been sought for Bertie. Eddy's parents
still treated him as a child. They were not alone among their
class in this respect. Daisy Brooke, Lady Warwick, later opined
that everyone in that set kept their children young for as long as
possible, 'for the younger generation, we knew, would date us'.[28]
Eddy's brother George was a young officer at the Royal Naval
College, Greenwich, in the summer of 1884 and the following
instructions were given to his mentor, Admiral Currey:

> It is His Royal Highness's wish that Prince George should not leave the neighbourhood of the College except to join in such sports as are undertaken by the members of the College as a body – or on the occasions when he will go from Saturday until Sunday evening to visit at such places as will be especially approved by the Prince of Wales (of which you will be notified), and His Royal Highness hopes that you will accompany Prince George at these times – unless some well-known friend is accompanying him...
> It will not be advisable that Prince George should accept any invitations to balls, dinners &c., while he is studying at the College without the sanction of HRH the Prince of Wales...[29]

No doubt Eddy's movements were similarly monitored, but he does not seem to have rebelled.

This, in any case, was the summer when Dalton finally left his side. At forty-five, he had been appointed Canon of St George's Chapel, Windsor, a post he would retain for the next forty-seven years, becoming Domestic Chaplain to Queen Victoria, King Edward VII and King George V. He did not marry the patient Kitty right away; perhaps their accommodation needed work. They would live in the Canon's House in the Cloisters at Windsor, a generously sized dwelling overlooking Eton, the Home Park and the river. Two more years passed before, in 1886, they were united in holy matrimony and the *Cruise of the Bacchante* was published to polite applause.

At the end of the summer, Eddy was packed off to Heidelberg to improve his German. While there, he corresponded with Harry Wilson, who gave him news of his – Eddy's – cat, and mutual friends, and wrote cheerful doggerel to entertain him. Lord Dupplin went to see him; he was an old reprobate, a friend of Bertie's whose only claim to fame was that he 'invented the dinner jacket'.[30] He was in the habit of lending his rooms (on the corner of Albemarle Street and Piccadilly) to the Prince of Wales for discreet liaisons.[31] His was an unexpected visit, the significance of which is hard to understand, but maybe he was at Homburg and deputising for the Prince of Wales. Eddy travelled back and forth to London as usual. On 10 August, the *Pall Mall Gazette* reported:

> Prince Albert Victor of Wales, who has been studying of late at Heidelberg University, will, it is reported, leave on Saturday, and will return to Heidelberg at the end of the vacation in order to resume his studies. The popularity of the Prince in the town was shown a few evenings ago by a serenade given to him by the Heidelberg Choral Society. The Prince, who expressed his great personal gratification at the charming music he had heard and at the honour done him, desired the serenaders to oblige him, in conclusion, with the *Wacht am Rhein*, a request which was naturally responded to with enthusiasm.[32]

His twenty-first birthday party, early in 1885, was spent at Sandringham. A group photograph taken in the grounds shows a dark, handsome young man, a head taller than the rest of the family, smiling directly at the camera from beneath a jaunty bowler hat. His father and George are wearing the same kind of hat, but while George slouches in tweeds and his father looks massive in a cape, Eddy is smart and townified in a high collar and a thick black raglan coat.

A week later, he was still there, and writing thank-you letters on engraved paper; there is a fashionably art-nouveau look about the stylised initials in an oblong panel – a tall serif E, with a C and a curly AV (for Albert Victor Christian Edward) inside. He wrote to his cousin Prince Louis:

Sandringham

Tuesday January 13th/85
My dear Louis
It was very good of you and Victoria to send me such a charming present for my birthday, for which I thank you both very much.

You may be sure it will remind me of our long cruise together and the many pleasant hours we spent in each other's company.

It is needless to say how many presents I had. I do not think I ever received so many before. Some will be most useful to me later on in life.

I was very sorry that neither you nor Victoria could come here for the festive week, as we really had a very pleasant party. Strange to say, all the relations got on wonderfully well together, and everything went off without a hitch. I had no end of addresses and deputations to receive, and I think it would have amused you to have heard some of them, as several of the old fogies could hardly read a word from nervousness. I must say I felt a bit nervous myself at first, but it gradually passed off. Then I had to return thanks to uncle George for proposing my health at dinner, which was a bit trying. We had the two expected balls which were a great success. The first night one wore uniform and I must say it looked very smart, quite like a court ball. The second was the tenants' ball which I really enjoyed most as we wore evening dress with red coats. The next day being Saturday, we had a lawn meet which was rather pretty as a great many people came first. But we had no sport although we found three foxes, which did great credit to our coverts. I have got some photos and will send you one, if you care to have it.

I have no end of letters to write, so excuse this not being longer.

I am going over to Osborne on Saturday so perhaps may see you at Portsmouth.

With best love to Victoria.

Believe me ever your affecte

Eddy [33]

Prince Louis had married Victoria of Hesse in Darmstadt nine months before. The Hesse girls had been brought up largely by an English governess, Miss Jackson – their mother, Bertie's sister Alice, having died of diphtheria in 1878.

The wedding day of Louis and Victoria had not been without its tensions.[34] The widower Grand Duke of Hesse, father of the bride, had a mistress, Madame Alexandra de Kalomine. Everyone except Queen Victoria knew about this, and they all trooped off to the wedding, dreading that once the Queen found out there would be a fearful fuss, for Mme Alexandra was a Russian divorcée. On the night of his daughter's wedding to Prince Louis, the Grand Duke quietly married Madame de Kalomine. The Empress of Prussia (Queen Victoria's eldest daughter, Victoria) was livid, and so was her mother, when she found out. The Queen (who was not there) insisted that Alexandra de Kalomine should annul the marriage at once – and Bertie was to tell her so. He did, of course, and she had to give way. The scandal was kept pretty much within the family, but the Queen went into a sulk.

To make matters worse, Princess Beatrice (who was now twenty-six, and on the shelf, having been made to turn Prince Louis down years ago) met Prince Henry, 'Liko', Louis's younger brother, at the wedding and fell for him. They decided they must marry. The Queen refused even to consider the question. Prince Louis, Bertie, and Grand Duke Louis of Hesse all had to plead with her before she would allow her daughter to marry Prince Henry, and then she consented only on condition that Henry and Beatrice lived with her.

Marriage was in the air, but a husband needs a role in life, and as yet there was no role for Eddy, any more than there had ever been one for his father. Bertie at least loved intrigue and pleasure and would exert himself in their pursuit. Eddy had as yet found no focus for similarly rewarding activities, although on 2 February he performed his first public engagement since attaining his majority: he opened a boys' club at 86, Leman Street, Whitechapel. It had grown out of the sixty-strong Shoeblacks' Society. These were teenage boys who, earning between £7 and £8 a year, had managed over a decade to save up £900 for a bigger, better club, supported also by subscriptions from prominent businessmen and local clergymen. It was called the Whittington Club, and still needed more money to furnish its dining room, reception room and library; there was even a gymnasium. Eddy made a friendly speech about doing whatever you do well and not doing wrong, and was cheered, and finished with a reminder that when the boys reached 'the age of discretion' they might want to look to the colonies – for 'there is plenty of room out there – ample air and larger aims; and here you seem rather crowded. May God bless you all whether here or there!' ('Loud and prolonged cheering', reported *The Times*.) Many of the boys' families would have arrived in England only a decade ago. Some did, in fact, make their fortune in South Africa and Canada. Eddy promised £20 to the library and as he and Dalton left in their carriage, to visit Toynbee Hall, the streets were lined with enthusiastic crowds.[35]

On Tuesday 24 February, he wrote to Prince Louis on Pitt Club writing paper, from Cambridge, about last weekend's visit to London for his sister's birthday party.

…The next morning at 7.30, beastly cold, we went to Wellington barracks to see the Foot Guards off. They looked very well in their London uniforms with everything to match, and most of them seemed keen on going. But it was a sad and painful sight to see their poor wives taking leave of them, a thing I dislike seeing more than anything.

We had several personal friends going, and I must say that I felt very lumpy in saying goodbye to them, as goodness only knows whether we will see them again or not.

Well how are you since I saw you last?… When is the happy event to come off? I hope Victoria is well, and does not smoke too many cigarettes. Write me a line when you have time, and with best love to Victoria

Your affecte

Eddy[36]

This letter, unhelpfully dated 'Tuesday night', dates itself from references in it to his sister Louise's birthday (20 February, the previous Friday) and the impending birth of the first child of the Battenbergs. This was a girl, born 25 February 1885, a Wednesday; it seems Victoria was going into labour just as Eddy was exhorting her not to smoke too many cigarettes (into which addiction her Prussian cousin Wilhelm had enticed her at the age of sixteen; his own sister Charlotte smoked long before it was accepted that ladies might do so).[37]

Eddy's handwriting is firm and fluent and the 'infinite sweetness of nature' is in every line. He may in some respects have been overprotected – what the derisive republicans would have called a chinless wonder – but he had those inestimably valuable qualities of kindness and compassion.

He became a Bencher of the Middle Temple in February 1885, while his father disported himself in Nice. In February, the American *United Irishman* announced that a $10,000 reward would be paid for the capture of the PRINCE OF WALES, DEAD OR ALIVE. Bertie did not let it perturb him. Early in March, he visited Eddy at Trinity. Ten days later, the whole family set out for Berlin to join in celebrations of the Emperor's birthday. 'The press is singularly reticent on the subject of the English princes here', sniffed *The Times*.[38] Perhaps, in view of the price on Bertie's head, that was all to the good. The whole lot of them – English princes, princesses and dukes – placidly travelled together, as a veritable royal circus, by special train all over Europe, and could presumably have been blown up like the unfortunate Russian Emperor anywhere along the way.

There was, as usual, another agenda in Berlin, for even Bertie could play matchmaker in the complicated dance of dynastic opportunity that made these royal get-togethers so interesting. He and the Queen were keen to see a union between Princess Victoria of Prussia, Eddy's cousin, and Sandro, the middle

Battenberg boy who had become Prince of Bulgaria. It would
be a love match, but was furiously opposed by the Princess's
brother Wilhelm. Bertie, who couldn't stand the conceited and
humourless Wilhelm, must have taken great pleasure in adding
to his annoyance.

In April of 1885, during the university vacation, the Prince and
Princess took Eddy with them on a state visit to Ireland. Bertie
hated going, and complained that since he was only making the
journey in the national interest, and not because he wanted to,
the government should pay for it. In the end they did, but it is
doubtful whether the national interest was served.

It began well enough, all things considered – all last summer
there had been a scandal involving English homosexual members
of the household at Dublin Castle, and, much more importantly,
the brutal evictions continued. There was a danger that hostile
crowds might demonstrate, but Parnell exhorted his country-
men to behave with 'dignified neutrality', and so they did – in
Dublin.

In Cork, it would be a different matter. Among the advertise-
ments for tea, horses, blacklead, manure and teeth-pulling in the
Cork Examiner at the start of April, one finds a running report
of the royal journey, beginning with news from the capital. The
Dublin City flag had been stolen by students in advance of the
visit, and they would keep setting off fireworks; the Prince of
Wales arrived looking 'a little wan but still fresh-looking for his
years'[39] (he was forty-six). Eddy's first steps on Irish soil – a slum
visit – were ignominious.

> On a visit to Golden Lane, Prince Albert Victor fell on getting out
> of the carriage in consequence of a heap of rubbish, but he sus-
> tained no injury beyond a soiling of his clothes on the heap.[40]

In a letter to *United Ireland*, the Archbishop of Cashel expressed
his fury with the lot of them. It was nothing personal.

Were they coming among us to restore our constitutional rights; to demolish Dublin Castle; to put an end to the Orange ascendancy and Freemason's rule; and above all to inaugurate an Irish Parliament in College Green, we should joyously strew flowers on their path.[41]

The National League decided to hold a big meeting in a park in Cork. In Dublin, Eddy and his parents attended a levee, 'were received at Trinity with enthusiasm' and danced at a ball.

Then began the whistle-stop tour, by special train, of towns down the east coast towards Cork City. Wherever they went, black handkerchiefs were waved derisively from bridges or people turned their backs or stood sullenly glaring at them. No member of the royal party was left in any doubt that the native Irish wanted rid of them. If they had to get off the train, they must be surrounded by troops: at Mallow there was an 'affray', in which hundreds of soldiers and police confronted Nationalist musicians playing *God Save Ireland*. The police belaboured members of the crowd with truncheons and drove protesting Members of Parliament into cattle pens.[42]

As the royal train approached, the *Examiner* complained about the expense involved in a complete redecoration of Cork station in honour of the visit, since it was shortly to be closed to passenger traffic for good. The royal programme was announced, minute by minute, in advance, so everyone who bought a newspaper knew where they were going to be and when. It was hardly a triumph of advance security.

A crowd of 20,000 turned out for the Nationalist League, and a speaker reported Parnell's view that:

If Ireland was engulfed tomorrow by a tidal wave, and we were all swept lifeless off this land, it would not give one single member of the Royal Family an hour's pain... He [the Prince of Wales] is coming here to conciliate you in the face of a great war with Russia.[43]

It was true that the Russians invaded Afghanistan in that same month. The Prince and Princess and Eddy duly arrived in Cork on 15 April and, despite cheering from some sections of the crowd, there was 'a full, deep undercurrent of hissing', and Hussars and police everywhere; the following day the *Examiner* reported that Alix had almost refused to come, so alarmed had she been by disturbances en route.

Eddy was largely ignored. He was there for decoration, to set the female West Britons' hearts aflutter, as he was 'not bad looking'.[44] As the visit continued with skirmishing, stone-throwing and groans, Bertie, Alix and Eddy raced through the set programme. They crossed Cork harbour to Haulbowline by steamer; a banquet – mock turtle soup, *pâté de foie gras*, veal with truffles, lamb chops, boar's head in aspic, asparagus, puddings, wines, cheeses – was demolished between ten to four and five o'clock; they inspected the harbour extension; and they were off. Away – to Killarney, where they were booed.

Bertie loathed every minute of it.

The army would be Eddy's next move, after Trinity. There was the May Ball, of course, and his tutor gave a further ball in the Prince's honour. A friend of Eddy's at Trinity recalled the morning after 'one of the most successful functions of a brilliant May Week':

> We had all danced till the sun was high in the sky and we could dance no more. Prince Albert Victor walked back to Trinity with my brother and myself and two or three other men, and when we reached the Great Court, the charm of the fresh summer morning made the thought of bed impossible. It struck someone that it would be a good idea to turn into the Bowling Green and have a final cigar before we separated. In a day or two we should all be going down, some of us for the last time... How clearly I recall the very sounds and scent of that delicious June day – the gay

squealing of the swifts as they circled around the old towers, and
the moist odours of the shaven turf at our feet. It was as though
the quintessence of our happy life at Cambridge had been distilled
into a golden cup...[45]

Cambridge had been a genuinely happy interlude for Eddy. But
he was gazetted to the Hussars in July, and public appearances
increasingly filled his diary: in the following months he was
made a Freeman of the City of London; he went to Sheffield
to attend a Cutler's Exhibition; and he was generally expected
to familiarise himself with the demands of public life. Also that
year, a number of important royal weddings took place.

Two were potentially of political significance. Princess Marie
of Orléans, a niece of the French pretenders the Comte and
Comtesse de Paris, married Alix's younger brother, Prince
Waldemar of Denmark. The Comte and Comtesse de Paris
celebrated another marriage even more gloriously – that of
Marie Amélie, their eldest daughter, to the heir to the throne
of Portugal. The French government – who had returned the
confiscated royal châteaux some years before – took umbrage
at these signals that the Comte was playing a kind of chess
game with his marriageable descendants and edging his way
towards domination of several kingdoms. He had gone too far,
and the House of Orléans was finally expelled from France the
following year.

The other wedding was more socially significant, and English.
Princess Beatrice married Prince Henry of Battenberg. All royal
Europe was there and, for the second time since last year, a
pretty bridesmaid caught Eddy's eye. She was, of course, much
too young for him; at thirteen, so young that she had had to get
special permission to leave Miss Jackson's strict course of instruction and come to Whippingham Church for the wedding. She
was his cousin, Alexandra of Hesse, otherwise called Alicky; he
had seen her at the wedding of her elder sister Victoria to Prince

Louis in Darmstadt. He had known her as a pretty child, but now everyone remarked that she would be a great beauty.

She returned to Germany, and Eddy joined the Hussars. Active military service was not an impossibility. People he knew had recently departed to fight in Afghanistan. He would have to work hard if he were to be put in charge of men, but he had some idea of what was required; he had been a cadet in the 2nd Cambridge University Battalion, and of course he had experienced naval drill and discipline. The 10th Hussars were his father's old regiment and Bertie, inexperienced, obese and of uncertain temper in a crisis, had only recently been rejected as a military leader. So it was Eddy's turn. Should he succeed in the army, his father would be reconciled to every disappointment that had gone before.

And Eddy might, against all expectations, turn out to have an aptitude for it; if style were everything, the Hussars would certainly be his milieu. He would adore the image of himself as an officer. His letters show that he had a strong visual sense. He loved pageantry and colour; he had been brought up with it, and with his father's appreciation of good tailoring. Bertie, not the easiest man to dress, was always suitably attired, and his immaculate appearance promoted the reputation of Savile Row all over Europe. Now Eddy had the chance to wear a uniform again.

6

Privacy in Public Life
1885–88

From July of 1885, Eddy's adolescence was over. He was to be first a subaltern and later an officer in the Hussars, with all the responsibilities that entailed. Captain the Hon. A.H. Fulke-Greville became his official companion. Their relationship was less that of guardian and ward (as in the case of George and Admiral Currey) and rather that of prince and equerry, although in military terms the 'companion' was a superior officer.

To the casual observer, Eddy had now made the transition from childhood to manhood. If the dinner parties of Trinity had engaged his attention at all, they would have opened his eyes to the political and social questions of the day – imperialism and the 'scramble for the world' in which Europe was embroiled; the poverty which afflicted a third of the population; Ireland. On the other hand, the military life upon which he was now embarking might rather narrow his focus. Army officers were traditionally glamorous and disreputable, known for their gambling, drinking and womanising, and total disregard of intellectual pursuits. As for the royal family, they rarely conversed about matters of national importance. The Prince of Wales was still excluded from much of the political information that mattered, and had he known more, would not have discussed it with his wife or children.

Did it matter if the heir presumptive, although he had seen the world, knew little of international politics? The vast gulf between the leadership that the royal family represented and the reality was expressed in a leader in the *Pall Mall Gazette* in April a year earlier:

> From being actors in the great drama of contemporary politics, and liable as such to be hissed and cheered by turns, [the royal family] have become as gods in a domestic Olympus, sharing the joys and sorrows of ordinary mortals, living a stately life before the eyes of all men, but incapable of exercising any authority over the course of events. [1]

This emasculation was judged a success. Whether or not it is strictly true is debatable; both Wales and his mother were quite capable of direct influence over political and service appointments, at least, and both to some extent set the tone of international debate.

The army that Eddy was now entering believed itself to be the most powerful military force on earth. But it had an image problem. Historically, the officer class were young men of the aristocracy and upper bourgeoisie, while the men were pressed rabble. Just as the mandarin class of government had been partly supplanted by professional civil servants, so, in the army, the stereotypes had changed somewhat since the Napoleonic Wars, with promising men receiving a service education and rising from the ranks by examination. Now only half of the officers were from titled families.

There remained a cultural divide between the army and polite society. Cockfighting and gambling were still favourite military pastimes. There were brothels, cheap and dear, around every barracks; the Wellington Barracks supplied eager customers for a trade which flourished north and west into elegant St John's Wood and south and east into raffish Marylebone and Fitzrovia.

The 'men' simply drank and became violent. A detective on the streets of Westminster in the early 1880s remembered that, 'Out of every dozen people you saw ejected from public houses, at least ten of them would be soldiers, and pretty well every riotous street affray was caused by their unseemly and often violent behaviour.'[2] Within a few hundred yards of every royal procession and display of military pageantry in Whitehall or the Mall were jails (Tothill Fields and the Millbank Prison), slums and scores of pubs. Ordinary soldiers were dangerous to the public, and frequently confronted similarly drunken Irishmen on the streets of London.

Eddy, however, spent every morning between July 1885 and early December – except when on official duties or on leave – being drilled at the Hussars riding school at Aldershot. If his horsemanship had been elegant before, he must have cut a fine figure after this. He began to play polo whenever he could. Like hockey, it is a fast and furious game of perfectly controlled aggression.

He had no difficulty in mastering the other military skills of an officer. Major Miles, who assisted with his training at Aldershot, said he 'learned orally' and there was nothing wrong with his capacity to retain information.[3] The Duke of Cambridge, Eddy's uncle, had been appalled on discovering a year or two earlier that Eddy, although 'as nice a youth as could be', knew 'nothing of the Battle of Alma!! He knew nothing about it!!'[4] Others had claimed that Dalton was a bad teacher; they may have been right, since in the army Eddy learned without difficulty. Like his father, he was quick on the uptake but found little time for books.

J.E. Vincent wrote of the prince: 'He had, it is said, a certain shrinking from the robust horseplay which is known to exist

among subalterns.' There was no physical chumminess. There
must always be a certain reserve. However friendly a royal personage became, there was a line that must not be crossed. One
catches a glimpse of that warm 'friendliness without friendship'
with which he and his brother had learned to treat their young
friends on the *Britannia* and the *Bacchante*. Eddy had learned
early on that he must command respect.

Early in February 1886, he wrote from Marlborough House
accepting his Trinity friend Harry Wilson's invitation to be
president of the Hockey Association at Cambridge.

> ...I think it an excellent idea to start an Association, which is likely
> to make the game more popular.
>
> It seems a long time since I saw you last, and I am glad to hear
> that you have settled to your reading at the Bar, and before too
> long I have no doubt we shall see you a prominent attorney. But
> I dare say you must find it a bit dull working in harness... I dare
> say you regret leaving Cambridge, in some ways, as much as I do,
> as I think, taking it all round, we had a very delightful time there,
> and the two years went by like lightning.[5]

He heartily hoped 'that old Jim Stephen is very flourishing... as a
better man never existed'. His letters were always affectionate and
friendly and quite urbane, although he was clearly a young man
who found it hard to keep up with all the demands on his time,
and constantly felt the need to apologise for not having written
sooner. Although the letters contain little detail of his army life,
the Hussars kept him extremely busy, and if ever a man needed a
private secretary, it was Prince Albert Victor. He appears to have
had none at all; even Gladstone's congratulations upon his twenty-
first birthday were answered in the familiar discursive hand and
style, although Gladstone complained that its imperfect grammar
must be edited before it could appear in *The Times*.[6] John Gore,
who saw all King George's papers, averred that in 1886:

Prince Eddy was not a very regular correspondent – he wrote on average one letter every two or three months to his brother – but he wrote at considerable length, usually beginning 'My dear boy', and was wont to supply very full details of his own intimate affairs among the reports of Sandringham sports and pleasures. His writing and spelling were both of a higher standard than Prince George's.[7]

Much of that year was spent in training, day after day, at Aldershot. 'You might come down here some time during the spring or summer and see what sort of a life I lead here, as I could easily put you up. You have no idea what a lot we have to do, and I am sure it would interest you to see Aldershot. Excuse this short scrawl, but I am rather hurried today, being on duty',[8] he wrote to Harry Wilson, who had invited him to Oxford to see a play. According to James Pope-Hennessy, Eddy's opinion of the army was not always so restrained; he thought his general was 'a lunatic' and found rituals such as 'jogging round and round the riding school in a very tight and uncomfortable garment called a stable jacket' tedious. A good many other young men of intelligence might have agreed.

Meanwhile, he was increasingly in demand for official duties such as state dinners and local shows and the distribution of prizes; he opened the new Union building at Cambridge, and at the end of July he presented colours to the Buffs. He was getting quite good at this sort of thing.

In 1886, the House of Commons was preoccupied with Ireland. A short-lived Conservative government, under Salisbury, had promoted a Bill which would deal severely with Nationalists, but at the end of January it lost an election to Gladstone, who had only recently come out in favour of Home Rule. The Queen was horrified. Gladstone tried to gloss over the implication of his ideas – as the Prince of Wales paraphrased him, to find:

some means… of meeting the wishes of [Ireland] and of preserv-
ing the integrity of the United Kingdom, under the paramount
rule of the Queen and Imperial Government.[9]

As Bertie said, though, that sounded like an Irish bull; he foresaw
disaster.

Either Mr Gladstone's government must go in for Home Rule, or
for coercive measures. I see no alternative.[10]

He, of course, favoured coercion, and slipped away to Monte
Carlo in February, as usual, to shake his head over the iniquities
of Fenian influence.

The Nationalist party in the House was nearly ninety-strong,
and was led by that riveting figure, Charles Parnell. But Gladstone's
solution to the Irish question was too extreme even for some so-
called radical members of Parliament, such as G.O. Trevelyan, who
made a spirited speech against it. The Home Rule Bill came before
the House in April, and was defeated, because over ninety Liberals
voted with the Conservatives; and soon afterwards the Tories were
back. The Prince of Wales had been in regular, direct contact with
senior statesmen ever since the crisis over Gladstone's election.
In fact, Eddy accompanied his father to dinner with Gladstone
at Downing Street late in May – not that there can have been
much of a meeting of minds between the two older men, and
Gladstone's opinion of Bertie's 'total want of political judgment,
either inherited or acquired' was well known.[11] Eddy probably
picked up more liberal opinions at university than he generally
absorbed at home. Certainly, when Harry Wilson, hearing of this
dinner date, sent him some verses about Home Rule, Eddy wrote
back: 'I thought the poems you sent me very good, and they
certainly do you great credit as they are only too true.'[12]

With the return of the Conservatives, contacts increased.
On returning to power, Lord Salisbury authorised his Foreign

Secretary, Lord Iddesleigh, to continue a practice, initiated earlier that year by Lord Rosebery, of sending copies of some secret Foreign Office despatches to the Prince of Wales to read.[13]

Sir Charles Dilke was no longer in a position to supply such material, because he had been disgraced in 1885. In another of those pungent scandals that somehow hung around Bertie and his circle like cigar smoke, Dilke's private life had come under public scrutiny. A Mrs Crawford, the young wife of a middle-aged MP, told her husband that she had enjoyed an affair with Dilke, beginning in 1881. In the divorce court, she revealed telling details about her encounters with the hapless co-respondent and thereby opened a window onto the fascinating world of a successful, unmarried man about town in late Victorian London.

He had begun the affair with Virginia Crawford when she was recently married and staying, alone, at Bailey's Hotel. There were romantic luncheons at the Hotel Metropole (a fashionable haunt; there must have been talk) and assignations at hotels 'off the Tottenham Court Road', and at his own home and hers. He and the MP's wife would ride together in the Row or visit picture galleries. In the absence of her husband in his constituency, Mrs Crawford would occasionally spend the night 'away with a friend', and reappear early in the morning; or the Member for Chelsea would visit before lunch, being entertained in the first-floor drawing room while his brougham was driven up and down the street. Her servants noticed *everything*, and remembered it all in court. As for Mrs Crawford herself, she remembered how Dilke told her he slept with his housekeeper, Fanny, and persuaded her to share his bed with both of them.

It was this revelation that finished him off. Throughout the two years' duration of the affair, Sir Charles Dilke had been part of the Prince of Wales's circle: he had often been spoken of as a future leader of the Liberal party. So repressed was the sexual atmosphere that the proceedings of almost any divorce case involving prominent people and adultery would – in this

age of almost universal literacy – be seized upon, written up and
sold as a scandal-sheet. The Dilke affair attracted more lubricious
interest than most. Frank Harris wrote many years later that
when he told Dilke that he would be able to recover from this,
Dilke said he doubted it – it was being put about that, since he
had had an affair with Mrs Crawford's mother many years before,
he had probably been committing incest.[14]

The Queen was particularly horrified. And yet, as Roy Jenkins[15]
seems to imply on her behalf: 'How gratifying to discover that
radical views and a republican past were associated with the
blackest moral turpitude.'

Wales called the sensational divorce Dilke's 'painful ordeal',
and sympathised with him. Although he had lost a valuable associate, the Foreign Office was now used to giving him sight of
most of their confidential material, and he continued to receive
it, and to take advantage of his new contacts in the Conservative
Party to obtain appointments for his friends.

Queen Victoria was more puritanical than ever. In this she
reflected middle-class opinion which:

> …was founded on a tradition that was wholly worthy of respect,
> the principle of which was that when the two sexes met together
> for social enjoyment they should preserve a certain outward form
> of dignity and politeness… Men did what they thought good, and
> saw what they chose, and said what they liked to each other, but
> women according to the code only saw what it was fit for them to
> see, and however vividly a domestic scandal or outrage was thrust
> in front of their eyes, the traditions of a certain class enjoined on
> them to assume in public a bland blindness to it… Any public
> recognition of it was unthinkable, and even more unthinkable was
> it that she should talk about it, or seek to protect herself against a
> domestic situation even if it threatened to ruin her life or render
> it intolerable.[16]

It was not so much what Mrs Crawford had got up to with Sir Charles Dilke that mattered; it was the way she had brought it out in open court, and the fact that even the servants knew. *Pas devant les enfants*; *pas devant les domestiques* – even *pas devant* the ladies – was the rule. After the court case, Dilke was allowed gently to subside from public view.

Upper-class women waited until they were married before they began to sleep with men, husbands or otherwise, and middle-class women must be seen to do the same. For two unmarried people of different sexes to be alone together at all, even in full view of the world, was indecent.

> When Uncle Frank was engaged to Aunt Ellen (his second wife) he was thirty-five, and she was twenty-seven, and a Fellow and lecturer at Newnham; and if any two people could be more respectable I would not like to know them. Yet when Miss Clough, the principal of Newnham, had been away for a few weeks my grandmother wrote: 'Frank will be glad that Miss Clough has come back, so that he can call on Ellen again.' He had not been able to go there at all while Miss Clough was away! She sat in the parlour with them herself; no-one else would do as a chaperon... One sometimes wonders how anyone was ever able to get engaged at all.[17]

The writer is Gwen Raverat, and Uncle Frank was another son of Charles Darwin. These were educated, liberal-minded people. How, in such a climate, was it possible that any decent young person could ever engage in any kind of sexual activity before marriage? Far less a grandson of Queen Victoria. Prince George's mentor, Captain Stephenson, received anxious letters from Alix in October 1886 reminding him that her son must avoid the 'disippations' of Malta; at the time, he was often seen with his uncle, the Duke of Edinburgh, and 'Missy', the well-chaperoned young princess Marie of Rumania. A crush he may have had, but 'disippation'? Hardly.

And yet both Eddy and George knew it was different if you were young, and rich, and willing to pay for sex. Such matters would horrify middle-class society, but among titled officers in the services, mistresses were looked upon with indulgence. Queen Victoria, who had been devastated at Bertie's seduction by a friendly trollope when he was twenty, was under no illusions. A policy of containment had worked for Bertie, more or less. Sir Henry Ponsonby began to make notes about possible brides for Eddy. The Tecks had a daughter but 'Princess May seems out of the question as the Prince and Princess of Wales have no love for the parents and the boy does not care for the girl'.[18]

The brothers had kept in touch by letter, and saw each other several times a year. George, in sailor mode, had grown a beard. Prince Eddy, who was spending Christmas at Sandringham, didn't like it, and wrote on 27 December 1886: 'I got your photos all right and thought them very good, but would have preferred you without a beard. I dare say it is more comfortable than shaving, which I now do nearly every day, but it makes you look so much older and I think you might take it off before you come home, if you feel inclined to. Old Curzon has taken off his and looks very much better.'[19] He liked not just uniforms but fashion; and he correctly perceived that the fashion for beards was over. (Wilde, who was as near as a corpulent thirty-something could get to being a fashion victim, would *never* have worn one.) A sketch made at York, a year later, of Eddy in the undress uniform of the 10th Hussars, shows him wearing a jaunty pillbox hat and clean-shaven but for a long thin black moustache, waxed and ravishingly curled at the ends. At Christmas 1887, George, at sea, received another letter from Sandringham, this time from Captain Stephenson.

> Prince Eddy is here and very cheery. Just the same with big masher collars. He tells me that he has become very keen about hunting and never misses an opportunity at York.[20]

Eddy and George were good friends, as they had always been, but their differences in temperament were more marked now. George was content to socialise largely within their enormous family. Eddy was different. George's official biographer, John Gore, pointed out that Eddy, unlike his brother, always cultivated friends beyond the royal circle. And later revelations indicate that he sometimes managed to evade the attentions of Captain Greville. The Prince's closest companion would have been expected to report back to someone, and Prince Eddy would have known that; but it has also been asserted that, in view of the numerous Fenian outrages of these years, and the increasing efficiency of Scotland Yard under A.F. Williamson, detectives were usually pretty close to key members of the royal family – without their knowledge. 'A Veteran', writing in 1930, says that there were always 'servants' with a secondary role around the Prince of Wales when he became king. He remembers an occasion when the King, on his way to the Duke of Devonshire's to dine, said how glad he was to have escaped his perpetually present plain-clothes snooper.

> The Equerry kept a grave face, although tempted to smile by his knowledge of the fact that the footman on the box was actually a Scotland Yard detective. His Majesty never knew either that all through the dinner there were two Scotland Yard detectives in the room, and at the very moment he was for the second time expressing his relief at the freedom from official observation a detective was standing within a few feet of him.[21]

Given the presence of spies, it is a relief to know that Eddy could, and did, have a private life, however disreputable it proved to be. What is more surprising is not that he had an existence beyond the officially approved one, but that it probably did not revolve around friendships with members of his own class. Had it done so, there were plenty of contemporaries who would have written about it. In the 1920s and even sooner, just about everyone who had known the Waleses in the 1880s and 1890s leapt into print and, if they were not always entirely open about what had gone on forty years before, they were certainly ready to drop thundering great hints. It seems, rather, that Eddy found friends not just outside his own family, and outside the Marlborough House set, but in social layers and parts of London previously unvisited by the aristocracy. He had spent his life answering to the demands placed upon him, and being found inadequate; perhaps he sought people who would make no demands.

Would he have been recognised in London's music halls and brothels? Probably not. He could not have convinced anyone that he was other than a 'toff' – the English upper class are marked right through, like sticks of rock, by their background – but as a vaguely identified Lord Algernon or Sir Percival, he could have got by. Other than the Queen and the Prince and Princess of Wales, whose images were everywhere, the faces of the royal family were not well known.

The way Eddy dressed is the clearest indication of his interest in life outside royal circles. In mufti, he wore high collars and big cuffs in the 'masher' style. The mashers and swells of the 1880s were compared by Roland Pearsall with eighteenth-century dandies, although:

> Unlike the dandies, whose mode of attire was an expression of their essence, the swells and mashers were orientated to an out-side object – to women. Their primary characteristics were that they were jaunty and not very bright, and although basically they belonged to lowly social groups, their equivalent could be found among the upper classes, as J K Stephen observed…[22]

Pearsall goes on to quote a poem written by J.K. Stephen which contains the lines:

> Its coat and waistcoat were of weird design adapted to the fashion's latest whim

I think it wore an Athenaeum tie.
White flannels draped its too ethereal limbs
And in its vacant eye there glared a glass.[23]

A music hall song of the 1880s by Charles Godfrey went:

I'm a don't care a figity, awfully bigity
Wonderful collarly feller
Five o'clock teaity, weak at the kneeity,
Kensington Gardeny sweller;
Bertie and Gusity, from University, do dear boy give us a call
A slasherty dasherty casherty masherty
Mashiest Masher of all.[24]

The Waleses, oddly, had produced a child of their times: he was drawn to the masher subculture. This short-lived movement was certainly oriented towards women. H.R. Ashbee, a dedicated collector of erotica and campaigner for better-written material, catalogued 'The Kaleidoscope of Vice – True Anecdotes etc. By A Masher' of 1884, remarking that it appeared to be fiction translated from *Les Tableaux Vivants, ou, Mes Confessions au pied de la Duchesse*. Well, at least some mashers knew French.

It must have been around now that Bertie saw fit to consult friends in Paris about a little local difficulty that Eddy had met with. Quite what it was, we cannot know, but the discussion can be dated to before 1888. George Sheffield was the lifelong companion and secretary of Lord Lyons, and it seems that only he, Laurence Oliphant and Julian Osgood Field were present one night in Paris when Wales asked Sheffield for advice. Field wrote, with fastidious discretion, thirty years later: 'I may not even hint at the nature of the advice asked for, given, and acted on; except, indeed, that it was closely connected with the late Duke of Clarence [Eddy]. Oliphant was a great favourite at the Embassy ...'.[25] Oliphant, the archetypal Victorian adventurer, had been *The Times*'s correspondent in Paris; he died at York House, Twickenham, at Christmas 1888.

So what, in terms of 'disippation', were the usual suspects? Prince George would write to his mother in 1888:

> I hope dear Eddy has quite recovered from his attack of *gout* (it sounds as if one was talking of an old man).[26]

Eddy was twenty-four. Was it really gout? Or had he caught gonorrhoea, as he later did – while somebody told Alix he had gout?

There were 'disippations' other than sex. Otherwise respectable young men, then as now, went in for drunken rowdiness. This is an 1885 diary entry of Alfred Fripp, medical student, after a rugger match:

> *Sat 14th.* Dined at Anderton's at 7. Then songs till 10 when we drove to the Gaiety and Alhambra in a party of twenty. Alhambra awfully full, only stayed about 20 minutes, then to Scotts to supper – but they would not serve us – so to Cavour – oysters and fizz. Drove to Euston to see them off – more fizz and a row. Here I parted from Trimmer, McKay, Coomer, and Beach-Hicks – all blind drunk, and walked home at 1.30. Beastly sick. Spotted by Mother but not by Father.[27]

Eddy, too, could have made a fool of himself like this, but it is not likely. Drink, gambling debts, women or men… There are no indications that Eddy drank or gambled or went with men. Mashers didn't. But he did have a girl in St John's Wood, whom he shared with his brother, according to George's diary, in which she is enthusiastically described as 'a ripper'.[28] And what would he have done, other than look for female company and affection? Under-educated and under-motivated he perhaps was, but his apathy indicates that, with the exception of field sports, he found little to excite him in royal social life. Outsiders made no complaint. The observations about his apathy, even deafness, came from Dalton, older courtiers or older members of the family. Even Bertie found little in common with his son. The Prince of Wales could follow French political life with interest, but he could share none of this fascination with Eddy, who would have had to read even the *Kaleidoscope of Vice* in English.

In March 1887, Eddy (who had passed his exam at the end of the garrison course of instruction) was posted to Hounslow, where he was promoted to captain. His public life continued. He paid a short visit to Gibraltar. Among many engagements at home, he opened the Hammersmith Suspension Bridge on 9 June. This was the summer of the Jubilee, to mark the fifty years of Queen Victoria's reign. Eddy and George would be her aides-de-camp. 'His youthful but well-knit figure, his excellent horsemanship, his smart and soldier-like appearance, attracted general attention', remarked J.E. Vincent later, and there was plenty of competition, for literally hundreds of princes and princesses and aristocrats from all over the continent gathered at Westminster Abbey on 20 June to celebrate with the Queen.

Late in June, Eddy went to Dublin to receive a degree at Trinity and other honours, and such an avalanche of invitations descended that the three-day visit was extended by a day. Prince George went too, and they appear to have enjoyed themselves, to have been a great hit among the Protestant ascendancy and to have caused little adverse reaction elsewhere. The Marquis of Londonderry reported to Queen Victoria on 1 July that they had been

> ...well and cordially received, in many parts with the greatest possible enthusiasm, especially on Tuesday in the Phoenix Park after the Review... when on their Royal Highnesses preparing to depart a large mass of the crowd adjacent to them (considerably

over 5,000) broke through the line and surrounded their Royal
Highnesses' horses, cheering vociferously...

It was not that Dublin was more pro-British than any other city,
simply that the Castle was the hub around which smart Anglo-
Irish social life revolved. Ireland was officially run by a Viceroy,
or Lord Lieutenant, who spent most of his time in England.
Day-to-day affairs were managed by the under-secretary to
the London-based Chief Secretary. The hated anti-Irish laws
were imposed and policed from London by Balfour – 'Bloody
Balfour', the Secretary of State. Rebellious types could aim at
much more relevant targets than a couple of young royals.

Bertie must have been pleased that there were princes other
than himself who could carry the flag. Faced with the brutali-
ties of Ireland, where local passions were incomprehensible, he
turned with relief to conflicts between the French.

In London he cultivated Georges Pilotelle, a refugee anarchist
cartoonist and artist for the French papers, who could be relied
upon to treat the Republicans, now in the ascendant, with derision. In 1887, he commissioned him to produce a portrait of the
Queen for the Jubilee. At least two distinct French refugee com-
munities, comprising every colour of the political spectrum, lived
in Fitzrovia and Soho at this time; many influential Frenchmen
frequented the Café Royal and Romano's. On the one hand,
there were Pilotelle, *Le Courrier de Londres*, and the royalists (who
of course included the King's friends the Duc d'Aumale and
the Comte de Paris, who had lived in style in or near London
for years). On the other, there were republicans prominent in
London from 1889: Henri de Rochefort, editor in exile, and
General Boulanger himself. Later, the two sides would come to
blows, and they too have a place in this story; but not yet.

Bertie's exotic private life meant he heard all about the infidelities and money worries of his contemporaries. Apart from his
official duties, which took up around forty days of the year, he

was constantly seen in 'evening-dress Bohemia'. He loved to play cards and to go racing (he had kept racehorses since 1877) and he was famous for the cut of his clothes, from Poole's the tailor, which so flattered his portly figure. He read the *Sporting Times* – the 'Pink 'Un', which could be rather gamey and 'indecent' – and was on good terms with its editor, Corlett, whose friends included Lord Rosebery, Lord Chesham, the Earl of Cadogan, Lord Chief Justice Russell of Killowen, Lord Brampton, the Duke of Beaufort, Baron Leopold de Rothschild, Lord Marcus Beresford (the Prince's racing manager), Lord Derry Rossmore 'and countless other well-informed personalities'.[29] We know this because they wrote letters. Before the telephone, people with busy lives had to communicate on paper; letters were delivered within hours. Corlett heard from everyone. 'Few editors have been the repository of more confidences, social, political, sporting, and merely personal.'

At the Marlborough Club, which was Wales's home from home in London, there was a basement room known to members as the Jerusalem Chamber, 'where money-lenders used to interview such members as necessity had made their clients'. Prominent among these was Sam Lewis, who knew everything about everyone and had become rich by being generous and well liked. By now, he was operating from his mansion in Grosvenor Square, and new contacts were referred to him by aristocratic touts.[30] Among his clients were 'Sporting Joe' Aylesford (until he died of drink in 1885), Lord Charles Beresford (one of the three Beresford brothers, said by Lillie Langtry to be 'as handsome as paint'), the Duke of Beaufort, the 8th Earl of Wemyss, Prince Henry of Hesse, Viscount Esher (Reggie Brett), and many others. While the Prince's finances never ran entirely out of control, the same could not be said of the debts his friends ran up through cards and horse racing. If you borrowed from a Rothschild or a Cassel, a Baring or Baron Hirsch, information might circulate in the City. There was no such problem with Sam Lewis. He had started out in Aldershot, advancing money to the troops, and remained a rough diamond. He and his wife Ada travelled to Naples once, and when they came back, a duke asked Sam how he had enjoyed it. 'Naples?' snorted Sam. 'You can 'ave Naples.' But Sam was the ideal man to visit if you wanted to hear all the latest news of London's political, racing and social world. He was charming and a gossip; but not about his clients. He simply knew enough to protect his own interests.

He must have had a small army of spies in society, chiefly among the servant class, for it was seldom that he did not know in advance the secrets which were worrying his would-be debtors. He seemed to know everybody's business, and the precautions he took to counter fraud seldom failed him.[31]

Should *emigré* circles and the Marlborough Club fail to keep Bertie up to date with what everyone was up to and with whom, then he was bound to hear it at Romano's restaurant, where Charles Piesse – partner in Piesse and Lubin, *parfumiers* of Bond Street – held court as a well-known off-course bookie and money-lender. He was a reckless bookie, and took money on cockfights and boxing as well as racing. Even more importantly, there was the Pelican Club. Founded in the Jubilee year of 1887, and owned by young Willie 'The Shifter' Goldberg, a racing man, the Pelican Club in Gerrard Street was aimed at those aristocratic bohemians who wanted to bet on bare-knuckle fights; it was the earliest incarnation of the National Sporting Club. Among the founding members were Lord Marcus Beresford, Sam Lewis, the Duke of Manchester, journalists and editors such as Labouchère, officers of the Brigade of Guards, lawyers (including George Lewis), General Boulanger, and several actor-managers. Wales, who was a member, liked to associate with actors and producers, which is how he had been able to assist Lillie Langtry in her early stage career.

And these years saw the apogee of the London music hall. The Duke of Manchester actually moved in with the wondrous Bessie Bellwood – she who had, only a few years before, been escorted home after the show by the young painter Walter Sickert, for whom she had cooked tripe and onions in her room in Gower Street. She was doing very nicely by the late 1880s, and the Duchess sent a note: 'The Duchess of Manchester presents her compliments to Miss Bessie Bellwood and wishes to state that if Miss Bellwood will permit the Duke of Manchester to return to his own home, the Duchess will pay all his debts and will allow him £20 a week.' Bessie wrote back: 'Miss Bessie Bellwood presents her compliments to the Duchess of Manchester, and begs to state that she is now working the Pavilion, the Met, and the South London, at £20 a turn, so she can allow the Duke £30 a week, and he is better off as he is.'[32] The upper classes had more fun, on the quiet, than the genteel denizens of Cambridge ever suspected.

Eddy, if he were to have a private life at all, must somehow evade attention. And with the Prince of Wales's thumb in every pie, that was no easy matter.

In March 1888, the old Emperor of Germany died. The Wales family, Eddy included, dined with Queen Victoria at Buckingham Palace on 8 March – 'the latest news was that the Emperor was not expected to survive the night'[33] – and on the morning of 9 March, the telegram came.

> Bertie, Eddy, Christian and Victoria S-H [Schleswig-Holstein] dined and directly after Bertie and Eddy drove to the station to meet Leopold of the Belgians, who was coming over on purpose for the Silver Wedding of Bertie and Alix, and they returned, bringing him about half-past ten. Leopold was, as usual, most kind. He understood that all festivities must now naturally cease on account of the Emperor William's death.[34]

His successor, Eddy's Uncle Fritz, reigned for only three months before he also died; and Wilhelm II, a cousin not many years older than Eddy, took charge with a vengeance.

As royal heirs of the same generation, the two could not have been more different. Wilhelm could be utterly charming, but the English royal family thought that behind the facade he was greedy and overbearing. Eddy's public life proceeded without controversy, because he did not take his duties as heir presumptive with anything like the same seriousness. Of course, he did not yet have a wife and children, as King Wilhelm did.

His round of public engagements trundled on; and yet one thing was different. From July, when he drew crowds on a royal visit to Bristol and performed several public functions in Yorkshire, where he was stationed, Major Miles (who had drilled him at Aldershot) accompanied him, rather than Captain Greville. No explanation appeared in the press. Eddy was made a Knight Justice of the Order of St John of Jerusalem, in Clerkenwell, and at Cambridge he was awarded an honorary degree. Harry Wilson wrote cheerfully:

> Five years ago! And yet to me
> It seems as if 'twere yesterday
> And I am now a staid MA
> And you, Sir, are an LL.D[35]

It is difficult to imagine anyone writing amiable doggerel to Wilhelm II, and still more difficult to imagine Eddy squaring up to the arrogant young Emperor, who was now annoying his mother, grandmother and above all his sister, Victoria of Prussia, by refusing to countenance her engagement to 'Sandro', Prince Alexander of Battenberg.

Bertie was nonetheless determined to start out on the right foot, and made it clear to Wilhelm that he would be in Vienna in September and was looking forward to seeing his nephew there. He arrived in the Austrian capital only to receive a grievous insult: there was no sign of Wilhelm II, and the Austrian Emperor had to confess that if the English Prince stayed, the German Emperor would not come. Seething, but patient, Bertie withdrew. He spent most of the following year biting his tongue and being nice, from a distance, to his dislikeable relation. The Queen was furious on his behalf.

Eddy spent the late summer and early autumn in Scotland, as usual. Early in November, it was announced that Captain George Holford would replace Captain Greville, 'who has resigned from the army'.[36] There may be a simple explanation for this, although it does seem odd that *The Times* made a mistake. Captain Holford did take over. But Captain Greville did not resign; in fact, he went on to become a colonel. He later travelled with Eddy down the Suez Canal, so perhaps when the announcement of the India trip was made on 11 June he simply went on ahead to make arrangements for it. Eddy's correspondence gives no clues; his mind was on other things. He wrote helpfully to Prince Louis on 7 October, from Abergeldie:

> ...respecting the man Phelps you wrote to me about. I did not personally know him for he was in some other squadron to mine, and one does not know all the men in other squadrons having constantly fresh recruits which is different to on board ship when one knows all hands. But I enquired about him and heard he was doing well. But he seemed very anxious to go out to India, and as the 5th Lancers are going out this month he was allowed to join them with some other men, for a man is qualified to go abroad after three years' service which he has. I only hope he may do well out there, for I believe it is a great change.
>
> I was so sorry to hear that your father had been so unwell, and papa told me some little time ago that he thought him looking very pulled down when he saw him. But I think that it is nothing really serious for Liko has not told me anything.
>
> When I received your letter I was staying at Balmoral where I had a very pleasant time, and we had lovely weather for ten days....
>
> I picked Mama and sisters up on my way back and found them very flourishing... Liko was full of his yachting trip round the

west coast when he seems to have had a very good time of it.
He came back looking quite the Ancient Mariner with a scrubby
beard which did not suit him a bit. So we made him take it off
in a day or two, and gave him no peace until he had done so. He
has been very deadly with the stags again, and I have also had
fairly good sport… Alicky is still here and is much grown. She's
looking prettier than ever, and will I am sure be very handsome
when she grows up. She and my sisters send you many messages.
I am sending you a small photograph you may care to have, and
would like one of you if you have a good one, some time.
Ever your affecte
Eddy[37]

This letter reveals an unfortunate misconception on his part.
His mother had brought him up to consider a girl of sixteen
(as Alicky was) as a child, not yet ready to be approached as a
young woman. But this sixteen-year-old was unusually pretty,
and a Princess of Hesse, and her political value was not lost on
more sophisticated observers. She had been invited to Balmoral
by Queen Victoria, with the express intention of promoting a
flirtation – indeed, an understanding, leading to an engagement
– between her and Eddy. 'My heart and mind are bent on secur-
ing dear Alicky for either Eddy or Georgie,'[38] the Queen had
written to her daughter Vicky as early as March last year, in a fit
of pique, after Alicky's sister Ella had married a Romanov and
her sister Irène had (contrary to Her Majesty's express wishes)
engaged herself to young Henry of Prussia.

Unfortunately, Bismarck was just as determined to see Alicky
married to a Russian. She had not spent the autumn of 1888 before
her Scottish visit at home in Darmstadt, but in St Petersburg and
Moscow, where she had been whirled around a gleaming dance
floor by the young Tsarevich Nicholas. Her head was turned
and her affections captured; and this bleak and icy castle, and shy,
gentle Eddy, were certainly not erasing the memory.

In the autumn of 1888, the man in the Clapham omnibus was not at all concerned with royal squabbles or royal calf-love. What riveted everyone's attention to the newspapers were the East End murders committed by the self-styled 'Jack the Ripper'. The brutality with which one streetwalker after another was despatched was horrifying enough; but what fascinated middle-class readers still more was the way people in Whitechapel – less than five miles from Kensington! – actually lived. Newspaper reports revealed a gas-lit world of squalor, drink, and shockingly immoral behaviour. In October, a section of what was claimed to be a victim's kidney was sent to Mr Lusk, of Mile End, who presided over a local Vigilance Committee. With it came a note about the other part of the kidney: *I fried and ate it was very nise.* In the very spelling, you could hear a sinister catarrhal whine. And this in the morning papers!

The Yard's brightest detectives were set to investigate. At first, it was difficult even to sort Ripper murders from the rest. A year later, the newspapers were still suggesting another crime by Jack the Ripper whenever a woman was found murdered east of the City.

There was nothing like terror for shifting newsprint. No one who read about these murders – so silent, so bloody, so *quick*, in the benighted alleys of this vast, ill-lit, foggy conurbation – could do so without a shudder. A random incident illustrates the pervasive nervous tension. Walter Sickert, the artist, who was only three years older than Eddy, was already building a reputation as a painter. He and his wife, between them, knew most of the artists, musicians and writers in London and a good many in Paris, too; and for several years he had been making etchings of the London music halls. When not escorting lady performers back to their lodgings, he would sometimes tramp home to Hampstead alone, dressed in his 'long check coat, long to the ankles [with] a little bag for his drawings'. It was on one such night around now that 'a party of girls who came across him in Copenhagen Street fled in terror when he said to them that he was "Jack the Ripper, Jack the Ripper!"[39] Their frantic reaction stuck in his mind; he told the story often.

Even the Queen tore her mind away from the Irish Nationalists, the stinginess of the government towards the royal family and the rudeness of her German grandson for long enough to wonder why the Home Secretary didn't *do* something (Mr Matthews, the Home Secretary, was 'not fit for the Home Office'.)[40] On 10 November, after the murder of Mary Jane Kelly in Miller's Court, a black hole off Dorset Street, she sent an agitated cipher telegram to Lord Salisbury from Balmoral:

> This new most ghastly murder shows the absolute necessity for some very decided action.
>
> All these courts must be lit, and our detectives improved. They are not what they should be. You promised, when the first murder took place, to consult with your colleagues about it.[41]

The Cabinet weakly decided that anyone providing information about the perpetrator (other than the perpetrator himself) would receive a free pardon. But in the minds of many people, Scotland Yard itself was suspect because it was corrupt. Sir Charles Warren resigned as Commissioner and Mr Matthews appointed James Monro, whose background was in the Indian police rather than the Metropolitan force, in his stead.

Changes at the top made little difference. With forensic science barely in existence, the Ripper investigators, led by an Inspector Abberline, had nothing to go on but hearsay. Every lead, however unlikely, was followed up. People came up with the oddest names – and went on doing so for over 100 years, long after the case was closed. One of them was Eddy's; and this is a matter to which we shall return.

7

Cleveland Street
1889

Eddy cut a fine figure in the spring of 1889. The Queen travelled from Windsor to Sandringham in April, and she was enchanted with her reception as she arrived at Wolferton station:

…there were great crowds. Alix, the dear girls, Lady Moreton, Charlotte Knollys, and Sir D. Probyn met us. The station was very prettily decorated, and just behind it there was a triumphal arch. The sun came out, and all looked very bright. I got into Bertie's large landau, open, with four horses and postillions, and dear Alix insisted on sitting backwards with Louise, in order that I might be better seen. Bertie and Eddy rode on either side, Sir D. Probyn in front, preceded by the Hunt, sixty in number, forty of whom were in their red coats. The road was lined with people, and numbers drove and rode. Great enthusiasm…[1]

There was a Guard of Honour of the Norfolk Artillery, and the Queen, who was almost seventy now, rested a little before 'we dined at a quarter to nine, Bertie leading me in, and Eddy sitting on my other side'. The new ballroom was converted into a theatre for the following night's play, with Ellen Terry and Henry Irving ('The hero [Irving], though a mannerist of the Macready type, acted wonderfully.') Altogether, the visit went off impeccably, and the Queen was delighted. How pleasant, how well-ordered, how *English* it all was. Continental monarchs suffered from such uncontrollable *passions*. Less than three months ago, the Austrian Emperor Franz Josef had lost his eldest son, who had married young, in a ghastly double suicide. Crown Prince Rudolf, the poor boy, had lost his mind – he pleaded with the Pope that his marriage be annulled so that he and another woman could marry and, when the Pope refused, ended it all. She was fortunate in her family. And Eddy would cut such a dash when the Shah of Persia came.

In London, two lawyers – one well established, the other just making his way in the world – had rather different business in hand. With Mr Monro as Commissioner, the West End was getting cleaned up. Policemen were refusing backhanders, at least until the heat went off again. Very early in the morning of Sunday 12 May, the police raided a couple of clubs where baccarat was played and charged everyone present with ownership of, or attendance at, a common gaming house. At the Adelphi Club, the owner tersely informed officers that yes, there was baccarat here, as there was in every other club in London. At Bow Street magistrates' court, on Monday morning, the Superintendent of Police could not adequately explain why, having on his own admission known of the Adelphi Club for four years, it had taken him this long to raid it.[2]

Stakes at the Field Club, at 7, Park Place in St James's, were high. According to the police, one defendant was nursing chips worth nearly £1,800 when they barged in at quarter past two in the morning. The services of Sam Lewis must have been in great demand – indeed, he never did business unless the banks were shut, as he valued the opportunity to cash cheques at high interest – and he was among thirteen men, including a croupier, a waiter and the owner of the club, who were taken to Vine Street to be charged. Great Marlborough Street court learned that he was a 'financial agent' of Grosvenor Square. George Lewis was solicitor to three young defendants: Lord Lurgan, the Earl of Dudley and Lord Henry Paulet. It would blow over, of course. As Mr Lewis would impress upon Mr Hannay, the magistrate, his clients had been merely occasional visitors.[3]

George Lewis had been busy for months defending Irish Nationalists. Last year, Charles Parnell had accused *The Times* of having published forgeries which made him and certain Nationalist colleagues appear to be inciting violence. Lewis had made weekly appearances in court on their behalf, and although the forger had now killed himself and Parnell was exonerated, the whole issue was still before a Commission. Alongside all this, he must continue to network energetically. The following Saturday, he would attend a dinner given by the Prince of Wales before a concert. His fellow guests would include the Duke of Beaufort, the Duke's third son, Lord Arthur Somerset, the Prince's medical man, Oscar Clayton, and Arthur Sullivan, the composer.

George Lewis's father had run the firm in Ely Place before him. George Junior had made his professional reputation with the Balham mystery – the mysterious fatal poisoning, in April 1876, of a young barrister, Charles Bravo. In the course of that notorious inquest, he had met the Queen's doctor Sir William Gull, who was a witness. Now he was lawyer to the aristocracy and, at thirty-eight, well on his way to a knighthood.

That even younger London lawyer, Arthur Newton, had been admitted to the Rolls only four years before and, having started his professional life in Lincoln's Inn Fields, had moved in 1888 to an office conveniently situated opposite Great Marlborough Street court. He had acted for the defence in several newsworthy cases, such as the Hoxton murder of 1886 and the trial of Mrs Hobbs, alias Travers, accused of keeping a disorderly house at 15, Belgrave Square. These professional highlights enlivened a parade of minor Soho outrages, such as dilution of beer by the proprietress of the Golden Lion in Dean Street and an attack on the owner of a fish and chip shop. He had yet to move into the big league. Now – the Monday following the Field Club case – the spotlight was upon him, and he was in august company. He was prosecuting before Mr Hannay, the court was packed with French political refugees of both sexes, and George Lewis confronted him for the defence.[4]

Mr Henri Rochefort, founder of *La Lanterne* in Brussels and now editing *l'Intransigeant*, had been sniping, in print, at Georges Pilotelle since January, when *Le Courrier de Londres* had carried his disrespectful cartoon of General Boulanger. So long as Pilotelle was a refugee in London, and Rochefort across the Channel, Pilotelle could do little – except send his seconds to Paris to challenge Rochefort to a duel. Sadly Rochefort, who had already fought fifteen duels, declined.

But honour could be retrieved, for Rochefort was soon to join the rest in exile. On the night of Saturday 18 May, the two men at last came face to face in Regent Street. Monsieur Pilotelle, on his way to Romano's, caught sight of Rochefort heading for the Café Royal, a lady on his arm.

> 'You miserable man! At last I have found you!' he cried [in French. We rely upon his own translation in court.] As a challenge he slapped his opponent's cheek with a glove.

Rochefort was unimpressed. 'I have something in my pocket and will kill you like a dog!' he responded fiercely, whipping a revolver case from his pocket and struggling to open it, for on this warm May evening he too was wearing gloves. Pilotelle ran off to get help and, dragging a policeman back to the spot, slipped and fell. Rochefort kicked Monsieur Pilotelle where he lay, and smacked him on the arm with the infuriating stuck revolver case.

It was all rather comic-opera. Mr Newton, prosecuting, opined that Rochefort's newspaper 'was opposed to the principles of order and Government'. Lewis, playing down the politics, growled that the paper was a tuppenny-halfpenny affair. Pilotelle testified that years ago he and Rochefort had been friends, but they had fallen out. Mr Lewis poked gentle fun at Monsieur Pilotelle and the crowd cheered for the lady music hall artiste sitting beside Monsieur Rochefort. As usual, it didn't matter much to the adversarial lawyers whether they won or lost; the point was to enjoy the game. Lawyers for prosecution and defence in the English courts traditionally hobnob together in the course of a trial, and they are more likely to be arranging dinner dates than plea-bargaining. Mr Lewis, like Mr St John Wontner, Harry Poland and several other distinguished attorneys whom Arthur Newton had now faced across a courtroom, was able to make a cool professional assessment of the young lawyer. He would have noticed that Newton employed a bilingual clerk, Augustus de Gallo, who would be useful in cases like this; there were so many French expatriates in Soho.

Newton, for his part, seems to have made the same observation as Rochefort, and stored it for future adaptation to his own ends. Rochefort wrote in his cuttings book:

> It's curious how much more attention you can attract by slapping a celebrity across the face than you ever could by producing a great work of art.[5]

As Mr Newton prosecuted the Prince of Wales's acquaintance Georges Pilotelle, Eddy was making an official visit to Belfast.

He returned when the royal family were looking forward to succeeding weeks of pleasure at Royal Ascot, the Windsor Horse Show and Henley Regatta. He was to tour India next winter; the announcement appeared in *The Times* on 11 June.

At the end of June, during a heatwave, the Prince and Princess of Wales announced the engagement of their eldest daughter, Princess Louise, to the Duke of Fife ('perilously near forty but always thought of as a younger man… It is thought none the worse of him that he is a partner in a bank', sniggered the *New York Times*.) The House of Commons argued over the amount of money which would be granted to Louise, and by implication to Prince Albert Victor, on marriage; the usual suspects – Labouchère, Bradlaugh – baulked at an increase.

On 30 June, the *New York Times* reported a rumour that Prince Albert Victor, 'Collars and Cuffs', might marry Princess Victoria of Prussia, 'a sister of William the Highflyer', but that the union would be unpopular – partly because they were cousins, and consanguinity was out of favour ('and Albert Victor is by no means an intellectual gladiator himself'), but mostly because the chosen princess was yet another German. The Queen alone must be pushing for this, because:

> Perhaps, after all, it may not be true about Albert Victor. Certainly the belief is that it will not be true if the youngster can be kept unmarried until the Queen dies. It is well known that when this event occurs the young man will immediately be styled Edward and the obnoxious German 'Albert' will be dropped from both his and his father's name.[6]

In fact, Eddy was in love, but with a different German cousin.

The *New York Times* misled its readers once again on 7 July, when it stated that Lord Charles Beresford was to resign from his post as a Member of Parliament and resume service in the navy, in order to prevent his rank from lapsing under the three-year rule. Lord Charles Beresford had been told to resign by the Prince of Wales not because he simply couldn't wait to command a ship again, but because his conduct had been, in the words of Philip Magnus, 'causing gossip and scandal'.

Charles Beresford was a handsome and amusing Irishman of uncertain temper. He and his brothers were notoriously mad, bad and dangerous to know, but he had managed to maintain his intimate friendship with Bertie, despite sending the famous telegram: 'Regret unable to dine this evening. Lie follows by post.' His wife had threatened to divorce him over his affairs, notably with 'Daisy', Lady Brooke. Lady Beresford and Lord Charles were reconciled, but his conduct as he waited to be assigned a ship, in the autumn of 1889, may indirectly have caused Eddy a great deal of trouble.

In July, the Postmaster General embarked upon the task of bringing Hammond, the brothel-keeper, and his associate Veck to justice. Eddy, so far as we know, had never even heard of Cleveland Street. He had been promoted to the rank of major and, with his father, was occupied with the Shah's visit, being part of the entourage that stayed at Windsor Castle with the Persian visitors in the middle of the month.

The royal betrothal was short, as was usual, and Louise became the Duchess of Fife on 27 July. The Shah's party stayed for the wedding. Upon leaving Buckingham Palace, the old gentleman presented extravagantly jewelled rings and boxes to those who had waited upon him. He was handsomely entertained by Albert Sassoon in Brighton for a few days, before leaving for France on 29 July.

No sooner had he steamed out of sight than the royal family steeled itself to greet the dreaded Wilhelm, or as *Le Courrier de Londres* sneered: 'the person we are supposed to call the Emperor'. Partly in order to keep this visitor out of the public eye, and partly to impress him with the might of the British fleet, which

far outshone the German, a royal contingent consisting of the
Prince of Wales, Eddy and George, Prince Christian and Prince
Henry (Wales's brothers-in-law) went out to meet Wilhelm at
sea on 2 August and to escort him onto English soil – or at least,
the Isle of Wight. The Emperor would stay with his grandmother
at Osborne, before spending a few days at Aldershot, where he
would review troops, some commanded by that hard-working
officer Lord Arthur Somerset.

Kaiser Wilhelm was not being allowed to forget that Britain
was a world power. The newspapers were full of Sir Edward
Watkin's plans for a Channel tunnel, through which a railway
would run from London to Gibraltar and thence by boat train to
Morocco, Egypt, the Persian Gulf and India. It was all mightily
impressive.[7] The French papers took the opportunity to snipe
at Germany. On 4 August there appeared a rumour about an
impending marriage for Eddy's sister Victoria, who, according
to the *Le Courrier de Londres*, knew her own mind: 'Let us hope
that she will employ this firmness in refusing all the German
princelings for whom her Grandmother seeks to find a bride.'[8]

When the Emperor left England on 7 August, it surprised no
one that Bertie was unfortunately indisposed, and could not say
goodbye. Shortly afterwards, he departed to Homburg to take
the waters.

Arthur Somerset, in all his military finery, was distracted by
private dread. Letters from Hammond, in Paris, to his wife
Caroline show that Veck's 'friends' had been asked for money
within ten days of the first Post Office interviews early in
July.[9] (Veck, the fake parson, was not immediately arrested. He
would be more useful to the police if he were kept under surveillance.) Veck's news – at the end of July – that a new round
of questioning had begun would have given Arthur Somerset
cause for concern. And now Somerset was interviewed, incon-
clusively, at Knightsbridge Barracks, on the very day when the
Germans left.

He must have known before the ceremonial Aldershot appearance that he was under suspicion, and that the authorities knew where Hammond was. Every clue that the police gave the boys during questioning would have been relayed to him through a long chain: from Thickbroom and Swinscow through Veck (who was handling the affairs of Hammond and the clerk Newlove) to Arthur Newton (solicitor, at this stage, for Hammond and Newlove only) and hence, via Reggie Brett, to himself. Reggie Brett was already, in August, communicating with Arthur Newton.

The demand for Hammond's extradition remained unpublicised. Lord Salisbury refused to grant it. It seems likely that he did so not out of any protective impulse towards Arthur Somerset, but rather because he was only too well aware that vulgar publicity could splatter mud indiscriminately, and incite class hatred.

One wonders why Newton was chosen to represent Somerset. He did not have a reputation with people in society; later, when he became known, he would represent Lord Alfred Douglas, but now he was simply a convenient solicitor for people in and around Soho. So why Newton? One possibility is that, having realised he was in trouble, Lord Arthur approached George Lewis, who pleaded pressure of work and recommended the young solicitor he had met at Great Marlborough Street. On the other hand, involving George Lewis at all would have been a red rag to the police – it would have added to their curiosity about the case. Another sequence of events seems more likely.

Hammond had disappeared before 19, Cleveland Street was searched on Saturday 6 July. He must have been tipped off either by one of the telegraph boys, or by a detective in the police or the Post Office, that he was wanted for questioning. He would have known of Newton, who handled many Great Marlborough Street defences; Hammond had made a seedy living in Soho for years and his wife was an ex-prostitute. He needed a solicitor, but more than that: he needed a solicitor who would quickly grasp that this client was in a position to extort enough money to get the case dropped, or at least to escape England for some years with his French wife and their son. As soon as Hammond, or Caroline Hammond, or Veck, gave the name of Lord Arthur Somerset as the person who would pay for his defence, then Newton would understand the implications, and encourage his new client to lie low while he got in touch with Lord Arthur to confirm what he said about bills being paid.

PC Hanks heard Veck promising to 'instruct a solicitor to defend Henry in the morning', on Tuesday 9 July. Hammond had left for France the day before. Veck and Newlove were not so successful in evading the law as Hammond was, although their cases took an unusually long time to come to court.

In the first couple of weeks of August, with the Kaiser departed, the Prince of Wales taking his annual cure on the continent and most of his friends in Scotland for the start of the shooting season, the only evidence against Lord Arthur Somerset was that of the telegraph boys and the brothel-keeper. Weighed in the balance against the Superintendent of Stables and Extra Equerry to the Prince of Wales, would anyone believe them? Although it was true that the police had only circumstantial evidence and sworn statements, he could not feel safe. So far as he knew, Abberline had no idea that more convincing proof of an 'unnatural' attachment existed – but Messrs Veck and Hammond did, and he had no reason to trust them, for they had not yet been bought off.

Inspector Abberline was in France until 9 August. Mr and Mrs Hammond had moved from their lodgings to a Parisian suburb, but still their every move was watched by the dogged John Phillips, Post Office detective. He could not persuade the French police to expel the couple on their own account, and nor could Abberline, who returned to London and talked to Hammond's former lover, John Saul. Early in August, the second round of statements by the telegraph boys was before the Attorney General, the Home Secretary and the Treasury Solicitor. No decision was forthcoming. Days passed. After an exchange of impatient letters, Lord Halsbury, the Lord Chancellor, decreed on Saturday 17 August that the new statements did not incriminate Lord Arthur Somerset, but only Veck.

Perhaps he, or Prime Minister Lord Salisbury, thought that by dealing with Veck they would somehow let Somerset's involvement subside from view, and protect the Marlborough House set. If so, they had completely misunderstood the situation. They failed to understand that Veck and Hammond were determined blackmailers, or that Abberline needed a high-profile success and Scotland Yard must be seen to be running an effective police force. There was already quite enough sneering about cover-ups and incompetence over Jack the Ripper.

On Monday 19 August,[10] at Great Marlborough Street court, a warrant was issued for Veck's arrest. At seven o'clock the following morning, the police raided his room at 2, Howland Street (just a few hundred yards from Cleveland Street) and found only a boy called George Barber. He told them that Mr Veck would be back by train from Portsmouth later. According to the official account, when Veck arrived at Waterloo station that evening and was arrested, he had documents in his possession which related to a 'Mr Brown' and Algernon Allies, of Sudbury. It is possible that he had retrieved papers from somewhere but, if so, they were never produced. It seems a lot more probable that the police threw the book at Veck, and that only then did he produce the ace up his sleeve – a curly-haired youth in Sudbury – in return for lenient treatment. By the time Arthur Newton was brought in to act for him, the damage was done. By Wednesday 21 August, Arthur Somerset knew it was all up. He negotiated leave of absence from his regiment (his commanding officer in the Royal Horse Guards – the Blues – was Oliver Montagu) and left the country.

There exists correspondence from early August onwards about efforts his friends were making on his behalf. Arthur Somerset was friendly with a brother officer called Binning; they had campaigned together in the Sudan in 1885 and were both among the close friends of Reggie Brett, Viscount Esher. Early in August (presumably soon after Somerset had been interviewed at the barracks), Binning wrote to Brett that the police had 'strong evidence on some point' against 'Podge', as they called Somerset.[11] Convinced that their entire circle would be subject to opprobrium, should Podge be prosecuted, Binning and Brett were anxious to settle the affair quietly. They knew it would be expensive. They were willing to pay for silence, but Arthur Newton – or the blackmailer, through him – was asking rather a lot.

Reggie Brett notoriously informed W.T. Stead, then editing the *Pall Mall Gazette*, of all the gossip he heard. Stephenson, the Treasury Solicitor, knew everything, and he had a brother at court. Lord Arthur Somerset knew in his bones that everything was bound to come out sooner or later; he was even more worried about that than he was about money. All his friends and solicitor could do was to limit the damage. However, by the end of August, despite Allies having been taken from his home by the police, no warrant had yet been issued for his own arrest, and he could still hope that it might never be.

Perhaps he thought that by going to Homburg he would be protected by proximity to the Prince of Wales. At the very least, he might prevent any rumours from reaching royal ears. He dreaded that above all – and it was constantly on his mind, because Reggie Brett had known Wales since university. How awful if Wales questioned him… They all had to lie. But if he made an enemy of the Prince of Wales, he would be finished: a pariah.

He stayed abroad for a month. Algernon Allies was brought to London and sequestered under police protection at the Rose

Coffee House. Arthur Newton sent his clerk to Sudbury, in a fruitless search for incriminating material that the police might have missed. Mr Matthews, the Home Secretary, insisted, in the face of expert opinion to the contrary, that there was insufficient evidence to issue a warrant for Lord Arthur Somerset's arrest.

At the start of September, the Prince of Wales arrived to stay at Mar, near Balmoral, with his daughter and new son-in-law, the Duke and Duchess of Fife. Eddy, having spent August in Scotland as usual, was now at the Cavalry Barracks in York. He wrote to Prince Louis as a lovelorn swain.

> September 6th/89
>
> My dear Louis
>
> I feel I should have answered your letter before, and to thank you for all you say in it, but I have been on the move so much of late that I have barely had time to collect my thoughts and to write to you in the mood I should wish.
>
> No letter I have received of late has given me more pleasure and hope than yours has. And it is indeed good of you to take the trouble and interest yourself on my behalf. We have always been I think the best of friends so I naturally understand why you interest yourself in my welfare, and especially in a case like this one, which is every thing to me. I most thoroughly appreciate all you say, and it gives me great encouragement. I thought you knew I was fond of Alicky. In fact I have been fond of her for years and have told no one with the exception of my parents, and that only a short time ago. But last year Grandmama [wanted to –] the subject, and was very nice about it; only I fear that someone else must have told Alicky, which was I think a great mistake, and as you say relations can only spoil my chance by mixing themselves up in the affair. I guessed that myself last year, and therefore was very careful how I approached Alicky,

and did not give her the slightest sign that I loved her, although inwardly I was longing to tell her so, but thought I had better wait my time.

Don't you think I was right in doing so? Another thing, I never knew until you told me that she thought I was ever fond of Irène, and that after she married I turned to her as the only sister left. I must say, that is not quite doing me justice for I never was really serious as regards Irène and never breathed a word to her on the subject, although I did say something to Ernie [Prince Ernest of Hesse, brother of Victoria (who had married Prince Louis), Ella, Irène and Alicky] about it at the time. In fact I didn't think I quite knew my own mind then, as it was at the time of your marriage, when I was a good deal younger than I am now. You may be sure I will do all I can to dispel the idea from her mind, and will tell her frankly all about it.

Unfortunately I have not had an opportunity of seeing her yet, but hope to go up to Balmoral in a few days.

I will have a good talk to Ernie about it, and as you say I am sure he will help me wherever no-one else could. I have been very anxious about the whole thing, and naturally too I think, for I [think?] what I have got before me is no light matter. But you may be sure I will do all I can to persuade Alicky that I love her for herself and for herself only, and that my parents and relations have had nothing whatever to do with it as far as I myself am concerned.

It will make such a difference to meet. I can only get her to give me some hope and encouragement if not more, that some day I may be her fortunate suitor. For I shall then go away quite happy, as I think you have heard I am going to India this winter. All you have said in your letter will be of the greatest help to me, and if I am successful in this, I shall know how much I am indebted to you for all the trouble you have taken.

I will write to you again and tell you how things go off, and till then must hope for the best.

I can't tell you what a happy creature I shall be if it only comes off
right, for I do indeed know what a prize there is to be won.
Ever yours very affectntly
Eddy[12]

It was terribly sad, but his affections were not returned. Alexandra
of Hesse had decided to marry the Tsarevich of Russia, if he
asked her and if religious difficulties could be resolved. Later,
he did and they were; and that story ended at Ekaterinberg.
But Eddy did not know this, and his romantic feelings seem
entirely genuine. It is hard to imagine the young man who wrote
with such self-effacing eagerness and warmth paying clandestine
visits to a brothel in order to meet small boys. If this were true,
he would by now have heard about the arrests at Cleveland
Street and have been in much the same frame of mind as Arthur
Somerset. If Veck and Hammond were capable of blackmailing
the son of a duke, one can see the kind of milch cow the heir
presumptive would have made. Yet there is nothing in his behaviour, or that of his family, friends or legal advisors, that implies
that any of them had – in the week when Eddy wrote this letter
– the remotest idea about this sordid affair.

This is not to say that there were no storm-clouds ahead for the
Prince of Wales. He, too, was rather fond of someone, and as soon
as he returned to London he had every excuse to see her. His latest
love was Daisy Brooke, the pretty, strong-minded and indubitably
married future Countess of Warwick. Husbands had never stood
in Bertie's way before, and Lord Brooke did not do so now.

Daisy Brooke's problem was not her husband, but her former
lover's wife. Lady Charles Beresford had come into possession of
a letter she had written to Charles. Lady Beresford approached
George Lewis with it, demanding that Lady Brooke be made
to stop all contact. Mr Lewis must have written to Daisy, for
she, who was at this point Bertie's favourite, told him and

pleaded that George Lewis be made to return the letter to her. If it compromised her in any way, then this was understandable. Wales asked George Lewis to show it to him. Mr Lewis ignored the rule of client confidentiality and did so. (Maybe it was because Lady Charles Beresford was only a woman; or maybe he wanted that knighthood very badly). Wales read the letter and announced that it must be destroyed. That was a step too far even for George Lewis, and he explained that he could not destroy it without his client's consent. Bertie called upon Lady Charles twice, asking her to take it back from Lewis and burn it; but she refused. He was used to getting his way, and her attitude annoyed him.[13]

At this point, somebody – and there are a number of candidates – told Lord Charles Beresford what was going on. He was angry with both the Prince of Wales and George Lewis, and moreover insisted that his wife retrieve the letter from Lewis and give it to him. Which she refused to do. However, she and her husband negotiated a truce. She agreed to retrieve the letter and send it to Charles's older brother William, the Marquis of Waterford, for safe keeping. Lord and Lady Beresford were once again reconciled, this time in mutual anger at the high-handed treatment they had received from George Lewis and the Prince of Wales. They sulked; Lord Charles did not take command of HMS *Undaunted* until after Christmas; and throughout the autumn they grumbled about the Prince and his behaviour wherever they went.

At the beginning of September, Hammond, *in absentia*, and Veck and Newlove were committed for trial at the Old Bailey on a number of charges, the most serious of which were procuring to commit acts of gross indecency, and conspiracy to procure to commit buggery.[14] *The Times* reported that they had been charged with 'conspiring together to induce boys to go into a house in Cleveland Street'.

Above left 1 The Prince and Princess of Wales (Eddy is at his father's feet), 1866.

Above right 2 The Prince and Princess of Wales with Princes Eddy and George and Princess Louise, 1868.

Right 3 The Prince and Princess of Wales with Princes Eddy and George and Princesses Louise, Maud and Victoria, 1870.

Above left: 4 Prince
Eddy, 1871.

Above centre: 5
Prince Eddy, 1875.

Above right: 6 Prince
Eddy, 1875.

Left: 7 Prince Eddy
and Princess Maud,
1875.

Clockwise from right:

8 The Princess of Wales with Princes Eddy and George, 1877.

9 Prince Eddy, 1876.

10 The Princess of Wales with her children George, Eddy, Louise, Victoria and Maud, 1876.

Clockwise from left:

11 Princes Eddy and George
as naval cadets, 1880.

12 Prince Eddy in naval
cadet's uniform, 1880.

13 The Princess of Wales with
Princes Eddy and George and
Princesses Louise, Victoria
and Maud, 1880.

*Clockwise from
above:*

14 The Princess of
Wales with Princes
Eddy and George,
1880.

15 The Prince and
Princess of Wales
and their family
on board the royal
yacht *Osborne*,
Cowes Week, 1884.

16 Princes Eddy
and George in
respective army
and naval officer's
uniforms, 1885.

17 The Princess
of Wales with
Prince Eddy, who
is in naval cadet's
uniform.

Clockwise from above left:

18 Inspector Frederick Abberline, 1889.

19 Marlborough House.

20 Prince Eddy in Hussar's uniform, 1888.

21 Prince Eddy in Hussar's uniform, 1888.

Clockwise from above left:

22 The Hon. Arthur Somerset.

23 Lord Arthur Somerset.

24 Somerset's solicitor, Arthur Newton.

25 Eddy as Duke of Clarence and Avondale, 1890.

26 Eddy as Duke of Clarence and Avondale, 1890.

Clockwise from above left:

27 Princess May of Teck among guests of the de Falbe's at Luton Hoo (the bishop of St Albans is in the centre).

28 The Wales family, 1890.

29 Eddy as Duke of Clarence, 1891.

30 Eddy and Princess May the day after their engagement at Luton Hoo, 4 December 1891.

31 Lady Sybil St Clair-Erskine.

Above: 32 Photograph claimed to be the Duke of Clarence in 1910.

Left: 33 Effigy of the Duke of Clarence, Memorial Chapel, Windsor.

34 'The last moments of the Duke of Clarence', January 1892.

Senior civil servants were aware that Lord Arthur Somerset had cut and run, but still enquiries met with no promise of action from on high. Sir Augustus Stephenson, the Treasury Solicitor, was angry and kept the pressure up. At last, on 10 September, with the Old Bailey trial ten days away, Sir Richard Webster, the Attorney General, gave Stephenson permission to move forward. Lord Arthur Somerset, wherever he was, must be summoned to appear before a court and the military authorities must be informed. Stephenson rejoiced, and passed on these instructions to the Home Secretary.

'If I could return in time before going to Newmarket it would certainly be all the better...', fretted Somerset in a letter to Reggie Brett, knowing nothing of this. The Prince of Wales wanted to meet him at Marlborough House later in the month to discuss arrangements for Eddy's trip to India, but he was not at all sure whether he dared return. 'For the first time in the memory of man the Stables don't know where the Master of the Horse is and they can't get a brush or an oat without my initials.'[15]

The second week of September: a flurry of activity. The Veck-Newlove committal was reported in the press. In Paris, a gendarme served an executive order on Hammond, telling him to get out of France. Reggie Brett and a stockbroker called Henry Weguelin were raising money. They both thought that Podge should come home to borrow whatever Newton required from Leo Rothschild, and they would pay it back.

Weguelin personally did not want to have financial dealings with Newton. On 9 September he wrote:

> Frankly, Reggie, the only person seriously implicated is AS... I think Eric Barrington, Howard Sturgis and one or two others should be called upon to assist... I shall be very glad with you or anyone else to 'back his bill', but I am not inclined to trust myself any further in Mr Newton's hands....

Sturgis was an American, a partner in Baring's Bank. Eric Barrington was Lord Salisbury's private secretary at the Foreign Office. (A fact worth bearing in mind: Barrington was in as good a position to 'assist' as anyone could be.) Also:

> ...we cannot blind ourselves to the fact that *he* is primarily in this mess and that principally through his own act. We are only hangers-on and there is only a distant probability involving an immense stirring up of mud of our being injured.[16]

Well, you find out who your friends are.

Hammond and his young companion, Bertie Ames, fled across the Belgian border to Halèzy, tailed by a Yard man and Mr Phillips of the Post Office. Mrs Hammond came home to their little son, Charlie. At the end of the week, the *Pall Mall Gazette* juxtaposed Somerset's name with a reference to some 'gross scandal'.

Surely now there must be a warrant for his arrest. But – no news. Two political appointees – Home Secretary Matthews and Lord Salisbury, the Foreign Secretary who was also the Prime Minister – would not be budged. Stephenson did not know this; all he knew was that the GPO and Commissioner Monro were blaming him for slackness or worse, and it was not his fault. He wrote an irate letter to the Attorney General. Children at work must be protected. Why was nothing happening? This letter had to pass through the hands of Cuffe, and he thought carefully before writing back to Stephenson on Monday 16 September:

> I am told that Newton has boasted that if we go on a very distin-
> guished person (PAV) will be involved. I don't mean to say that
> [I] for one instant credit it – but in such a case as this one never
> knows what may be said, be concocted or be true.

On the same day, Arthur Newton received £1,200 in fees from Weguelin: a remarkably generous amount.[17] The trial of Veck and Newlove was scheduled for that Friday, 20 September, at the Old Bailey.

On Tuesday 17 September, Stephenson wrote back to Cuffe:

> ...the Home Secretary may know, or may have information which may lead him to believe that he knows, more than we do – also that Mr Newton the solicitor may know more or may believe that he knows more than we know. He [Newton] is a dangerous man and he may – or his clients may – make utterly false accusations against others – with respect to whom so far as our information goes – or the descriptions given by the boys – there is no shadow of grounds for imputation. Still such imputation may be made. We must not lose sight of such a contingency but whether anything will be gained by abstaining from including LAS in the charge – with the evidence we have against him – is a serious question.[18]

He instructed Cuffe to send his memo on to the Attorney General, regardless. He was pretty sure that the 'dangerous man', Newton, was bluffing, and was determined to call his bluff.

On Thursday 19 September, Veck's counsel having plea-bargained and the Attorney General having agreed to bring the case forward, Veck and Newlove were brought before an Old Bailey judge at four o'clock. The case was not listed and no reporters were present. Both were charged with minor indecency offences, the conspiracy and procurement charges having been dropped, and both received light sentences (Veck nine months' penal servitude, Newlove four). Arthur Newton was delighted; and, on the continent, Lord Arthur Somerset packed his bags for a quick trip home.

As Stephenson intimated, there had been not a whisper of any involvement on Eddy's part from the telegraph boys, or Veck, or Hammond. There was nothing in the observations kept on Cleveland Street, or on any other homosexual haunts in London, to indicate that Eddy had ever visited such places. There had been no talk of any romantic or physical attachment on his part to men or boys, ever – even when he was in the navy, the service most famously tolerant of homosexual affairs. He was attractive enough to make Oscar Browning fall at his feet at university, but that was merely a silly old man's snobbish crush, and even E.F. Benson, who was homosexual, cringed with embarrassment on the Prince's behalf. Weguelin, writing on 9 September to Reggie Brett, had not the remotest idea that Eddy's name might be brought into this.

So did Arthur Newton start the rumour? Almost certainly. Yet the politicians – Salisbury, the Prime Minister, and Matthews the Home Secretary – were more craven than Stephenson. They fell for Newton's bluff. They were nervous, and saw the hierarchy of power rocked to its foundations. The civil servants reacted calmly, like the lawyers they were. They looked at the facts, and judged that there would be no case to answer. But they had less power, in this case, than the politicians; and perhaps less to lose.

Somerset must have believed that the course of justice had been stopped in its tracks, because he was confident enough to return to England on Saturday 21 September and visit his parents at their grand Palladian stately home, Badminton.

According to James Lees-Milne, the Duke and Duchess of Beaufort were 'good but simple country people'. Well, hardly. The Duke had an expensive fondness for young girls. Gossip had it that there was a lady who kept a house off Regent Street and always informed him when she had a fresh batch in 'from the continent'. His wife knew of his tastes and turned a blind eye. It was famously related that one day, when she was about to entertain guests at luncheon, she heard that a picture had just been delivered. Gaily, she took the company along to see what it might be. The butler pulled away the wrapping, and there was a portrait of Beaufort's latest love. No one knew quite what to say. She calmly gave instructions for hanging it and then changed her mind. On second thoughts, she said, the Duke might prefer to admire it privately, and it should be put up in his own dressing-room. [19]

Somerset had a sister (Blanche, who was married to the eldest Beresford, the Marquess of Waterford) and three brothers – among them Henry, exiled to Monaco since his wife caught him with the footman. The Duke was a convivial old gent, a great racing man, and if Somerset had known that his father had borrowed £29,000 from Sam Lewis last January and topped it up with another £6,000 in July, then maybe he would have asked for help with his legal bills. Apparently, he could not bear to tell his father anything just yet; this was more in the line of a flying visit to see his parents and borrow money and go to the Newmarket Sales on Wales's behalf. He also met the Prince of Wales, as arranged, and received instructions on the saddlery and other riding kit to be got ready for Eddy's tour of India. He promised to meet Bertie and Eddy together a week later, on 1 October, just before they left for Denmark.

In France, Hammond got Bertie Ames to write to his sister-in-law, Florence. He was being followed still, even in Belgium, and was fed up with it: 'it makes me feel so ill I can scarcely eat my meals'. [20]

In Houndsditch, Algernon Allies remained under house arrest in rooms above the coffee-house. Perhaps he thought sometimes of Mr Brown. How surprised he would have been to know that Mr Brown was thinking of him, too. For on the Wednesday following Somerset's clandestine return, a visitor came. It was a young man Allies did not know, who bought him lunch and offered him a free passage to America, some new clothes and £15 to get him started in New York. But supposing he couldn't find work? Not to worry, explained the young man; he would

get £1 a week until he did. Algernon Allies said he would think
about it and meet the young man that night in a pub in the
Tottenham Court Road. He thought about it and told the story
to Inspector Abberline, who told him to go ahead and keep
the appointment. That night in the pub, Abberline and his men
watched Mr Taylerson, Arthur Newton's clerk, arrive with Allies
and hand the boy over to Augustus de Gallo. PC Hanks thought
he saw Newton himself slip away once Allies had arrived.[21]

They followed de Gallo and Allies as they took a cab to
Arthur Newton's office. Inspector Abberline was in a quandary.
If charges were pending and Somerset was a wanted man, then
Allies was the star of any future trial, and Newton was trying
to nobble a witness. But were charges pending? He still did not
know. He and his men could do nothing. The next day he asked
for permission to charge Newton and his clerks with conspiracy
to pervert the course of justice.

Cuffe and Stephenson were beginning to think their cause
was lost. Cuffe wrote:

> It is possible similar offers will be made to others… and if ulti-
> mately instructed to proceed we may find ourselves without wit-
> nesses… Those who are in danger have every reason for putting
> them out of the way and plenty of money to do it.[22]

The Attorney General instructed Cuffe to send all the papers
on the case to Lord Halsbury, the Lord Chancellor and final
legal arbiter.

Newton knew that Abberline was fully aware of his attempt
to get Allies away. He protested that he was working on behalf
of Allies's father, who objected to Allies being kidnapped and
kept away from him. Since Allies's father could not raise the fare
to London, the idea that he could buy a passage to New York
seemed a little far-fetched, even for Newton.

On 26 September, Newton wrote to Reggie Brett:

I do not think it advisable in writing to go into details but when
I was at home in the country last night at 11 o'clock I received
information of the most reliable nature that on Friday (tomorrow)
a warrant will be applied for against your friend. I immediately
came up to town and was up till 3 this morning trying to find his
whereabouts and sent down at 6 o'clock this morning to find you.
Kindly let me know where I can see you tomorrow.

Somerset, in Newmarket, was tipped off and, after an immediate,
accident prone, circuitous journey by back routes to Newhaven,
arrived in Dieppe the same day. To the Prince of Wales, who had
asked to see him before he himself left for Denmark on Tuesday,
he telegraphed that he was unavoidably detained. Later, he wrote
that he wished he had known, as Newton later told him, that
the tip-off about the warrant came directly from Algernon Allies,
who was 'the biggest liar in Europe'.

The police began to leak. On the weekend of 28–29 September,
accounts appeared in the *North London Press* and the wide-
circulation *Reynold's News* which were based on the first statement
made by Newlove to PC Hanks, back in July. They named 'the
heir of a duke, the younger son of another duke, and an officer
holding command in the Southern district'.[23] Euston, Somerset
and Jervois, in other words (Jervois, according to Newlove, was
a colonel at Winchester Barracks). To make sure that Newton
knew he meant business, Abberline also served a subpoena on
Allies and the telegraph boys to appear as witnesses at the Old
Bailey on 21 October, when the session opened. If Newton could
bluff, so could Abberline. His real hopes of getting Hammond
and Somerset brought to trial seemed pretty slim.

Abberline knew that Somerset could come and go through
the Channel ports and he could do nothing about it. He did not
have permission to make an arrest. He was also well informed
about the movements of Hammond, and was apparently unable
to act. On Monday 30 September, Newton sent a telegram telling

Hammond to move closer to Brussels. He met him there at the Hotel Bordeaux and negotiated the price of silence. On Thursday 3 October, while Somerset was writing reassuringly to his friends on Marlborough House paper, Hammond was dictating a letter home from the Hotel de l'Europe at Anvers to tell Caroline and Charlie and Caroline's sister Florence to get packing. He had held out for £800 and first-class fares to New York, and expected to get it. He and Bertie were booked to leave the day after tomorrow, and he instructed his family to follow within weeks – to ship the piano and 'sell the birds'. He sent his brother Ted at Gravesend an address in Seattle where they were going to stay.[24]

Newton, back in London at the end of a busy week, told Henry Weguelin that he could not settle 'the man in Paris' (Hammond) for less than £2,000. He had already bought the tickets at considerable expense to himself, and trusted that all would be settled.

On Saturday 5 October, Hammond and Bertie Ames steamed away from Antwerp in the SS *Pennland* under the names of Mr Charles and Mr Arthur Boulton. Mr Taylerson went with them.

On that very same Saturday, Somerset came back to England; Commissioner Monro knew that he was back and told Cuffe he needed a warrant. Stephenson told Cuffe to telegraph for an opinion to Lord Halsbury; but the Lord Chancellor was visiting a remote part of Scotland, and it was Saturday, and the precious missive would have to be carried across miles of heather to a place called Kinrockit Cottage before it got to him. For once, the Victorian post and telegraph system, which seems so astonishingly fast, failed.

On Sunday 6 October, Monro sent another note – he must be able to get at least an extradition order against Hammond – at this rate the man might get away! On 8 October, the funeral of the Dowager Duchess took place at Badminton and the police stood by and watched as Podge took his place among the mourners. PC

Luke Hanks was on graveyard duty, and telegraphed to London halfway through the day asking for permission to arrest his quarry. He got no reply.[25]

Oliver Montagu, who had to grant or reject an application from Somerset for four months' leave, contacted Commissioner Monro on Wednesday 9 October to ask whether the police had a strong case. Monro had no idea that Eddy's name had been raised and was guardedly confident.

That same day, Lord Halsbury's (mis-addressed) opinion belatedly arrived on Cuffe's desk.[26] It was the Lord Chancellor's opinion that pursuing the case would cause more harm than good; the offence was no more than a misdemeanour and evidence was weak, because the witnesses were of such bad character as to make them unconvincing. Cuffe wrote drily to Stephenson that. 'If identification by respectable witnesses is a condition... it comes to saying there shall be no prosecution. People do not do these things in the presence of persons of respectability as a rule.' He suggested that at least the dossier should be passed to the War Office, and the Attorney General agreed – but, once again, Cuffe had to wait for permission from Halsbury. It was refused three days later.[27]

The day after the funeral, Somerset returned to London. On 10 October, he received a kind letter from the Prince of Wales (now at Fredensborg), asking why he had gone to Dieppe just when he had asked for a meeting. Somerset wrote to Brett: 'I saw Probyn today. He evidently knows nothing and asked me to go to Sandringham tomorrow which I shall do. Anything to get away from here.'

That evening, he met Newton and the counsel keeping a 'watching brief' for him. Counsel was Charlie Gill, who had defended Veck and would later prosecute Oscar Wilde. He had often worked for Newton in defence of minor indecency cases, and was later renowned for remarking that when the lighting was improved in Hyde Park he lost £2,000 a year.

Newton and Gill talked to Somerset until two in the morning. They told him to leave the country, as there would be a
warrant unless he resigned and did so. He was determined to stay
and fight, as the witnesses were not as credible as he was.

At Sandringham, he saw Lord Marcus Beresford, a brother
of Charles, who worked there in his capacity as the Prince of
Wales's racing manager. Oliver Montagu, his CO, sent a telegram saying he would like to have a meeting. On Wednesday
16 October, Somerset was back in London, where he found
fellow members of his clubs (the Marlborough and the Turf)
supportive. He complained, however, that rumours were being
spread about him. He thought that the police were among those
who were talking.

By now, Somerset was beginning to convince himself of the story
planted by Newton with such effect nearly three weeks before. He
was interviewed by Sir Dighton Probyn, Private Secretary to the
Queen, and Sir Francis Knollys, Private Secretary to the Prince of
Wales. He wrote to Brett from the Marlborough Club:

> Sir Dighton and Francis Knollys met me at 9.15 this morning and
> I suggested they should see Newton. They agreed and I sent for
> him. He told all just as he had told Colonel Montagu and they
> went off to Monro. He told them nothing but they hunted him a
> bit and told him it was a scandal that these rumours were entirely
> circulated by the police. He denied it, whereupon Sir Dighton
> said they were and as evidence he knew that Abberline had been
> to the *Pall Mall Gazette* and tried to make them write up the case
> and that two inspectors had told two gentlemen in society in the
> street all about the case.

'I suggested they should see Newton.' Why would he have
made such a suggestion unless his vindication – that if the case
were pursued Hammond, or Veck, would name Eddy – was
thin, and he could not corroborate it? It had to be something

that originated with Newton; and Newton could tell them that Hammond had told him just about anything.

Probyn and Knollys were not impressed by Arthur Newton. On that day, 16 October, they tried to persuade Somerset to dump him and hire George Lewis instead. Stephenson's assessment of Newton as 'dangerous' may have been widespread already; or maybe they just did not believe everything he told them.

Knollys and Probyn had a busy Wednesday. Commissioner Monro passed them on to Cuffe (whose superior Stephenson, for family reasons, had been forced to work from home throughout the affair). Cuffe made notes of their meeting, which are mostly illegible, but in his note 'for the record' he says 'the P of Wales didn't believe a word of it and wished he could come himself to clear LAS – and must have something settled'.[28]

Cuffe listened to what they had to say and promised to get back to them when he had taken advice. When they had gone, he wrote his note of the meeting to Lord Halsbury and hurried away to see the Attorney General. What was he allowed to tell them? Sir Richard was instructed to say, politely, that he had seen the Attorney General and was allowed to say nothing. Clearly 'loyalty to the institution of the crown was more important than loyalty to the person who might be king'.[29]

On Thursday 17 October, Somerset wrote from his office at Marlborough House to Brett:

> I had half a mind to go and see Lewis but Newton spontaneously
> entreated me not to. I have a very strong conviction that Newton
> is very nervous about any trial on his own account but of course
> I know nothing. He is certainly not the man he was. He is and
> looks worried and repeats himself.

Somerset did not, as they advised, give up Newton. But after seeing Knollys at the Turf Club in the afternoon, he wrote to Brett again:

The Treasury refuses all information at present... Can anything
be done? What on earth are they waiting for? To try and catch
someone else or what? I have a very shrewd idea that our legal
friend [Newton] must have overstepped the ordinary etiquettes
or something of that kind. Meanwhile I suppose we can do
nothing...

Sir Dighton Probyn and Knollys were very strongly impressed
against my legal adviser yesterday and if Lord Salisbury refuses
information want to take me to see Russell tomorrow and get
him to squeeze the Government. All this is very difficult and
unpleasant.

With Hammond gone, Newton was the only person in London
who could know for sure that the rumour which was already
protecting Somerset was without any foundation in fact.
Influential people clearly suspected that, by lying about Prince
Eddy, he had gone too far in defence of his client. But they
could not be sure.

When Stephenson returned to his post in London on Friday
18 October, he confided that he was now dreading a personal
approach from the Prince of Wales, who knew him (his brother
was an equerry).[30] The likeliest implication is that Eddy had been
mentioned. Arthur Somerset was important, but not important
enough for such an unprecedented move by the Prince. Both
Knollys and Probyn had dealt with blackmailers on the royal
family's behalf before this, and they had in the past favoured a
cover-up at any cost.

And what were these rumours, exactly? The vaguer they seemed
to be, the more noble Arthur Somerset seemed. 'I couldn't possibly comment' would only warm up a fomenting heap of
innuendo. Most people heard that Eddy had been to Cleveland
Street, and some may have assumed that he had been caught
there; exactly what was said to have happened is unknown,

except that Arthur Somerset was rumoured to be covering up for him.

The Beresfords had been sniping at Bertie for months over his falling-out with them, and their main complaint was Wales's hypocrisy about mistresses. They had been part of his circle for years, and now that he had taken the part of Lady Brooke against them they felt betrayed. Gossip had always seethed among the Marlborough House set, but in the autumn of 1889 there was a sense of battle lines being drawn.

The eldest Beresford son was the Marquess of Waterford, and his Marchioness was Blanche, Arthur Somerset's sister. Perhaps Marcus Beresford, running the racing stables at Sandringham, heard Arthur Somerset repeating Newton's hint which seemed to be so devastatingly effective, and certainly Arthur Somerset also spoke to Blanche, whose husband – his brother-in-law – had known what was in the Daisy Brooke letter. What more natural than that Somerset, whose entire identity was bound up with his honour as a gentleman and a soldier, should seize the opportunity to recast his role? In the latest version of events, he was the noble victim of his own honourable conduct. And what more natural than that gossip, fanned by resentment, should become malicious?

Eddy and his father left England on 1 October for Denmark, where they would join Alix and the others. Two days after Hammond sailed away from Antwerp, Eddy was writing to Prince Louis from Fredensborg, his thoughts a million miles from any scandal. Just weeks before, Alicky's brother Ernest had tactfully made him aware of her true feelings.

October 7th/89
My dear Louis
When I answered your kind letter which I told you gave me so much pleasure as well as hope, I little thought what I had to expect,

and to hear, on my arrival at Balmoral. For as you advised me I saw Ernie soon after my arrival and had a long talk to him on the subject. You will most probably hear all about it before you receive this, as Grandmama is sure to tell you everything, as I hear you are going to Balmoral for a day or two on your arrival in England. I don't think it is necessary to tell you every detail for you will probably hear that from Ernie, and besides I have little to tell you, beyond that I said nothing to Alicky, through Ernie's advice; but now begin to regret I did not, for I might have explained things a little better if I had. For I can't really believe Alicky knows how much I really love her, or she would not I think have treated me quite so cruelly. For I can't help considering it so, as she apparently gives me no chance at all, and little or no hope; although I shall continue loving her, and in the hope that some day she may think better of what she has said, and give me the chance of being one of the happiest beings in the world. For I should indeed consider myself so, if I would only call her my own.

I am almost certain, as certain as most people are who are in love with a girl, that I could make her happy, if she would only give me a chance of doing so. Don't you think I may say so, for I certainly feel it. I am sure you will feel for me in my great disappointment, or you would not have taken the trouble to write me such a nice letter as you did and interest yourself in me. Grandmama was extremely nice about it all and said some very kind things to me, for as you know, she was always in favour of a union between me and Alicky, and spoke to me on the subject last year. Perhaps later you might be able to find out if there is any real reason why Alicky does not care for me, and if I have offended her in any way. For Ernie said there was none, which makes it all harder for me to understand.

I fear you will have just missed seeing her and Ernie unless you met them on their way home.

I was very glad to hear you had been given a ship at last, and it is the first time you have your own command which I should think is what you wished. I am very sorry not to see you before I start for India, for it is a very long time since we met, and I shall be away for at least five months. But perhaps on my way home next year I may come across you, for I should very likely stop at Malta and go home over land, as I have never been there as yet.

We have been here since last Monday and remain until the end of the week when we start for Venice where we stay a few days on our way to Athens. I should be very pleased if you would send me a line sometime to tell me what you think of my prospects, and whether I shall have a chance again with Alicky. For what has happened entirely alters what you said in your first letter.

Ever your very affectte cousin,

Eddy[31]

The Queen was not at all happy about Alicky's adamant reaction – 'she refuses the greatest position there is!'[32] – and yet she admired the girl's strong-mindedness (or her gambling streak, for we must not forget that she had no formal understanding with the Tsarevich Nicholas). But one aches for Eddy, who seems to be so shy, so unassuming and so trusting. Could it be that the navy and Cambridge and the Hussars had left him awkward when faced with girls – at any rate, girls of his own class? He is unassertive, as well as unassuming; dependent on advice; happy to let others make the running on his behalf. None of this is surprising, given his background. The son of a notoriously sophisticated father, he seems emotionally more like a fifteen-year-old than a man of nearly twenty-six. The Princess of Wales is often blamed for the infantilisation of both her sons, but the Queen expected all of her family to do her bidding throughout their adult lives, and as for the Prince of Wales, his behaviour was so ripe, so notorious, that the Marlborough House set can never have felt fully at ease in Eddy's company, and talk among his brother officers must have been guarded.

He seems baffled by the complexity of people. Everyone agrees that he was friendly and charming, but in his 'voice' there is all the vulnerability of the innocent. He had not been completely taken up by contemporaries of his own class, so nobody knew how he spent his time, and it is this widespread ignorance of his true nature that allowed gossip to thrive. The letter to Louis was written on Monday 7 October 1889. Bertie wrote his kind letter to Somerset on 9 October. He heard the rumours shortly afterwards, and brought out the biggest guns he had. He could do no more without being accused of blatant interference.

He preferred not to set foot in England himself, for he was acutely embarrassed financially at this time and moneylenders – not honourable ones, like the Rothschilds, or understanding ones like Sam Lewis, but loan sharks – were conspicuous wherever he went. As a prince, he received hospitality and gifts everywhere, and was expected to return the favours. He was also expected to support a family and large household in a style to which others could only aspire. The government money he received was inadequate to keep even a careful man in his position, and he was not a careful man. The Queen, while demanding that he carry out most of the public duties which otherwise would have devolved upon her, declined to supplement his income. In France, in mid-November, the British Ambassador wrote to Lord Salisbury explaining that he had instituted a police enquiry, 'with a view to the protection of HRH' from 'the abuse of his name and position' by disreputable moneylenders. The French police reported that after months of unsuccessfully trying to borrow money, he had got it from the Rothschilds; the British Ambassador thought they were wrong, and he had got it from Baron Hirsch.[33] Whoever was right, the Prince of Wales was in recurrent financial trouble. This was nothing new. It meant, however, that he had, to some extent, the sympathy of Henry Labouchère, the rich editor of *Truth*, who as a radical believed that if there must be a royal family at all, then at least the reigning monarch should pay for it. Labouchère's sympathy would be of real value to him in the months to come.

8

Under the Carpet
1889–90

Eddy and the Prince of Wales left for Denmark on 1 October 1889. Eddy would not return to England for seven months.

After a few days, the Prince of Wales left the family in Fredensborg and proceeded to Venice. Eddy, with his mother and unmarried sisters, followed in the second week of October. The whirlwind of activity from Knollys and Probyn on 16 October indicates that information about Arthur Somerset, and possibly even Eddy, first reached the Prince of Wales during the time he spent in Venice: 'I don't believe it. I won't believe it any more than I would if they had accused the Archbishop of Canterbury. Go and see Monro, go to the Treasury, see Lord Salisbury if necessary.' It was on 16 October that Sir Dighton Probyn and Sir Francis Knollys met Newton, approached Scotland Yard and the office of the Treasury Solicitor, and urged Arthur Somerset to engage the Prince's own lawyer, George Lewis.

On 17 October, Knollys telegraphed to Lord Salisbury making an appointment for Probyn to see him the next day.

On 15 October, the Waleses embarked on the *Osborne* for a ten-day cruise to Piraeus. In Athens, they would spend a few days at a gathering of the clans – the wedding of Crown Prince Constantine, Duke of Sparta, to Princess Sophie of Prussia. The fact that their own eldest son was not as yet spoken for would not have been lost on the Waleses. The Prince must have felt extremely confused. He was horrified by the talk about Arthur Somerset. He found it almost impossible to believe that his friend had been keeping such sordid company, and the very idea that it could be true made him think that Somerset had gone mad – a 'lunatic', he called him. But he could trust Knollys and Probyn to sort something out.

Friday 18 October saw royal influence exercised in the subtlest of ways. Sir Dighton Probyn and Sir Francis Knollys had arranged to meet Lord Arthur Somerset in the afternoon, before Probyn's early-evening appointment with the Prime Minister. They arrived at the Marlborough Club and found that Somerset was not there, although they noticed a luggage-laden cab waiting in the street.

Lord Salisbury was on his way back from France, and would travel across London on his way to Hatfield House. He expected to be at King's Cross in time for the seven o'clock train on the Great Northern Line, and met Probyn at the railway station. He had time enough in which to answer Probyn's enquiry, which was, in his own words quoted by H. Montgomery Hyde: '…whether there was any ground for certain charges which had been made in the newspapers against sundry persons whom he named', including, apparently, Prince Albert Victor and the Earl of Euston, as well as Lord Arthur Somerset.

The Prime Minister intimated that only Somerset was involved, and that there had been insufficient evidence to issue a warrant, although, 'I think,' Salisbury later told the House of Lords, 'I added – but of that I am not quite certain – that rumours had reached me that further evidence had been obtained, but I did not know what its character was.'[1] Salisbury had seen the evidence against Somerset, which Probyn had not. Sir Dighton Probyn was shocked that even Somerset was truly implicated; he had until that moment believed him entirely innocent and the whole affair a matter of mistaken identity.

Somehow, between 17 and 18 October, Arthur Somerset was given to understand that storm clouds were gathering. According to his later letter to Reggie Brett, it was Oliver Montagu who helped him get away quietly.[2] The morning after Probyn's interview with Salisbury, he was in Boulogne. The *North London Press* was not fooled for a minute.

> My Lord Gomorrah sat in his chair
> Sipping his costly wine;
> He was safe in France, that's called the fair
> In a city some call 'Boo-line';
> He poked the blaze and he warmed his toes
> And as the sparks from the logs arose
> He laid one finger beside his nose –
> And my Lord Gomorrah smiled.
>
> He thought of the wretched, vulgar toys
> Of his paederastian joys,
> How they lay in prison, poor scapegoat fools;
> Raw, cash-corrupted boys –
> While he and his pals the 'office' got
> From a friend at Court and were off like a shot
> Out of reach of Law, Justice, and 'that – rot'
> And my Lord Gomorrah smiled.[3]

Athens had not seen anything remotely like it for centuries – the massed fleets of England and Germany and several other countries banging thunderous salutes in the bay; cheering crowds of picturesquely costumed country folk; long processions of carriages full of ladies in froths of lace from Worth and gentlemen, pink from the heat, in tailoring from Savile Row and the Rue de Rivoli; everyone jostling and swarming and chattering under a late summer sun, as the crowds, on foot and on wheels, progressed to the cathedral. In magenta prose, *The Times*'s correspondent compared the show of naval force to Barbarossa, with 'labouring sloops and high-pooped caravels', and expressed his fascination with 'black-eyed islemen from the sunny Cyclades'. The Orthodox ceremony had been shortened by special request of the King, but still took hours and hours, and Eddy and George had to take turns holding a heavy golden crown over the head of the bride. There was a Protestant wedding immediately afterwards. The bridal couple, exhausted, soldiered bravely through.

Bertie snatched a moment in which to write a gracious letter to Lord Salisbury, thanking him for allowing Somerset to flee and asking that the 'unfortunate lunatic' might perhaps be able quietly to slip into the country to see his aged parents from time to time. He was nice to the Kaiser, who came aboard the *Osborne* and told him how to reorganise the fleet. He and Eddy slipped away to Port Said on the morning of Monday 28 October. The Princess and the girls came, too, just as far as Salamis, but the weather had changed by the time they trans-shipped from the *Osborne* to the *Dreadnought* for their trip back to Athens for luncheon. How convenient to have a warship on hand for such eventualities. Eddy and his father ploughed on in the *Osborne* across choppy seas.

Was anything said? It seems likely that Knollys and Probyn preferred not to consign Newton's threats about Eddy even to the diplomatic bag; after all, Salisbury said there was nothing in it. Even if the Prince of Wales had heard rumours as early as this, it would have been more in character for him to evade confrontation, with a good Burgundy and reminiscences of his tiger hunts in '75.

By 31 October, Eddy and his father had parted, his father to return to Europe and avoid his creditors in Paris while Eddy made his way with Captain Holford overland by train to Cairo. There, they embarked upon a delightful journey down the Suez Canal with friends (including Captain Alwyne Greville, who had been equerry until June) and a party of about a dozen whom he knew, among whom only one unmarried female is listed (perhaps a lady's maid). Sir Edward Bradford was among the most colourful of the party. A vicar's son, awarded a cadet-ship with the East India Company as a boy, his brilliant military career had been cut short in 1863 when he lost an arm to a tiger. He was appointed to the Indian police force and specialised in investigating sedition and serious criminality, but continued to enjoy boar-hunting with the reins held between his teeth.[4] No doubt this would be a working holiday for him, as he would have a security function besides being able to explain to Eddy the many new customs and people he would come across in India.

Eddy had two cabins knocked into one, but the accommodation aboard ship was still airless. At Aden on 5 November (according to Vincent, who took notes from Holford's diaries), he 'received a deputation of Parsees and Jews', but there were few other official duties. The party proceeded across the ocean to Bombay, amusing themselves with concerts, banjo-playing and cards, like a rather warm and sticky house-party. They arrived in port on 9 November.

Bombay, that gloriously seething city, would tax the descriptive powers of the most ambitious *Times* correspondent, and even Eddy, so notoriously undemonstrative, must have been bowled over by new impressions. He was greeted by his uncle, the Duke of Connaught, and whirled through the colour and life of the city to stay in the hills at Poona for a few days. On 15 November he arrived at Hyderabad, 'the most truly Oriental city in India, and perhaps the only one in which the spectacle of Europeans and Asiatics meeting in friendly and unrestrained social intercourse may be witnessed'.[5] We are indebted to J.D. Rees, a senior member of the Indian Civil Service, for this description and for the thoughtful, liberal voice of British rule which pervades his account of the Prince's travels. Generally, he writes, people are better off under the British and protected 'native' rulers than they were 100 or even fifty years ago. He approves of government by Indian rulers, 'when once their position is assured by the protection of the British power', believing that the locals prefer it to rule by the British. At least, he says, their revenues stay in the country and their gods are respected. Native territories tended to be dirtier and less well organised, but according to Rees, the Indian population hated paying taxes for better sanitation and irrigation and were happier when 'the government, though less scientific, is capable of producing more of that repose and quiet content so congenial to the native mind'. Like all of his class, he had read Gibbon and compared India with lands of the Roman Empire, which he thought were deplorably over-ruled from afar. There could be dispute about how much social progress had been made in the state of Hyderabad, but 'lady doctors are being educated'.

Hyderabad was ruled by a Muslim potentate, His Highness the Nizam, a hereditary ruler two years younger than Eddy. The Prime Minister was His Excellency Sir Asman Jah, his brother-in-law; somebody at Reuters got his name wrong and the Nizam of Hyderabad had to write a brisk correction to *The Times*, which appeared on 16 November – the day after Eddy's reception and the incorrect news report. Communications crossed the Empire at lightning speed, if you knew the right official.

Lady Grant-Duff, accompanying the English party, described the magnificent Nizam as:

…below the middle height and slightly made, with handsome, regular features, more European than native in character. He wears whiskers and a moustache, and his hair is somewhat longer than is the fashion among young Englishmen. He wears a black coat like an undress uniform, a gold belt with a diamond clasp, and magnificent diamonds on his cap.[6]

He was famously charming and pro-British, and very rich indeed; he was said to have spent £200,000 on his welcome to the Prince. The party arrived by train and 'on the way had dined, slept and breakfasted in the luxurious railway saloons of HH the Nizam, which no Pullman car, or any other kind of *wagon lit*, can equal'. The Prince was accompanied by Captain Holford and Captain Greville and the Resident Sir Dennis Fitzpatrick, the staff of the Residency and officers of the 7th Hussars. The Nizam's ADC was Nawab Afsar Jung – 'one of the best riders, pig-stickers and tent-peggers in India'. The lovely weather, cool in the morning and hot in the day, was much appreciated by the large English party. At every station, there were big levies of troops: Eddy reviewed 7,000 in Hyderabad. One of the Hussars fainted. All the city's nobility turned out: Parsees, Hindus, and Muslims. The Prince rode in a carriage through the city towards the Char Minar, or Four Minarets:

…in one window, a venerable Mussulman sits smoking his hubble-bubble pipe; in another, a veiled lady peeps timorously out; here, a boy toys with a pet bird, or a man takes a fighting partridge from his pocket. In the shops of the armourers are knives, swords and long guns, whose thin barrels are bound with brass, inlaid with ivory, or ornamented with silver. In the flower-shops there is a wanton exhibition of roses without stalks, and of garlands of heavy and sweet-smelling jasmine, such as pleasantly asphyxiate the wearer…[7]

In the teeming crowds, Eddy noticed a few placards gently pleading for better educational facilities. And then they arrived at the Nizam's palace, with its raised lakes, pillared halls, chandeliers, royal yellow carpets, and neverending series of courtyards and quadrangles surrounded by high walls. And back to the Residency for a ball. There was a ballroom and exotic garden; and among the Nizam's party was a racing man, Ali Aboola from the Persian Gulf, an importer of horses and supporter of the Turf. With so many Hussars in the party, polo would be played soon, and in no time all the talk was of hunting.

In the morning they would start early for Sirunagar, where HH the Nizam had a large deer park.

> The prince and the Nizam shot a buck apiece. The hunting leopard ran down another. No sooner was he un-hooded than he disappeared in a deep ravine, and was soon among the deer, which fled before him. He marked down his quarry, however, and sprang upon it, and when the party rode up he was sucking the blood from his victim's throat. He was hooded by his keeper while continuing his sanguinary draught, and immediately let go the antelope, and was taken back to his cart, and given a bowl of buck's blood as a reward for obedience and good behaviour.[8]

They took luncheon to the music of a private band, in a magnificent palace. In the afternoon, there was snipe shooting; and, in the evening, a state banquet for 400 hosted by the Nizam. Eddy had not a minute's rest.

In England, the rumour mill was grinding loudly. According to one account:

> The 'responsible' rumour had it that Lord Arthur was an innocent victim of the malevolence of the lower orders determined to drag the aristocracy into the mire. The 'irresponsible' rumour had it that

Lord Arthur was the sodomite-in-waiting to the royal family, the medium through which Prince Albert Victor was able to indulge his unnatural lusts.[9]

Arthur Somerset, alias Short, alias Lord Gomorrah, resigned his commission at the end of October. Before all this began, he and Marcus Beresford had recommended a fellow officer for a job as Master of Horse to the Sultan of Turkey. He now wondered whether he might not be able to take up the post himself, if it were still vacant; he could find no employment in France even as a clerk, since he lacked references.

N[ewton] tells me that he fears it is certain that several people will be prosecuted. In case any of those mixed up in this case have to go abroad, I wish they would come here or I would go to them. It would be so much less dull.[10]

On 10 November, the *New York Times*, in an article headed 'November London Gossip', alleged that another 'extremely painful and revolting scandal', of the same nature as the one at Dublin Castle in 1884, was the talk of the town; and, as in that case, the minnows would be prosecuted while the sharks got away. Having named Lord Arthur Somerset as the only one of sixteen to forty possible culprits, including royal ones, to be named – and allowed to get away – it goes on:

Current rumour says that Prince Albert Victor will not return from India until the matter is completely over and forgotten, but there are certain stubborn moralists at work on the case who profess determination that it shall not be judicially burked, and the prospects are that the whole terrible affair will be dragged out into light.[11]

The long-dreaded warrant for Podge's arrest on charges of gross indecency was not issued until 12 November, by which time he had

joined his brother in Monaco. The Duke of Badminton pleaded
with him to come home and face the music, and did not know
what to tell the Duchess. In the end, he came up with a cock-
and-bull story about some nasty men having caught Arthur in a
house of ill fame and blackmailed him.[12] The Duchess listened
sceptically. Arthur's sister Blanche, the Marchioness of Waterford,
had every sympathy for her brother and travelled to Monte Carlo to
comfort him. She wrote protesting at the rumours about Eddy.

> Please correct any impression that Arthur and *the boy* ever went out
> together... Arthur knows nothing of his movements and was hor-
> rified to think he might be supposed to take the Father's money
> and lead the son into mischief of ANY kind. I am sure the boy is
> as straight as a line... I am so glad – dear nice boy.[13]

She also expressed utter disbelief in stories that George Holford
would have taken Eddy to the place. There were so many different stories. Arthur Newton's original – the one he told Knollys
and Probyn in the presence of Somerset – is unknown, although
it seems to have concerned some kind of appointment book
kept by Hammond.

Christmas loomed. Somerset, having grown a beard as a dis-
guise, moved on to Constantinople in high hopes of working
for the Sultan, only to discover that for legal reasons the British
Embassy were impelled to arrest him themselves. He had to
leave at once. He scuttled onwards to snowbound Budapest,
wondering how he would find work. He had very little money,
and nothing to do except walk and read. He wrote a self-pitying,
self-serving letter to Reggie Brett. Somerset freely admitted that
he hardly knew Eddy. He might not have quailed at lying to
his good-hearted sister in November, when he heard what the
Beresfords and others were saying, but on 10 December 1889
he was writing in terms that implied he believed what he had
heard about Eddy being involved.

I can quite understand the Prince of Wales being much annoyed
at his son's name being coupled with the thing but that was the
case before I left – in fact in June or July... It had no more to do
with me than the fact that we (that is Prince and I) must both
perform bodily functions which we cannot do for each other. In
the same way we were both accused of going to this place but not
together; and different people were supposed to have gone there to
meet us... Nothing will ever make me divulge anything I know
even if I were arrested... It has very often, I may say constantly
occurred to me that it rests with me to clear up this business, but
what can I do? A great many people would never speak to me
again as it is; but if I went into Court, and told all I knew, *no one*
who called himself a man would *ever* speak to me again. Hence
my infernal position... At all events you and Newton can bear
me witness that I have sat absolutely tight in the matter and have
not even told my father anything.[14]

'Nothing will ever make me divulge anything I know' – on the one
hand, he admits that he barely knows Eddy; on the other, that he
'know[s]' something. There is a difference between knowing, and
believing because it suits you. A letter of 23 December acknowl-
edges this. The newspapers in England and America had made snide
references (untrue) to Eddy's imminent recall from India under a
cloud. And the police were after Newton. Somerset wrote:

I should think they have tackled a strong and dangerous man in
N. If they put him in a corner he will very likely give them a
nasty one... I feel sure that with all this virulent prosecution of
everybody they will end by having out in open court exactly what
they are all trying to keep quiet. I wonder if it is really a fact or
only an invention of that arch ruffian H[ammond].[15]

No statement could be clearer; any story about Eddy must have
come to him from Newton, who had cited Hammond.

An indignant defender of Eddy, whose letter appeared in the *New York Herald* on 22 December, had – like him – concluded that the truth would out.

> What is quite clear is that the authorities are now determined to go on, and that sooner or later the real culprits will stand revealed to the public eye, even if they manage to escape the hands of justice.

This anonymous letter-writer was believed to be close to the Prince of Wales. Now that Somerset was away, Bertie was anxious that a full enquiry should be held. Evidently the true story was that:

> This man, Hammond by name, knew most of his customers and had kept a list of them. That list is now in the possession of the police, unless it has mysteriously disappeared with certain other papers which passed between police headquarters and the Treasury.[16]

From being a blackmailer's list, this had become – in the mind of certain gossips – a kind of Visitors' Book. Genteel number 19 may have been, but not quite as genteel as that. If Hammond knew his customers' true identities, he would have found out largely by having them followed. Street directories, and servants, were good sources of information once an address was known.

As further fuel to curiosity about Cleveland Street, another titled person was publicly named, directly in the context of 'Eddy' rumours. On 16 November, the *North London Press*, informed by a police source, printed Somerset's name, and that of the Earl of Euston, who had 'gone to Peru'.

> These men have been allowed to leave the country, and thus defeat the ends of justice, because their prosecution would disclose the

fact that a far more distinguished and more highly placed personage was inculpated in these disgusting crimes.[17]

Lord Euston had been mentioned by Newlove, and now he
had become, in one version of the story, the person who had
allegedly taken Eddy to Cleveland Street. As it happened, he
was famously amorous of women; he was livid, and instructed
George Lewis at once. Apart from anything else, he said, he
hadn't gone to Peru.

Parke, the editor, got up a defence fund. Newton sent
Charles Gill a watching brief on behalf of Somerset. Lord
Euston appeared at a preliminary hearing and explained that
he had gone to Cleveland Street once, believing it to be a house
where he could see girls in *poses plastiques*, and upon realising
as soon as he got inside that it was not, had left in disgust. The
full hearing was delayed, by one thing or another, until after
Christmas, the result of which was merely to let gossip spread
like a brush fire.

Oliver Montagu, who according to Somerset had helped him
to get away, was now furious with him for staying abroad, and
wrote to tell him so. In a letter to Blanche Waterford, he said he
had told her brother:

> [that] I felt he could not be aware of the irreparable harm he
> was doing by still persisting in his silence as to the real cause of
> his leaving the country and insinuating that it was for the sake of
> others that he had done so thereby leaving people here to draw
> their own inferences and drag innocent people's names through
> the mire.

Somerset protested to Brett:

> I have never mentioned the boy's name except to Probyn, Montagu
> and Knollys when they were acting for me and I thought they

ought to know. Had they been wise, hearing what I knew and
therefore what others knew, they ought to have hushed the matter
up, instead of stirring it up as they did, with all the authorities.

Probyn, Montagu and Knollys were not 'acting for him', except
in the couple of days before he fled on 19 October, when they
may well have believed him innocent. Thanks to Newton, the
story had started to get about in the few days before the trial
of Veck and Newlove, over a month earlier. Somerset continued backtracking, via his sister, Blanche Waterford. In a letter to
Reggie Brett, in December, she wrote:

> Arthur does not the least know how or where the boy spends his
> time, and [says] that he never went out with him except twice
> to Jubilee fireworks and a smoking concert where my Father was
> – and that nothing in the world would distress him more than that
> his going away should throw the smallest doubt upon the boy.[18]

Days later, she asked whether her brother should write to Sir
Dighton Probyn 'or someone', explaining that 'he believes the
boy to be perfectly innocent, but that the man (Hammond)
threatened to *chantage* [blackmail] him as a stronger inducement
to extract hush money from Arthur'.

Word reached Blanche Waterford that she was supposed to have
been gossiping, and she wrote to Oliver Montagu in December,
knowing that he had been at Sandringham and that she was suspected by the Prince and Princess of rumourmongering about
their son. He wrote back that their Royal Highnesses had never
thought so:

> …though I fear there is no doubt that some female members of
> your family have done so, and I confess that I think it the most
> cruel and wicked shame on their part.

Blanche had no sisters, and her mother knew little of the affair, and would have been at pains to cover it up anyway. H. Montgomery Hyde says Montagu is referring to Henry Somerset's estranged wife, and that she was 'obsessed with the subject of homosexuality'. She was Blanche's sister-in-law. Lady Henry Somerset had been *persona non grata* in society for over a decade, was living in Shropshire, and was at this time entirely occupied with doing good works.[19] She was charming, earnest, and a talented writer and artist who had made a meaningful life for herself among people of a quite different stamp, who did not mix with the Beauforts. She had no one of influence with whom to gossip. An impossible contender, in other words.

A much likelier culprit was Lady Charles Beresford, that other sister-in-law, who trusted Blanche's husband well enough to deposit Daisy Brooke's letter with him. She was throughout the autumn of 1889 still extremely angry over that affair, and had, in her own mind, every reason to repeat whatever she heard about the Wales family. Undoubtedly, this was the conclusion reached by the Prince of Wales, casting about in his mind for someone malevolent enough to spread such stories.

Bertie was adept at divide-and-rule tactics: just a word – that if Lady Charles Beresford were invited, he would not be present – would be quite enough to effect a social boycott. And, indeed, she was shunned. On 12 January 1890, Lord Charles and the Prince of Wales had an enormous row about Beresford's wife's ignominy. The Eddy rumours may not have come into it; but in any case arguments between friends usually raise an accumulation of small grievances, and as Wales was now entirely fascinated by Daisy Brooke, he may have resented her former affection for the younger, handsomer Beresford. Beresford, who was about to go to sea in the *Undaunted*, felt that his wife was being cold-shouldered because she had refused to do the Prince's bidding and destroy Daisy Brooke's letter. He lost control of his temper, shouted and called Bertie a blackguard and a coward,

and stormed off.[20] These tactics improved neither his friendship
with the Prince, nor his wife's social position. George Lewis was
invited to Sandringham, where – Lord Euston's case having been
successfully concluded the week before – he played baccarat
with the Prince of Wales.[21]

On the Saturday following Eddy's arrival in Rangoon for
Christmas, Rochefort's *La Lanterne* and the *New York Herald*
printed a report that there was no truth in the rumour that
Prince Albert Victor would be recalled early from his Indian
tour. *The Times* also insisted that he would return in March, as
decided 'nearly a year ago'.

> We are requested to state that there is not the slightest founda-
> tion for the report which has appeared in certain newspapers
> to the effect that Prince Albert Victor will return from India at
> an earlier date than was originally settled... The Prince of Wales
> terminated his visit to the Danish Minister and Mme de Falbe
> yesterday morning and, attended by the Hon Tyrwhitt Wilson,
> returned to London. The Princess of Wales and Prince George
> of Wales, with other of the guests, remain at Luton Hoo two or
> three days longer.[22]

There is a strong impression of a face like thunder. The French
and American papers were fanning the flames, deliberately.

    There is a curious note in one account of Reggie Brett's part
in the affair, that same Saturday, 21 December. At Brett's home at
1, Tilney Street, he and John Oswald – another friend of Podge's
– interviewed Arthur Newton and, according to James Lees-
Milne, 'vindicated Mr Newton from police charges that he had
endeavoured to obtain false evidence from telegraph boys who
had frequented the Cleveland Street brothel'.[23] This statement
by Brett's biographer raises more questions than it answers. What
'false evidence'? It would certainly suit Newton if the telegraph

boys implicated Eddy. But common sense suggests that Brett and Oswald were in no position to 'vindicate' or exonerate Newton. What passes between a client (several of the telegraph boys were his clients) and a solicitor is supposedly confidential.

The police certainly charged Newton, but not with trying to elicit false evidence. In the absence of their main suspect, they were going to expose as much as they could about Cleveland Street. Newton, De Gallo and Taylerson were accused of attempting to pervert and defeat the course of justice by offering money to various boys to leave England and go to America, and by hustling Hammond away to America. The preliminary hearings were recorded in *The Times* from 8 January onwards; Arthur Somerset was named as Allies's friend Mr Brown, and Taylerson (for whose conduct Newton took responsibility) was pointed out as the person who had approached Allies. A reader who did not know the ins and outs of the case would be hard put to make sense of it all; it was all something to do with telegraph boys, and Cleveland Street, and people going to see Inspector Abberline and complaining that they had lost their job. Charlie Gill, defending Newton, with truly breathtaking nerve blamed Inspector Abberline, saying that if he had prevented Hammond from escaping overseas none of this would have happened.[24] He produced witnesses who had been at a dinner party which, according to them, took place at Mr and Mrs Newton's house at New Malden on 25 September – the day when, according to PC Hanks, Arthur Newton slipped away from the pub when Allies turned up. According to Mr Samuelson, an accountant at the *Daily Telegraph*, Arthur Newton was happily dining with him, and his other guests, until Taylerson arrived at ten and took him back to town on urgent business. Cross-examined by the prosecution, 'he thought the 25th of September was a Tuesday; no, wait a minute, it was Thursday or Friday'.[25] It was a Wednesday.

Newton's case dropped from view, and continued unresolved throughout the spring. Not so that of Ernest Parke of the *North*

London Press, who on 15 January appeared at the Old Bailey in
order to defend himself on charges of criminal libel against Lord
Euston. He pleaded justification: that Lord Euston, according
to his information, had committed indecent acts at Cleveland
Street from May 1887 onwards with John Saul and Frank Hewett
– Hewett being one of the telegraph boys. Cross-questioned
by the formidable Sir Charles Russell, Parke's witnesses might
well have collapsed anyway, but since most of them swore that
they knew Lord Euston well, by sight, and that he was a man of
middle height, there was no hope for the benighted editor. Lord
Euston was six feet four, and none of Parke's witnesses knew
him from Adam. They had all been paid by an incompetent
detective agency to make statements of recognition. Hewett was
not there, as he had 'gone abroad'. When Saul was called as a
witness, he claimed to have told Abberline about his meetings
with Euston last August. This allegation worked rather in favour
of the prosecution, for it was impossible for a jury of property-
owning men to believe that the police would not have taken
immediate action, had that been true; and they had done nothing. Otherwise, Saul, who made no secret of his trade, made the
worst possible impression. The jury's deliberations took less than
forty minutes, and Parke, pleading the inviolability of his sources
to the end, had to serve a prison sentence of twelve months
without hard labour.

After Hyderabad, Eddy's party travelled onwards to Madras,
where there was a ceremonial greeting from Lord Connemara,
umpteen military and government officials, the Maharajah of
Vizianagaram and the Prince of Arcot. At Chingleput they shot
snipe – 'The Prince and Captains Holford and Harvey bagged
between them 49 and a half brace in the day…'. There was a state
reception for over 1,000 people 'and as many as possible were
presented to His Royal Highness, who wore the uniform of the
10th Hussars'. The excellent band of the Governor of Madras

played, among other things, an original composition entitled 'a welcome to Prince Albert Victor', by Monsieur Stradiot.[26]

At Mysore, they saw the prison in which Tippoo had kept Englishmen; and moved on to a nearby estate for an elephant hunt. From Bangalore – most of these journeys were by train – they proceeded to Trichinopoly and back to Madras, where, despite the extensive preparations which had been made to receive them, they carried straight on, on medical advice, because of a cholera scare. There was more hunting at Travancore, dancing by Nautch girls and a juggling show. Eddy was showered with rose petals and met nabobs galore, and was earnestly informed about social questions and education and history between shoots. A typical maharajah was the proud owner of a circus, in which his sons were trained to ride, besides

> ...a covered and barred enclosure, where pearls, diamonds and rubies, silver cords and golden bowls worth in all perhaps £300,000 are spread out for inspection on a carpet embroidered with pearls and other precious stones, itself worth £20,000.[27]

The monsoon rains were upon them by the time they embarked, on 16 December, at Madras for Rangoon. Captain Holford, groaning into his diary, complained that the cooks on SS *Kistna* persisted in cooking rich French dishes throughout their rough passage across the Bay of Bengal.[28]

After Rangoon, they spent an enchanting Christmas season in the warmth and sunshine of Mandalay, with boat races and a garden party with a tug of war. A boat trip of several days up the Irrawaddy was followed by horse-racing. At all these events Eddy was meeting new people – in Mandalay, largely British ones. In the first week of the New Year, the party was back in Calcutta for polo, steeplechasing, snipe shooting, a 'native' entertainment on the Maidan, and a grand ball, besides a meeting with the Maharajah of Cooch Behar. Then they were off to Benares to see the burning ghats. J.E. Vincent, scrutinising Captain Holford's diary, writes:

> The striking point about all these days is their interminable length. The one on which my eye now rests began at 6.45am, and ended with the native play, which did not begin until after dinner at 8pm.[29]

At a tiger hunt in mid-January, hosted by a maharajah, the Prince killed cheetah and sambur. The shoot was judged less than successful, as 5,000 beaters had been employed in the maharajah's determination to corral a tiger which would take up its position in Eddy's line of sight, but it had proved too clever for them. They progressed to Lucknow, where a British survivor of the siege explained exactly what happened, and where, to the Prince. There were more grisly recollections at Cawnpore, where a massacre of British women and children was marked by a garden barred to 'natives'.

Considering the royal party's size, the distances to be travelled, and the complexities of packing, Eddy and his companions were covering an enormous amount of ground with remarkable speed. Every starched and polished and bay-rummed gentleman had at least one British batman or valet. The Duke and Duchess of Connaught, meeting Eddy at Bombay, had been overwhelmed by the volume of luggage that accompanied him; like his father, he was punctilious about being correctly attired for every occasion. Unseen logistical support came from armies of local washerwomen and cooks, drivers, and animal-keepers. Packing every item of luggage, from gun-cases to huge leather trunks and writing cases and bootboxes and solar topees, into leather or metal hatboxes must have taken hours. And yet the party descended, like locusts, and moved on again within days.

At Bhartpur, on 22 January, they bagged a large number of animals and would have shot even more, except the day's sport was spoiled, 'as has been the case many times and will be the case many more times, by dalliance over luncheon'.[30] The next day was spent sightseeing at Agra, where the Taj Mahal is situated, after which they returned to Bhartpur for pig-sticking on 24 January. The Prince stuck a few, and a horse was stuck too; there is no mention that they paid the maharajah for it. At Lahore, the Prince and companions rode through the city in a silver howdah on the back of an elephant. And so it went on: meeting Prince Adolphus of Teck, May's brother, and Afsar Jung many times, and inspecting troops, sightseeing, and participating in a 'buffalo wallow' in which a man (unnamed) broke his neck. Military receptions, presentation of medals, an expedition along the Khyber pass; and on by midnight train from Peshawar to Rawalpindi where, after a grand review of troops, Eddy met Ayub Khan. 'He lives here partly as a prisoner and partly as an honoured guest,' Holford noted in his diary, adding 'We allow him £30,000 a year.'[31]

The party returned to Lahore, and continued to Delhi, sticking pigs and hunting at every opportunity. In Jaipur, they rode through the town on elephants, 'beautifully caparisoned and painted, the Maharajah and the Prince being on the first'. At lunch the next day, they heard there was a tiger within reach. 'There was no more thought of ladies or of luncheon' – and all the men raced off to hunt. With the assistance of 2,000 beaters, five elephants and a smoking fire, they bagged it.

In February, they visited Mayo College and drove '72 miles along a sandy track in frightful heat' to Udaipur, where the maharajah had provided 'a drive of pigs and hyenas, and fights between firstly, a tigress and a wild pig, and secondly, a panther and a pig', After this they rowed home to Udaipur across the illuminated lake, and Holford wrote 'this was by far the most beautiful sight any of us had seen'.[32]

At Jodphur, they got two days' pig-sticking; at the 'Nepal Terai' where (after an inspection of troops) they hunted tiger and leopard, they shot 'two hog deer, and some peacock'. Further on, the Prince killed a tigress and one of her cubs, which had been ringed ready for him. On and on, day after day, tigers and bears were shot. As for partridges, they killed too many to count.

In London, the rumours continued. The Prince of Wales had been delighted by the long letter in defence of Eddy which had appeared in the *New York Herald* just before Christmas, but ultimately it silenced no one; and when Parke got his long sentence, insisting to the last that he stood by his allegations but was protecting a source, many supporters thought he had been unjustly punished. If Saul had lied in the witness box, why had the authorities decided not to prosecute him for perjury? If he had told the truth about his way of life, why was he not prosecuted for indecency? Newton was doing all he could to keep his own case out of the public eye, and in March got it transferred from the Old Bailey and deferred to a later date. There had been no last word, and Bertie correctly perceived that, until there was, Eddy's name would not be cleared.

Support came from an unlikely source. Henry Labouchère, the editor of *Truth*, was determined to see injustice righted. Back in November, he had started running a series of articles about the Cleveland Street affair in his magazine – 'some of the greatest hereditary names of the country are mixed up in the scandal'.[33]

Labouchère was a republican, with strong feelings against the institution of monarchy, but no animosity towards the royal family personally; he simply disapproved of unequal treatment before the law. He was a rich man, a radical member of the establishment and the heir to a Huguenot banking fortune, with the networking talents of Bertie himself. Naturally, they knew each other, and both were liberal-minded. Ironically, it was Labouchère's amendment to the criminal law that was partly at the heart of the Cleveland Street affair. His insistence, in the House of Commons in 1885, that boys and men should be protected from homosexual advances by legislation, as in France, had resulted in that bodged law that became known as the Blackmailer's Charter.

Reggie Brett wrote to Labouchère in February, asking that he cease the relentless attacks in *Truth*. Labouchère agreed that too much was being made of the matter and, as far as he had heard, through a friend, Lord Arthur Somerset had indulged only in 'gentle dalliance' at Cleveland Street.[34] He was in touch with Knollys, and through him with the Prince of Wales, and went on to do his very best to defend Eddy against the slanders against him. In his capacity as Member for Northampton, he decided to reopen his attack on the cover-up of the affair. He directed his attack upon Lord Salisbury and the Home Secretary, Matthews.

At twenty past five on 28 February 1890, in the House of Commons, he rose to his feet and began to drive home his demands. 'There is no doubt that of late years a certain offence – I will not give it a name – has become more rife than it ever was before...'. He alleged that Newlove and Veck had got away with a light sentence in an effort to hush up the involvement of powerful people. He wanted to know why nobody had detained Lord Arthur Somerset, even for questioning, at any point; and why Hammond had been allowed to escape to America on a ticket bought by Mr Arthur Newton's clerk. These things he considered a travesty of justice, and he blamed Lord Salisbury for what amounted to 'a criminal conspiracy by the very guardians of public morality and law with the Prime Minister at their head'. Lord Salisbury's actions had in every respect aggravated the scandal. He was 'absolutely certain' that there was no foundation for what was being said about Eddy, and wanted to point out that Wales had done his best to get the whole affair brought out into the open. Despite his well-known views on royal grants, he believed the Prince of Wales was as anxious as he was to expose the true story.

I have seen the name of a gentleman of very high position mentioned in foreign newspapers in connection with the case but
having, as I have just said, looked very narrowly into the whole
matter, I am absolutely certain that there is no justification for the
calumny. In connection with this I may add that I know that a still
more eminent gentleman, closely connected with the gentleman
to whom I have alluded, has used all his efforts to have the fullest
publicity given… I protest against the good name of any man, be
he prince or peasant, being whispered and hinted away… I only
allude to this in order to show how incalculable are the evils that
might have arisen from this system which the Government has
adopted.[35]

He demanded an investigation. In 1888, the party opposite had
jeered at Parnell for not demanding an investigation into the
letters he was wrongly accused of having written. His not having
asked for an investigation, in that case, had been taken as an
indicator of something to hide – yet Parnell was later proved
innocent, and the letters forgeries. They could hardly deny
Labouchère an investigation now that he *was* asking for one.

The Attorney General defended the Veck/Newlove plea-
bargain. Sir Charles Russell's role in defending Newton was
brought up. On benches on both sides of the house, lawyers
who had had some part in the affair muttered and shrank from
the attack, while more Members filed in to watch. Labouchère
alleged that Probyn, having heard from Salisbury that October
night at King's Cross that a warrant would be issued almost at
once, tipped off Somerset. This may be true: no one will ever
know, and it does not matter – but it mattered to Labouchère,
who was asked to reveal his source. He told the Attorney General
that he would write the source's name on a piece of paper so
that he, Webster, could read it out. This offer was evaded (the
source was Knollys) and the Attorney General insisted that Lord
Salisbury (who was in the Upper House) denied ever having

put a date on the warrant. Labouchère said he did not believe Salisbury, and he was asked to withdraw. He refused, and was suspended from the House at ten to eight that evening.

The question was, had Lord Salisbury, or had he not, indirectly tipped Somerset off? He put speculation to rest (or so he hoped) in the House of Lords on Monday 3 March. He explained about the hurried meeting at King's Cross (he was late for his train) and how Knollys had asked whether there was any ground for the charges.

> My reply was that so far as I knew there was no ground whatever for them, no vestige of evidence against anyone except one person, whose name it is not necessary I should mention, and I said that as against that person I understood that the evidence was not thought to be sufficient in the judgment of those whose business it was to decide… That is all I recollect of a casual interview for which I was in no degree prepared, to which I did not attach the slightest importance, and of which I took no notes whatever… the rest of the conversation principally consisted of expressions on the part of Sir Dighton Probyn of absolute disbelief in the charges which were levelled against the person whom I have indicated, and of answers of a more reserved character on my part… I am quite certain that I never said, as has been imputed to me, that a warrant was about to be issued the next day, because such a statement would have been absolutely inconsistent with… [my assertion that] in the judgement of the legal authorities the evidence was insufficient.[36]

Since writing to Louis from Fredensborg, Eddy had been travelling for nearly six months. In March, after a 700-mile railway journey from Bareilly, they met the Gaekwar, who invited them to enjoy

> a hunt with cheetahs in the early morning, a conjuring entertainment, [and] an inspection of the Gaekwar's new palace and of his

marvellous jewels, including the diamond known as the Star of the South, for which the Gaekwar's father had given £80,000. Here too they saw carpets wrought in seed pearls for Mecca; and in the evening there was a great banquet, at which both the Gaekwar and the Prince made speeches.[37]

As ever, he laid foundation stones and planted trees. He visited a leper hospital and hunted lions. And in the middle of the month, his Indian tour complete, he spent six days attending ceremonial and official functions in Bombay: 'but even at Bunder,' writes the sympathetic J.E. Vincent, 'there was a final address to be read, and a final answer given by the Prince.'

As Eddy left India on SS *Assam* bound for Cairo, preparations were already being made for his next stage of life. The royal family were now determined that he must marry. In March of 1890, the Prince of Wales travelled to Germany with a list of possible brides. His first choice was 'Mossy', Margaret of Prussia, who was the new Emperor's sister. His wife did not approve of a Prussian bride, but what alternative was there? Eddy knew Mossy, as all the cousins knew each other; she had shared his carriage through the streets of Athens last October. She was not pretty and he did not want to marry her. The Prince of Wales did not know this, but he had no better ideas and the Queen certainly would not have her grandson marry anyone who was not royal. It was unthinkable that Prince Eddy might marry a lady in society. Louise had married a mere duke, which was bad enough, but at least he was rich. The Tecks still suffered from the Duke's father's morganatic marriage. However popular they were (and the fat Duchess was popular, despite being rather trying at times), they were never quite *comme il faut*: Princess May was penniless and would be awkward to place because of her tainted ancestry. Perhaps it was fellow-feeling – a feeling that she too was, in some way, an outsider now – that drew Princess Louise, the Duchess of Fife, towards May of Teck. They were quite close at this time

(East Sheen Lodge, where the Fifes lived, was within easy walking distance of White Lodge) and there is an account of a day in February 1890 when Louise came to call in a pony carriage and 'the two young things drove off in great glee'.[38]

In April, Prince Eddy spent eight days in Egypt. Arriving on a Monday, he was greeted by Sir Evelyn Baring, with whom he was to stay. Baring was the astute British agent and Consul-General who ruled Egypt through the Khedive Tewfik, about whom opinions are mixed. A contributor to Baring's entry in the *Dictionary of National Biography* regarded the Khedive as 'sagacious but not forceful', while Lord Randolph Churchill, who objected to Gladstone's support for Baring, called him 'one of the most despicable wretches who ever occupied an Eastern throne'. No doubt he was charming when Eddy spent the whole of Tuesday 9 April as his guest at the legendary Ghezira palace, on its island in the Nile. On Wednesday, free of official duties, Eddy shot quail; on Thursday he visited Saqara; and on Friday he attended a gymkhana, a dinner and a reception with senior British administrators, before leaving, on Saturday, for Athens.

Crown Princess Sophie, his newly married cousin, spent the next week with him and wrote to her mother 'poor boy he looks still dreadfully yellow and thin! He is such a dear and so good and kind!'[39] That 'still' could only refer to the last time they met – at her wedding over six months ago. And yet he seems to have had energy for what most people would consider an extremely active life, physically and mentally. He had been surrounded by 'old India hands' and old friends throughout his Indian trip, had been constantly stimulated and constantly on the go, had been accompanied everywhere by Holford and Captain Harvey, and no word reached London of any worsening in his health. It is hard to reconcile his robust acceptance of duty, and enjoyment of sport, with chronic illness of any kind. And yet illness there was.

On the last leg of his journey from India, Eddy paid his respects to President Carnot in Paris before taking the London train. Cheering crowds, a red carpet and an address by the mayor greeted him at Folkestone on 2 May. At Charing Cross, his parents, his sisters and the Duke of Fife were assembled on the platform to meet the 'thin' young prince, and he returned with them to Marlborough House.

Two weeks later, Newton having taken the unusual, and expensive, step of having his trial moved by writ of *a certiorari* from the Old Bailey to the Queen's Bench, in order to foil the bloodhounds of the press, it finally took place. Sir Charles Russell protested on Newton's behalf that he was terribly sorry; he had only been trying to protect clients from a blackmailer. The Attorney General, prosecuting, rolled over. He might almost have been speaking for the defence. In conclusion, he 'accepted the plea of guilty on the last count, and did not offer any evidence in regard to the earlier counts, and it was with great satisfaction that he found it unnecessary for him in public to go into the case, because the mischief done by discussion of such matters could not be over-exaggerated'.[40] Newton was to serve six weeks in prison, but it seems he never did. So ended the Cleveland Street scandal – for about eighty years.

9

Indisposed
1890

Eddy was the most susceptible of young men. Not simply because he admired prettiness and good clothes, but because he was sensitive to an undertow of feeling in the older generation that he was not quite good enough, and he wanted to be loved. So when his sisters told him that Hélène, the daughter of the Comte de Paris, Duc d'Orléans, was enamoured of him, he naturally became interested in her.

You probably know through the girls, who told me that dear Hélène had been fond of me for some time. I did not realise this at first although the girls constantly told me she liked me, for she never showed it in any way. Well, soon after you left and as I knew my chances with Alicky were all over, I saw Hélène several times at Sheen, and naturally thought her everything that is nice in a girl, and she had become very pretty which I saw at once and also gradually perceived that she really liked me...[1]

According to a French writer, she was 'tall, pretty, athletic and interesting, with a bubbly personality and enormous style'[2] and her family had been friends with the English royals since before the Revolution – and had been welcomed with open arms every time they were driven out of France into exile. Hélène was darkly pretty; she was as royal as could be; she had been brought up in England; and she adored him: what more could he want? Within a fortnight of his return from India, Eddy was smitten. Alicky had written him a final regretful letter. The Queen informed her eldest daughter sadly:

> All hopes of Alicky's marrying Eddy are at an end. She has writ-
> ten to tell him how it pains her to pain him, but that she cannot
> marry him. Much as she likes him as a cousin, that she knows she
> would not be happy with him and that he would not be happy
> with her and that he must not think of her.[3]

By 19 May she knew that Eddy was attracted to Hélène – a Roman Catholic! This would not do at all. Far too wily to put her foot down, she summoned all her talent for gentle guidance and reproof and took up her pen.

> I wish to say a few words about the subject of your future marriage.
> I quite agree with you that you should not be hurried and I feel
> sure that you will resist all the wiles and attempts of intriguers
> and bad women to catch you. But I wish to say that I have heard
> it rumoured that *you* had been thinking and talking of Princesse
> Hélène of Orléans! I can't believe this for you know that I told
> you (as did your parents who agreed with me) that such a mar-
> riage is utterly *impossible*. None of our family can marry a Catholic
> without losing all their rights and I am sure that she would never

change her religion and to change her religion merely to marry is a thing much to be deprecated, and which would have the very worst effect possible and be most unpopular, besides which *you* could not marry the daughter of the Pretender to the French throne. Politically in this way it would also be impossible.[4]

According to this, Eddy had already been warned off. This is interesting because one wonders in what context the subject would have arisen. Maybe it has something to do with the fondness George had expressed for Julie Stonor two years before. She was also a Catholic and probably the love of his life; yet 'it cannot be', Alix told her younger son sadly. George, who had a priggish, bossy streak yet somehow expected to be taken seriously as the more mature of the two sons, undoubtedly meant well when he warned his parents not to be in too much of a rush to marry their children off. Marrying too young, he warned them, could have dreadful consequences: look at Crown Prince Rudolf! Which may have been overstating the case, rather.[5]

However, if the Queen thought that a mere letter would be enough to deter her elder grandson, she was wrong. Eddy and Hélène continued their clandestine flirtation all summer at East Sheen Lodge, the home of his sister Louise near Richmond. Hélène was not a recent acquaintance. The Prince of Wales was quite friendly with the Duc d'Orléans, who was slightly deaf, and hard to get to know – 'astonishingly German in general bearing', according to Julian Osgood Field.[6] They were both at a dinner given by Lord Randolph Churchill on 21 July. All the French royals – the Duc d'Aumâle and the Comte and Comtesse de Paris in particular – were friends of the Waleses, and Hélène had been brought up partly at Sheen House, less than a mile from East Sheen Lodge where the Fifes lived. Rosa Lewis, the famous Edwardian hotelier, was a young cook in the Orléans household in the mid-eighties and admired her employers very much.

The Comtesse de Paris was the most interesting woman in the world. There never was a better brought-up family than hers. Every child had its two nurses, and every child was made to learn something – something useful: to make a boot, cook a cake, and so on.

The Comtesse was the best shot and the best rider imaginable. She was very masculine. She used to smoke big cigars. She was methodical, too. Why, she even put on her chemise at the same hour every day of her life… She was very particular about one's appearance. The Queen of Portugal and Princess Hélène, who were her children, and all the rest of them, would come into the kitchen to see me; and if you had a round back, when the Comtesse passed through, she would give you a whack, and tell you to stand up straight.

She told me to keep my back straight, just as she told her daughters – with a whip!

All the Comte de Paris's children were talented… I was overwhelmed with admiration for them in my early days. I liked their appreciation, and the economies they made to give to the poor.[7]

The House of Orléans had had the misfortune to produce, at the time of the Terror, a duke ('Philippe Egalité') who supported the Revolution but was nonetheless guillotined. His son, Louis Philippe, fled to Richmond, bought York House, and renamed it Orléans House; he returned to Paris as a 'citizen King' in 1830. There, the Comte was born. In 1848, when he was ten, the family was driven into exile once more. Orléans House having been sold, Queen Victoria gave them Claremont, near Esher, to live in. The family were allowed to return to France in 1870. All the French royal châteaux were restored, and two of the Comte's uncles went back to Paris as members of the National Assembly. The Comte was bringing up his children in England, so he stayed put.

There had traditionally been enmity between the House of Orléans and the House of Bourbon, but in 1883 the Bourbons relinquished their right to the throne; the Comte therefore took precedence and became the acknowledged Pretender. He was forever intriguing, and, in 1886, saw one of his daughters married, in unashamedly monarchist pomp and glory, to the Crown Prince of Portugal. This offended the Chamber of Deputies and the Senate to such a degree that they threw out all former French royalty for good. Undeterred, the Comte supported General Boulanger, that anti-government, anti-republican leader who lost courage after his own overwhelming popular victory in the Parisian elections of 1889 and fled. First the General, the 'damp squib', went to Brussels, then (in April 1889) to London, to join the Comte and the Prince of Wales in membership of the Pelican Club and become a regular at the Café Royal.

The Comte went on to see his niece married to Prince Waldemar, a nephew of Alix's in Denmark. Were he now to accept the future King of England as a son-in-law, the Quai d'Orsay would suspect some kind of royalist pincer movement.

In June of 1890, Eddy was made a duke. The Queen had mixed feelings about the whole issue. She understood that it was necessary to make him a peer, in order that he might take a seat in the House of Lords, but felt that a dukedom was rather a comedown for a prince. If it had to be (and the politicians seemed to think so), then at least she would decide on his title. She would not have him become a Duke of York. She had dreadful memories of one of her own dissolute uncles, who had held that title and whose interests in life had never included his wife. So Eddy became the Duke of Clarence and Avondale, Earl of Athlone. 'The only Duke of Clarence who is known to history is the numbskull who was deservedly drowned in a butt of malmsey, and during the present century the title was associated with the aberrations and extravagances for which William IV was enviably notorious', growled Labouchère. Clarence was an ancient Irish title. It was true that most of its holders had caused scandal in one way or another, but for some reason the Queen chose it, and this 'supreme distinction', said *The Times*:

> …marks his accession to the full privileges and responsibilities of his position. In their exercise he will count upon and receive the cordial sympathy and good will of a nation over whom, in the course of nature, he is one day destined to rule.

Thus began what J.E. Vincent in all seriousness called 'the brief period of laborious ceremony which he passed as an illustrious personage in an age when princes of the blood work at least as hard as common labourers'. Perhaps it was not quite so bad. Certainly the Duke of Clarence, as he was now called, had to take his seat in the House of Lords, besides accepting high office in the Berkshire freemasonry and the colonelcies of several regiments. But most of his time was still engaged by the Hussars, and his love life. It seems there was more to this than innocent flirtation at Sheen.

There are entries in Prince George's diary[8] for 1890 about a mistress George kept at Southsea, and another, in St John's Wood, whose favours he shared with Eddy. We know nothing about her. All the same, future generations have concluded that Eddy was suffering from a sexually transmitted disease.

In the middle of July 1890, Mr Dalton's godson Alfred Fripp – who had passed his exams, and was now a young doctor at Guy's – was looking forward to his summer holiday. The hospital was sometimes approached by doctors looking for a *locum tenens*, and in this case, the letter came from a Dr Jalland of York, who needed someone to take his place almost at once. Fripp did not want the job – he wanted a holiday – but the friend with whom he intended to travel halfway around the world had failed to find the money, and his brother-in-law, Hale-White, who was a lecturer at Guy's, insisted that he should take this opportunity of general practice. So he did. He arrived in York by train on Saturday 19 July, and the following morning Dr Jalland took him to meet key patients. At the Hussars' barracks he met Clarence, who remembered him at once. He was apparently completely well, but was leaving the following weekend to begin a period of convalescence at the Royal Hotel, Scarborough.

The cure was not complete, and Fripp was called to Scarborough. He wrote to his father:

> You would be amused to see me dancing attendance on HRH... I sent him to bed at once, he has a sharpish attack of fever. I was over there again today. He is going on fairly well. It is an awful nuisance for me having to go every day. I start at 2.30 and get back at 9, then dinner, then a two-mile drive to Lord Downe, HRH's Colonel, to whom I have to report... Then another mile to another patient. I don't get back until 11 and then I am tired.
>
> HRH seems to take kindly to me. We get on very well together, but sometimes my ingenuity is sorely taxed to exhibit the right mixture of firmness and politeness. You would be amused to see Colonel This and the Hon That dancing around and asking me the most minute directions – what time he is to take his meals; then the menu for each meal is submitted to me. I have to have long talks with each of them privately, and then again with HRH who pours out all his little woes and always makes me smoke in his room. He smokes himself until he is stupid. I have knocked him down to three cigarettes and one cigar a day...
>
> Don't mention HRH's illness outside our house, as the Prince of Wales particularly wants it not to get into the papers. He is afraid the public will get the impression that his son is a chronic invalid. The Scarborough aristocracy is wild – it was quite enjoying itself making a lot of him.[9]

According to his biographer, Fripp was 'born with the gift of evoking loyalty and admiration, and he could always draw the

best out of others... Tall, robust, tanned, with an infectious smile,
a ready laugh, and a great fund of common sense. His whole
manner suggested confidence, his voice and smile brought hope.'
Eddy certainly liked him a lot. But what was the matter with the
royal patient? Was it 'a fever'? According to Theo Aronson,[10] who
does not give his source, Fripp was treating him for gonorrhoea.
Writing thirty years after these events, Frank Harris – the voice
of the 1890s in many ways – confidently stated that in such a case,
bed rest along with 'unlimited drinks of strong barley water and
no sign of wine, spirits or beer should bring about a complete
cure in a month' (although that month would be both sordid
and painful).[11] There were no antibiotics and no penicillin, and
the clap was everywhere. Just about any prostitute working at a
house frequented by officers or men in the Hussars could have
passed it on.

The newspapers got hold of the story that a doctor had
been called in, but said the Prince had fallen from a horse
and dislocated his ankle. As to the 'fever', there was, of course,
professional discretion as well as a social taboo to prohibit any
mention of venereal disease. It would be unthinkable that Fripp
should write home about it, but it would be unrealistic to
expect the young man to keep quiet about where he was and
whom he was treating, especially since he now leapt nimbly
across the social gulf and came to attend upon Prince Eddy
in the Highlands. When Dr Jarrold returned to York, Fripp
followed Eddy to Scotland, where he, his mother and sister
Victoria ('Toria') were staying with the Fifes. Fripp was put up
at the Fife Arms – Mar Lodge was crammed with courtiers and
royalty – but was invited almost daily for lunch and dinner at
Mar. Somebody at the hotel tipped off a correspondent of one
of the London papers, who wrote:

> There is a young doctor at the Fife Arms named Fripp, who goes
> over to Mar Lodge once or twice a day ostensibly to play lawn

tennis with Prince Albert Victor. The real fact, however, is that he is here at the instance of a well-known Court Surgeon, and is in constant medical attendance on HRH who, while driving through to Sir James Mackenzie's funeral, certainly looked very ill.[12]

Dr Fripp and Eddy would take long walks together in the afternoon. Otherwise the afternoon was spent in fishing, and doubtless the princesses appreciated the presence at their picnics of this good-looking, jovial young man. One night there was a picturesque ghillies' ball, and another night a torchlight dance, with the guests all in Highland dress. The weather was glorious, in the Dee the salmon were jumping, and then over they all went to the Highland Games at Braemar.[13]

On Monday 25 August, Fripp wrote in his diary: 'Prince confided to me his love affair.'

Now, this could have been a tactful way of saying 'Prince confided to me how he caught this ghastly disease.' Or 'Prince confided to me that he had a tremendous passion for a girl he wasn't actually seeing at the moment.' Or 'Prince confided to me that he was in love with Princess Hélène.' The latter is much the most likely, but it was hardly news. The Princess of Wales and Princess Victoria had arrived at Mar and the Paris family were there; Louise, Duchess of Fife had spent all summer promoting the affair at Richmond; and there must have been some whisper, with two of the Wales sisters having nothing better to think about. And their mother was entirely in favour.

Quite why Alix was so keen to marry Eddy to this French princess is obvious; the girl was sensible, accomplished, elegant, attracted to Eddy – and all the other contenders were German. Even to Fripp, she said 'I hate the Germans.'

There ensued a direct appeal to Queen Victoria's sentimental side. On Friday 29 August, Eddy and Hélène rode off in a carriage, with a hamper, to picnic at Balmoral and to call upon the Queen.

They approached the meeting with trepidation, but it worked remarkably well. Queen Victoria wrote a memorandum to Salisbury:

> Soon after I went upstairs a message came that 'Prince Albert Victor' wished to speak to me. I of course said certainly and he came in and said 'I have brought Hélène with me' taking her by the hand and bringing her up to where I sat, saying they were devoted to each other and hoped I would help them. I answered they knew it was impossible, on which he said she was prepared to change her religion for his sake. I said to her would it not be very difficult for her to do this and she answered in a most pathetic way with tears in her eyes 'For him, only for him. Oh! Help pray do' and he said the same and that 'She has been attached to me for years and I never knew it', that he was sure I would try and help them. I assured them I would do what I could to help them but it might be difficult. He told me she had not told her parents of it – she had done it all of her own free will. 'I thought I would come straight to you. I have not told Mama even,' he said.[14]

He took Hélène to the door and returned alone to his grandmother, who was touched by the appeal, and he told her that Alicky had never returned his affection, but Hélène had loved him for a long time and 'had grown quite thin from anxiety' over changing her religion, and had struggled over it. Her father would be angry, but would get over it, and 'her mother winked at it'.

> I said I must tell the Govt that there might be political difficulties, to which he replied he thought there would not be: 'she knows that her father will never succeed there'... I never saw him so eager, so earnest... It was difficult not to say yes at once.

She added a postscript:

I must not omit to say that their meeting at Mar was accidental. The Paris' had been asked some time ago by Louise Fife and AV would have been at Aldershot had he not been ill.[15]

A.J. Balfour enclosed the note with a sardonic note of his own to 'My dear Uncle Robert' (Lord Salisbury). He was enjoying the royal predicament no end. Alix was somewhat discomfited, he felt, by the Queen's tacit reproach: why had she allowed the young people to meet? It seemed the Princess disclaimed all responsibility; it was up to the Comtesse de Paris to look after her daughter, but the Comtesse spent every daylight hour stalking deer. Everyone was tremendously sentimental, without seeing the anomaly – 'that at best it is the sacrifice of religion for love, while at the worst it is the sacrifice of religion for a throne: a singular inversion of ordinary views on martyrdom'.[16]

Balfour blamed the parents. He was convinced that the Princess of Wales had put them up to it, and as for the Comtesse de Paris: 'in the intervals of deer-stalking… she is more certain that it is good to be Queen of England than she is that it is bad to marry a Protestant'. And he acknowledged that the royal grandmother was certainly wavering:

> …sentimental considerations are much strengthened by her desire to see the young man married, and by the dearth of suitable Protestant princesses. All the little German princesses of a marriageable age are, according to her, totally ignorant of the world and utterly unfit for the position. In Princess Hélène she thinks she sees a clever woman – healthy withal – who will be the making of her husband. She feels to a certain extent the political difficulty with France – but she thinks it can be got over by making it a condition of the marriage that the young lady should break with her relations![17]

One can almost hear Balfour gasp. He 'did not say much [to the Queen] beyond pointing out the extremely awkward position everyone would be placed in if, after an abortive attempt on the French throne, the Duc d'Orléans were to take refuge at the court of his sister the Queen of England'. He was just as amazed by the Queen's apparent willingness to believe that the public would not react badly to a recusant bride for Eddy.

> Her frame of mind in short is this: on personal grounds she has
> been absolutely won over to the marriage, the political objections
> a little frighten her, but she is in process of persuading herself that
> they may be ignored. I need not say that I shall do my best acting
> on the lines of your telegram to arrest any further movement in
> this direction.[18]

Salisbury's telegram (which he must have written immediately upon an earlier communication from Balmoral) instructed Balfour to emphasise the difficulties and urge the Queen to communicate at once with the Comte de Paris.

> Prevent any Royal consent being given. Time will enable
> Canterbury to work on the Princess and I doubt perseverance
> of the young Prince.

Balfour spent the Saturday afternoon with her, and wrote again to Salisbury.

> According to her there are but three marriageable Protestant prin-
> cesses at this moment in Europe, besides the Teck girl and the
> Hesse girl. The Teck girl they won't have, because they hate Teck
> and because the vision of Princess May haunting Marlborough
> House makes the Prince of Wales ill [Balfour means Princess
> Mary Adelaide: the Prince of Wales constantly made remarks about
> her enormous girth]. The Hesse girl won't have him. There remain
> a Mecklenburgh and two Anhalt Princesses (I am not sure that I
> have the names right.) According to Her Majesty they are all three

ugly, unhealthy, and idiotic; and if that be not enough, they are also penniless and narrow-minded – or as she put it, German of the Germans! They might do perhaps (as she said) for a younger son, but &c &c... Here we have (she went on) a charming and clever young lady – against whom no legal objection can be urged, who has loved Prince Eddy for three years (NB she is only 19 now) to whom he is devoted, and who will fill her position splendidly – how can it be stopped? The Prince will never marry anyone else – his health will break down – and so on.[19]

He had been perfectly right about Alix's attitude; she already saw the couple as unofficially engaged, and had no idea of the political implications. 'Nothing on earth could have given me greater pleasure than to see those two dear children united,' she wrote to the Queen. Bertie loved the idea; the girl's mother was pleased; but the Comte would almost certainly prove difficult. This, one day after the young lovers' impulsive plea to the Queen, was the only straw at which Balfour and Salisbury could still clutch.

Balfour had to admit that he was impressed by Alix's cunning. He was convinced that the interview had been all her doing.

My opinion of the Princess of Wales' diplomacy is raised to the highest point... She accepts... the theory that for three long years (i.e., since the heroine was 16) Prince Eddy has been the object of a hopeless affection – (a theory let me say in passing which, whether true or false, would appeal with overwhelming force to a boy who like Prince Eddy has always felt himself unsuccessful and uncared for); and she has set her seal to, if she has not invented, the ingenious theory which makes apostasy the conclusive mark of disinterested love.[20]

Their only hope was that the Comte would refuse. Otherwise... Balfour had a plan 'which would both test the constancy of the lovers and remove some of the objections to the match', but with luck, it wouldn't come to that. In any case, nothing could be done until the Comte had been consulted, and at this moment the Paris family were on their way home.

As the guests left Mar, the Waleses went on to their home at Abergeldie, and Fripp had been invited to stay there with them. Prince Eddy came with George's old mentor Admiral Stephenson to pick him up from the Fife Arms; the Princess of Wales and Princess Victoria came in another carriage; and the retinue and baggage trundled along in a series of vehicles behind. At Abergeldie, they found that the Prince of Wales had just arrived with an equerry and his friend Christopher Sykes.

> The Prince very soon came walking into the smoking-room to see me and was extremely nice in every way. Not so fat as I expected, looking very well, in boisterous spirits and the best of good tempers... He had lately seen Oscar Clayton so he knew all about Prince Eddy and his illness and progress, but he extracted a detailed account from me, questioned me on every point, said he was very pleased with the way Prince Eddy had got on and with the good control I had had over him, especially pleased I had got him to reduce the smoking. Also he said Oscar Clayton had a very high opinion of me and all I had done.[21]

A few miles away at Balmoral, Balfour was thinking hard about Eddy's affection for Hélène. The next day he wrote to Lord Salisbury again ('How sick you must be of my handwriting!') to say that the whole thing *might* come off, if it must,

> ...by patiently carrying out a well considered policy for some years... If *he* showed for a sufficient length of time that he would look at no one else, and *she* began to advertise her conversion by attending the parish church...

A grateful letter from Eddy to the Queen was enclosed. Unfortunately, it revealed a certain political naivety on his part.

> I am rather distressed from what you say is Lord Salisbury's answer… But forgive me Grandmama for saying that I believe that in this case it is quite sufficient to have the Sovereign's concent [*sic*] and that the Prime Minister need only be told of her decision.[22]

'So now you know your true position under the constitution,' Balfour added wrily.

The Queen didn't know the half of it. There was not much that did not come to the ears of the Prince of Wales, and if his son were not only thinking of marrying, but thinking of marrying the daughter of a friend of his while in the throes of a raging infection, then it must be cured. Fripp's reports at Scarborough went directly from Lord Downe to Sir Oscar Clayton, and it is now clear that at Mar he had been able to meet Sir Dighton Probyn, Alix's Private Secretary. On the very day of Eddy's approach to Queen Victoria, his father wrote to Probyn, now back in Norfolk:

> So you had a long conversation with Mr Fripp about my son, and I am glad he told you his candid opinion about his health, which I regret to hear is not satisfactory, and the future will have to be considered very carefully. I should be glad if you would ask Clayton down to Sandringham for a couple of nights, and talk the matter well over with him, i.e., as to the present and the future, and whether a sea voyage would not be advisable, as hunting this winter seems out of the question. Also, I want you to write and tell Dr Fripp to ask to have an interview with the Princess, and tell her candidly what he has said to you, so that she may know how matters are, which are far more serious than she has any idea of.[23]

Probyn accordingly wrote to Fripp, instructing him to tell the
Princess everything, and adding that what was required was a
lasting cure.

> The gout and *every other ailment must be completely eradicated* from
> the system, and until that is done, the young Prince must be
> prepared to submit to any system of dieting or what he may think
> discomfort ordered by his medical advisors.[24]

Self-prescription, and picking and choosing one's remedy to avoid
pain, are common patterns of behaviour among royalty even today.
The Prince of Wales certainly took his doctors' advice lightly. He
barely drank at all, but nothing on earth would make him eat less;
he believed, as his mother did, that food was always good for you,
and a short annual regimen at some spa would enable him to start
feasting again like a boy of twenty. It seems unfair to expect that
Alfred Fripp, who was a year younger than Prince Eddy, would
have the authority to make his royal patient do as he was told.

Maybe when Sir Oscar Clayton had seen Probyn he realised this. At any rate, he wrote to enlist the help of Sir Henry
Thompson.

Sir Henry had made his name, and his career, by curing King
Leopold of the Belgians of kidney stones a year or two before
Eddy was born, using a crushing technique – 'cutting for the
stone' had been, in the years before antisepsis, a route to death,
and Thompson's skill at lithotrity became justly famous. He
always said he could have cured Napoleon III, had the old man
not refused to be treated until it was too late. He was an authority on diseases of the prostate and 'his practice was chiefly limited
to diseases of the lower urinary tract'.[25] On 3 September, while
on holiday at Stratford with his wife:

> I received a letter from Sir Oscar Clayton stating that TRH the
> Prince and Princess of Wales, who were staying at Abergeldie

Castle and leading a quiet country life, had expressed by letter to himself a wish that I would visit them and spend four or five days. Sir Oscar asked me to come up to Town and learn from him the Prince's object – for of course there was an object.[26]

It seemed that the Duke of Clarence was in excellent health, but they wanted an opinion 'relative to a local affection which gave rise to a little uneasiness'. Sir Henry treated the great and the good for diseases which were not, in those days, mentioned. As an indication of this, his 'octaves' (dinners attended by eight remarkable men) were well known, and Frank Harris (who admittedly is not to be trusted on every point) has an account of a dinner at Sir Henry's when he met Lord Randolph Churchill, then in the tertiary stage of syphilis and perceptibly mad.[27]

Thompson's invitation to Abergeldie arrived on 15 September, and he accepted; he would be there the following weekend.

Fripp had been chosen – the word is used advisedly – to accompany the Prince and Holford on a four-day tour of Wales in the week of 15 September. There was a feeling that Eddy must be kept within sight of someone in authority at all times, and the new young doctor was both liked and trusted. His patient had not ceased to think of his absent love. Sir Henry Ponsonby wrote to Balfour on Wednesday 10 September:

> The Queen asks for your opinion as to [to] whom the succession would go if the Duke of Clarence married a papist but had children who were Protestants. His Royal Highness saw the Queen yesterday and was depressed at the aspect of affairs. He told the Queen that if consent to the marriage was refused he would marry PH and lose his rights to the throne. But that his children would be Protestants and he imagined would therefore succeed.[28]

The courtiers, the Queen, and the politicians puzzled over the Act of Succession, while for Prince Eddy and his doctor the days passed pleasantly, punctuated by large meals served by 'huge, red-coated, overfed men' (the description is Fripp's), conversation, shooting, and games of halma. There was a tea at Balmoral (without the Queen), a musical performance by Madame Albani who had been invited as a guest with her husband, and endless shooting parties. Fripp enjoyed shooting grouse but had never done it before in his life, and nearly killed a lord by accident. Prince Eddy shot his first stag of the autumn. The head, he said, would be Fripp's. There was already masses of venison in the larders, so:

> The Duke of Clarence said – 'Send some of it to Fripp's nurses at Guy's.' So I was asked how many they could do with. I pointed out that there were three or four separate messes, the sisters, two batches of day-nurses and night-nurses, to say nothing of the residents and others at Guy's. The matter was talked over and John, the faithful servant, was instructed to despatch six haunches (there must have been fifty in the larders) to Guy's Hospital.
>
> We were sitting in an L-shaped hall which was used by the entire party except when anybody wanted to be private. Our group broke up and John went away to carry out his order but was called back. In my position I could not help overhearing what the Duke whispered to him. 'John, three will do!' And later 'Oh, John, one will do!'

Fripp thought Eddy truly Scottish. A couple of days afterwards, when a telegram was handed to the young doctor at lunch, he put it in his pocket. The Princess of Wales, looking concerned, told him he must open it. So he read it, and must have grinned, because she teased him to read it out. He did.

Venison returned as carriage not paid. Matron. Guy's Hospital.[29]

On the way to Wales, Holford and the Prince called at the barracks in York, so Fripp was able to meet the Dr and Mrs Jalland for breakfast before proceeding to Hereford and Abergavenny. Royal addresses were presented, handshakes given, speeches made; they drove in procession through cheering crowds, met lords and ladies, and attended grand dinners and receptions and so forth. Fripp had brought some books, thinking he would be able to swot up on anatomy during the tour. He was supposed to take a post teaching it at Guy's in just two weeks' time. He was living through an extraordinary experience, but even at Mar he had begun to feel 'what everybody speaks of; that when with Royalty you never can call a moment your own'. Not only was he guide, philosopher and friend to Eddy, whom he liked, but he had been called upon to treat any number of small ailments and sprains in the rest of the royal family and household. Now, on the tour, he and Holford were fully engaged in taking turns to write Eddy's speeches. It must have been pretty funny; anyway, it was the start of a lifelong friendship.

The three young men returned from Eddy's round of official engagements on the Friday and found that the most distinguished surgeon of the day had been invited to spend a few days at Abergeldie as a guest. Fripp's biographer does not mention the presence of Sir Henry Thompson at all. This discretion is surely no accident, as Sir Henry's specialism was well known, and inferences might be drawn. Sir Henry recorded that when he arrived Fripp was already there, and so was Holford, 'who had temporary charge of the young Prince'. Prince Eddy was out shooting, but the Princess of Wales and young Princess Victoria took the two doctors out on a drive to Balmoral Castle, where they left them. Fripp and Thompson walked back to Abergeldie deep in discussion.

In the evenings, Sir Henry discovered, the royal family dined at nine and the ladies retired before midnight, while the Prince and his friends stayed up smoking and talking and playing cards.

For a man of seventy, it was rather trying. On the Saturday after-noon, he examined Eddy thoroughly in young Fripp's presence. Sir Henry then had a private interview with the Prince of Wales. The next day the Prince saw him again, early in the morning. It seemed that 'The Queen was anxious to hear my opinion and he desired me to tell HM what I had said to him.'[30]

The family met the Queen at the morning's church service at Balmoral, and then there was Sunday luncheon, and Thompson spent the afternoon writing a long letter about the case to Sir Oscar Clayton. Later, Her Majesty drove up for tea at Abergeldie, with the family only. He was summoned into the presence; they were all there. She told Sir Henry she had often heard of him from

> …her old friend Sir James Clark, and also from Sir William Jenner, and especially from her uncle Leopold the First. When she paused I said I should never forget the King, and she remarked that 'no-one ever did who had the opportunity of seeing much of him.'… All this took place in the room with the rest of the royal family present. She never asked any question about the Duke as I had fully expected her to do. On my asking the Prince in the evening why HM had not named the Duke's case he said the Queen had previously asked him to tell her my opinion, adding 'it was her wish you should feel your visit to be that of a guest and not of a professional advisor.'[31]

So no invoice, then. On Monday, Bertie went shooting,

> …having arranged with me to have a chat with the Duke and give him some good advice. I had expressly stated to HRH that I thought the Duke's great love of smoking had led him quite unconsciously no doubt to indulge in the use of tobacco so largely as to lead me to fear that it would exert a prejudicial effect on the brain. The Duke and I, followed by Fripp, sat out of doors under a

big tree in the garden, and the subject just named was the theme
of a serious but kind lecture such as a man of experience might
address to his son. I kept his attention for an hour, making it interesting by illustrations and certainly made an impression, reminding
him of what he might do and enjoy if he would greatly curb the
habit in future. He expressed himself as much pleased and hoped
I would attend him in future, but I reminded him that he came to
me by Sir Oscar's advice, and any professional attendance must be
in consultation with the latter. Fripp said to me afterwards 'That's
the way you give your lectures at the hospital, I suppose, isn't it?'
'Very much,' said I, 'only it is vastly more difficult to address a
single hearer than a crowded theatre.'[32]

Thompson was to leave on Tuesday, but before he did there was
another interview with the Prince of Wales. Bertie promised that
he and Holford would keep an eye on his son when Fripp had
to return to Guy's.

Smoking alone (Bertie smoked) cannot have necessitated such
guardianship. Did 'smoking' mean something else, as 'fever' did?
Certainly one is left with the strong impression that if released
for an instant from supervision, Eddy would get into a 'scrape'.
Whatever the Prince of Wales promised, any hope that he would
keep an eye on his son seemed remote. Bertie's life was with
his own friends, not with Eddy, and that could not change, for
Eddy's first loyalty had always been to his mother.

Eddy certainly seemed to be in love with Hélène in the
autumn of 1890. He wrote to his brother 'you have no idea
how I love this sweet girl now, and I feel I could never be happy
without her'.[33] In a rash moment, he had even said he would
relinquish the crown rather than be parted from her.[34] But in
this year and the next, he had troubles which, had they become
known, would have undermined all his plans. Patricia Cornwell
mentions two letters (apparently in her possession) from Eddy
to George Lewis, thanking him because he had 'gotten himself

into a compromising situation with two ladies of low standing, one of them a Miss Richardson'.[35] It seems from the first of these, written in November 1890, less than three months after his betrothal to Hélène, that he had recently paid £200 for the return of some compromising letters and the girl – Miss Richardson – was asking for £100 more.

Alfred Fripp's astonishing summer did not quite end when he took the London train home at the end of September. At the end of his first week back at Guy's, he took the night train back to Abergeldie and stayed briefly, taking a long Saturday afternoon walk with Eddy and treating Admiral Stephenson's lumbago. In London the following week, he called at Marlborough House, went for a walk with the Prince and took a Turkish bath with him, then lunch.

On another side of St James's Park, the notion of this marriage had meant a great deal of dusting off of old volumes by Lord Salisbury and his researchers. On 9 September, the Prime Minister wrote a memo to the Queen to explain the legal position. First of all, the Princess obviously required her father's consent, for she would not come of age until she was twenty-one. Secondly, the marriage would not count in France, where she could not marry at all until she was twenty-one, and thereafter for four years any ceremony would be valid only after special pleading from the girl to her father. Thirdly, the Act of Succession was clear enough: no person should possess the crown who married a Papist. And it could be read to imply that once a Catholic, always a Catholic.

> When, at what point, does she cease to be a papist? Unless her ecclesiastical superiors excommunicate her, which they are not likely to do, no avowal of opinions, no attendance at our services, will separate her from the communion of the Church to which she now belongs.[36]

Prince Eddy had been right in that, technically, if the Queen gave her permission the marriage could go ahead without consultation with her government; but of course 'her consent to this marriage is a State Act of the greatest gravity'. In England, the Catholics would despise Hélène's apostasy while the Protestants would not believe in it. The French would growl at the monarchists and the Germans would feel threatened.

The Prime Minister, in short, was not keen. Everything depended on the Comte de Paris. If by any chance he gave his consent, then Salisbury urged the Queen that the whole matter must be aired in full Cabinet.

In the second week of September, within days of this letter, Hélène's father flatly refused to countenance his daughter's engagement. A week later, the young Princess was resolved to seek an audience with the Pope, to try to obtain a special dispensation. It was already clear that Prince Eddy threatened to renounce his claim to the throne and marry her in the expectation that their children, brought up as Protestants, could eventually somehow inherit the crown anyway. The Pope's likely decision was impenetrable to speculation, and Salisbury asked the Lord Chancellor how exactly to interpret the Act of Succession – just in case Eddy was right again. He was. An unprejudiced observer might almost suppose that the young prince had been reading the Act for himself. Salisbury added:

> I have also referred to [the Lord Chancellor] the question as to whom will succeed if Prince AV becomes incapable. My impression is that the Act clearly gives it to his children being Protestants.

He used the words 'becomes incapable' rather than 'dies or becomes incapable'. There were precedents for incapacity in the monarch, not least that of George III, who had died of porphyria only seventy years before. In 1890, Lord Salisbury already suspected that Prince Eddy might later in life become irremediably unwell.

10

Resolution
1890–91

For an army officer, Eddy spent remarkably little time on duty; he seems to have been convalescent for the better part of a year, from July 1890 onwards. Early in October 1890 he was still at Balmoral, where on 11 October he danced with his grandmother. The old lady was most gratified by his handsome bearing, as well as her own nimbleness of foot. From Fripp's meetings with Eddy that autumn, it can be inferred that Admiral Stephenson was unofficially keeping an eye on him. (This is the Admiral Stephenson who was Bertie's equerry, whose brother was the Treasury Solicitor.) On 4 November, Stephenson came along with the pair of them to dinner and to see *Sunlight and Shadow* at the Avenue Theatre. Afterwards they went back to Marlborough House, and Fripp didn't leave until quarter to four in the morning. One imagines the two young men gossiping over brandy and cigars while the Admiral creeps away with relief, feeling his duty done. The following month, staying at Windsor for a few days with his godfather, Canon Dalton, Fripp (who had put in his bill; the patient must have been cured) again met Eddy with Stephenson.[1]

The Prince of Wales had deputed his supervisory role from the start, which is a pity, for a few months devoted to stern guardianship might have kept him out of trouble. In the second week of September, while the rest of the family were still at Abergeldie, Bertie had made yet another misjudgement.

For once, the matter was only tangentially to do with mistresses, but the light that would now flood in upon the Prince's social life revealed him in the act of gambling – a scene that, to many middle-class Victorians, was quite as shocking as adultery or violence.

He had spent Monday 8 September until Wednesday 10 September 1890, St Leger week, in Yorkshire as the guest of Alfred Wilson, a shipowner. (This was the week before Prince Eddy, Holford and Fripp left Abergeldie for the four-day Welsh tour.) Normally, he would have stayed at the home of his friend Christopher Sykes during the Doncaster races, but poor Sykes had pretty well ruined himself in his efforts to keep up with his royal friend, and was in no position to play host this year. So Bertie had accepted an invitation to Tranby Croft, the Wilsons' home near Hull, and Daisy Brooke, among others, had conveniently done the same. But on Saturday 6 September Daisy Brooke's stepfather, the Earl of Rosslyn, died; so she could not be present.

On the first evening, baccarat was played long after midnight, and the son of the house, Arthur Wilson, saw Sir William Gordon-Cumming cheating. Alerted, five other members of the party witnessed what was going on. The following evening, the matter was reported to Bertie, who kept the bank and had been the main loser. Gordon-Cumming (who denied that he had cheated) was told that if he promised in writing on his honour never to play again, nothing more would be said.

And there the matter rested: a document was signed, every-one was embarrassed, the culprit was shamefaced, but all went on their way, sworn to secrecy. Bertie was advised to keep the signed statement, witnessed by himself, which he did. He left Tranby Croft on the morning of Wednesday 10 September and, according to the official account, watched the day's racing from the cavalry barracks at York, where he spent the night with the 10th Hussars. According to Daisy Brooke's stepbrother,[2] Bertie and Lady Brooke met on her way north, at York station. She was travelling to Dysart, the Rosslyns' castle in Scotland, for the funeral on 11 September. Perhaps they snatched a few hours together. Bertie did not leave York by special train for Abergeldie until the following day.

Within the next few weeks, it became evident to Sir William Gordon-Cumming that something *had* been said. Society inferred that Wales had told Daisy Brooke about the cheating as soon as he saw her, and it was she who had passed on the news. Wits immediately renamed her Babbling Brooke. This seems unfair, since her brother Harry, who saw her at the funeral, was absolutely certain[3] that Lady Brooke did not mention the scandal to anyone at Dysart. Besides, Wales was a notorious gossip. However the talk had started, it increased when Gordon-Cumming was duty bound to decline a game of cards at his club. He was mortified by the knowledge that he would henceforth be cut by the Prince of Wales. He felt aggrieved and denied any guilt. By January of 1891, everyone knew he was determined to sue his five accusers for slander. Wales, whose signature was on the document that incriminated the plaintiff, would have to appear in court yet again.

The timing could not be worse. The nonconformists, Gladstone included, were turgid with self-righteousness this winter. Charles Stuart Parnell, the Irish Nationalist Member of Parliament, had been cited in the divorce of his agent, Captain O'Shea, from Kitty O'Shea. Where the great and no-better-than-they-should-be were concerned, the press were ready to seize on almost any transgression of accepted standards and make political and financial capital out of it.

In February of 1891, Bertie tried to keep Gordon-Cumming out of the civil courts by encouraging a military enquiry into the Tranby Croft case. He failed. The proceedings would go ahead at some unspecified date later in the year. The matter hung over all of them, particularly Bertie, throughout the spring. Alix was fiercely defensive of her husband, so fiercely defensive that while he undoubtedly appreciated her loyalty he cannot have found very much to say in response. Queen Victoria seized the opportunity for reproof. Any mention of baccarat would cause scandal. It was illegal, and, according to a shocked visitor at Sandringham: 'they have a real table, and rakes, and everything like the rooms at Monte Carlo'.[4] Revelations about card-playing did not go down well with Her Majesty, who thought that the principal duty of the royal family was to set a good example or, failing that, to be seen to set one.

Bertie continued to spend as much time as he could with Daisy Brooke. Her young stepbrother Harry was the new Earl of Rosslyn. He had married only six weeks before his father died, and inherited £50,000 in 'tangible assets'. With an annual income from the family estates and coal mines of £17,000 (his army pay had been £250 a year, and he was already borrowing from Sam Lewis), he set about spending money on horseflesh and betting. The horses were not all slow ones, although his inheritance began to disappear at a frightening rate. The young earl had a younger sister, Lady Sybil St Clair Erskine, whom he adored, and of whom he said 'there was no more beautiful face, with the most wonderful laughing eyes'.[5] She had a 'rollicking jollity and devil-may-care life'. Harry, Sybil, their siblings and two stepsisters had grown up together at Easton, the house Daisy Brooke inherited as a child. Sybil Erskine had not the 'depth' or political passion of Daisy or the literary talent of another sister, the Duchess of Sutherland. But she would become the next passion of Eddy's life.

Christmas having been spent at Sandringham as usual, Eddy was invited to Osborne in February. There were 'theatricals'. The Queen loved these amateurish performances, although Eddy privately told his brother how tiresome he found it all: 'It is extraordinary how pleased grandmamma is with such small things for she is quite childish in some ways about them. It was the same thing with the tableaux in Scotland this autumn. But I suppose it is because she has no other amusement that she takes such interest and pleasure in these performances.'[6]

The 'tableaux' included such static enchantments as 'The Arab Encampment' (with Her Majesty's Indian servants playing the Arabs), a scene from *Faust*, with Prince and Princess Henry of Battenberg posed as Faust and Marguerite, and 'Ellen Douglas, Lady of the Lake', played by one of the maids of honour, and accompanied by the overture to *Rob Roy* played by Her Majesty's musicians.[7] All this was by candlelight, for there was no electric light in the tall stone halls of Balmoral. Only giggles would have relieved the tedium, and no one would have dared.

No doubt he wished to be with Hélène, but in April Eddy was back with the Hussars in York, and in May they were to leave for a summer tour of duty in Ireland.

The Queen recognised that her grandson would probably never marry his French princess. She half hoped that Princess Marie, the eldest daughter of the Duke of Edinburgh, would make a suitable bride. The Prince of Wales was not in favour; 'Missy' had an overwhelming personality. Also, she had a German governess who disliked the English. There seemed to be no hope and, indeed, in June her engagement was announced: 'Missy' was destined one day to become the famous Queen Marie of Rumania.

Whether Eddy and Hélène maintained anything but a fitful correspondence during the autumn of 1890 and spring of 1891 is unknown. Her mother was sometimes said to be the stronger parent, but it is certain that her father would not have looked kindly on a stream of letters from Windsor, Marlborough House, Sandringham, Sheen, Osborne, Abergeldie and even, finally, the barracks at York. In any case, Hélène conceded, after months apart, that she could never marry Eddy. Pope Leo XIII would not allow it for political reasons, reinforced by the obvious religious ones. She wrote sadly telling him that he must consider himself released from his vows, and that he should marry a Protestant princess.

Eddy was naturally upset. This was a second rejection. His friends were an insensitive bunch, as well. In J.E. Vincent's account of his life there is no mention of his blighted love affair at all, but 4 May 1891 stands out as the occasion of a dinner in aid of the Royal Hospital for Women and Children, Waterloo Road, at the Hotel Metropole – at which Prince Eddy made a speech. At least, *The Times* was provided with a copy of what Holford had written, but Vincent explains that on the night, the text was stolen away and passed down the table amid much suppressed hilarity, and the bereft prince had to ad lib. He made quite a good job of it anyway.[8]

Later in the month, a long-standing invitation promoted by his grandmother brought his cousin from Germany, Margaret of Prussia, to stay at Sandringham in May. If the Queen expected him to fall for this girl (who even she conceded was 'not regularly pretty') on the rebound, she was sadly mistaken. Poor Mossy must have felt very left out, with Alix trying to be nice and her potential suitor preoccupied. He was at Marlborough House, cheerful and talkative, when Sir Henry Ponsonby called. Sir Henry was surprised and relieved that Prince Eddy seemed to have recovered from Hélène's letter. He had been led to believe that he would find the young prince emotionally devastated.[9]

Alix thought he was. She wrote to George about Hélène's decision: 'to me too it is a horrible grief, I own, as she would have made the most perfect wife for Eddy in every way'.[10] But the Princess was consoled by the birth of her first grandchild; Louise of Fife gave birth to a daughter. Fripp visited the Fifes at Sheen and signed his name in the book, perhaps reminded that this had been the scene of Eddy's love affair, such as it was, with Hélène last summer.

Eddy knew he must marry. He would never have his own establishment until he did. Once married, he would no longer have to put up with people reporting back to his father. The Admiral, his Commanding Officer, his doctors – even Fripp, a friend of his own age – were essentially on his parents' side, and it did rather take the edge off friendships when even people you liked were expected to spy on you.

At the beginning of June 1891, the Tranby Croft affair came to court. For the Prince of Wales it was a nightmare. He had to appear every day except the last, and Sir Edward Clarke, the Solicitor-General, on behalf of Gordon-Cumming, did not spare him. Bertie was virtually accused of using Gordon-Cumming as a scapegoat for his own self-indulgence and bad judgement. There had been, thundered the Solicitor-General, men who were willing 'to sacrifice themselves to support a tottering throne or prop a falling dynasty', but Gordon-Cumming was not among them.

Gordon-Cumming was not vindicated. The verdict went against him and he was socially finished, but the damage had been done. Bertie had been depicted as a rich, selfish gambler capable of caddish behaviour. He was deeply hurt, and spent most of the summer resenting the 'bitter and unjust' attacks of the press and resorting to the self-victimising royal complaint that he was powerless to defend himself.

His eldest son was in love again already, and enjoying the summer season. Eddy was everywhere. He was at Ascot; he was at garden-parties, dances, at a levée – he presented Fripp with a black pearl tie-pin and, incidentally, paid his bill (a six-month delay being prompt payment for royalty, as the young doctor discovered later in life). He was hardly with the Hussars at all. Nor was he at the music hall, or he would have taken to heart the popular song:

> When courting don't write spooney letters
> To your fair one for love or for sport
> For should you but break any promise
> They are sure to be read out in court.[11]

On 21 June he wrote to Sybil Erskine (in terms which suggest that the flirtation had started before Hélène's letter):

> I thought it was impossible a short time ago, to love more than one person at the same time [a contention that his father had already disproved]... I can explain it easier to you when next we meet, than by writing. I only hope that this charming creature which has so fascinated me is not merely playing with my feelings... I can't believe she would after all she has already said, and asked me to say... I am writing in an odd way and have no doubt you will think so but I do it for a particular reason...[12]

He pleaded that she must cut out the crest and signature lest 'someone got hold of the letter by any chance'. Who could he have had in mind? Surely not Daisy Brooke, his father's current love?

Sybil didn't cut anything out, though. A week later he wrote:

> I wonder if you really love me a little? I ought not to ask such a silly question I suppose but still I should be very pleased if you did just a little bit... You may trust me not to show your letters to anyone... You can't be too careful what you do in these days, when hardly anybody is to be trusted.[13]

He was light-hearted, charming, affectionate and a flirt – and there was no precipitate proposal of marriage this time. The Rosslyns were of long and honourable lineage and the right religion. But it seems that since the enormous fuss and distress over Hélène, Eddy had resigned himself to his position. The few girls who might match the demands of his elders as well as himself were either too young, like Marie of Greece, or too old. He must marry whoever his parents chose for him, or cease to be the heir presumptive; and he correctly assessed his chances of success in another walk of life as nil. Certainly Sybil Erskine had a title, but nothing less than a princess would satisfy the Queen as a partner for her grandson. As for Alix, she would certainly be upset if she suspected Daisy Brooke might become part of the family. And had Bertie ever suspected Eddy's fondness for Sybil Erskine, he might have opposed it, because her twenty-one-year-old brother, the Earl of Rosslyn, was already losing the family fortune to bookies (a course of events that ended in his bankruptcy in 1897), and he would despair if Eddy began to consort with that set.

Until a princess was found for the prince, he would have to settle for love affairs conducted in secret. It was not at all satisfactory.

In July, Kaiser Wilhelm II arrived as the guest of Queen Victoria for a stay of almost a fortnight, and Prince Eddy was in constant attendance. From 4 to 8 July, Windsor was full of so many Germans (the Emperor arrived with a suite of nearly 100) that every room at the White Hart, besides most of the other hotels in the town, was occupied by minor Prussian army Vons and Grafs. Prince Eddy was fortunate in being accommodated at the castle.

Back in London on 9 July, the sun shone on a garden party at Marlborough House. Lord and Lady Brooke were accompanied by Lady Sybil St Clair Erskine.[14] It was an opportunity to meet, and no doubt it was taken.

As usual, the British were determined to impress the Kaiser with pomp, pageantry and displays of military might. Before a vast Guildhall dinner on 10 July, he reviewed nearly 30,000 volunteers and regulars, who marched in from special camps at Richmond Park and Wimbledon Common. The visit was rounded off with a visit to Lord Salisbury at Hatfield from 11 to 13 July.

Just one thing about Eddy had been noticed, at any rate by *The Times* correspondent, again and again. For nearly a fortnight, the entire royal family had glittered at one state occasion after another – including even a royal Anglo-German wedding at St George's Chapel. Bertie had appeared in a succession of vivid uniforms, bristling with braid and medals. But Prince Eddy almost always wore his Hussars outfit. Smart as it was, it was not imposing. The Prince of Wales was dressed to impress in a way his son could not be, for he did not hold high rank. Prince Eddy was still a major. Other men who had entered the service at the same time were by now lieutenant-colonels.

Prince George was no further advanced in his naval career; at twenty-seven he had not yet made commander. But sooner or later he would, as his future lay in the navy and his father would brook no argument about that. Prince Eddy was altogether a more difficult customer, apparently capable of an apathy that amounted almost to dumb insolence. He had to have a role that suited him.

The subject of his promotion had come up before. His uncle, the Duke of Cambridge, who was commander-in-chief, had asked Lord Wolseley whether it would be advisable. Lord Wolseley (on whom was modelled 'I am the very model of a Modern Major-General' in *The Pirates of Penzance*) had sent the following kindly answer:

HRH has far more in him than he is often given credit for but I should describe his brain and thinking powers as maturing slowly.

Personally I think he is very much to be liked, thoughtful for others, and always anxious to do the right thing. He is, however, young for his age and requires to be brought out.[15]

Prince Eddy's career was not ignominious. It was not that interesting. In fact, it was barely a career at all; apart from some time at York in the spring, he had hardly been in uniform, except on ceremonial occasions. The Hussars had been stationed in Dublin all summer, yet he had managed to attend every major event of the London season. The Prince of Wales, aglow that July with medals and feathers and the flattering effects of military tailoring, noticed that Eddy's career was going nowhere and came to a decision. Keeping the boy in the army, he decided impatiently, was a 'waste of time'.[16] Besides, he was still annoyed at him for getting into bad company, as he must have done to require the services of Sir Henry Thompson.

Prince Eddy finally left for Dublin in August, leaving his father seething with frustration. There would have to be a plan. Suggestions were sought.

The Queen, who had seen quite a lot of Eddy at dinners and luncheons at Windsor during the German visit, was bewildered and annoyed that neither he nor his brother spoke a foreign language. It limited their circle of acquaintance and their political understanding. They were 'dear good boys but very exclusively English' and Eddy, in particular, had spent barely any time in Europe. Of course he had been to Germany and Denmark, but he had spoken English there, and 'of Italy, Spain, Austria, Hungary, Russia, Turkey and Holland (very interesting) he knows nothing'.[17] France was conspicuously omitted. But she urged that Eddy should spend some time in each of the main European capitals, going about socially, getting to know people, broadening his outlook.

The Prince of Wales was not at all in favour of this. He, who had broadened both outlook and acquaintance on the Continent to a degree his mother never imagined, was determined that his son should not disport himself in the same way. Besides, from a purely selfish viewpoint, it would cramp his style to have the boy popping up all over Europe. He did not want to stroll out of the Hotel Bristol with Lady Brooke on his arm only to meet Prince Albert Victor's heavy-lidded stare from a passing cabriolet. No: the colonies, that was the answer, and for as long as possible.

Both ideas were put to Alix. She was happy for the prince to remain in the Hussars, for she would see so much of him. But she had to admit that Eddy himself was not at all keen on soldiering. She wanted him at home, but doing what? He did not want to marry anyone who had been suggested. Given the choice between Europe, and another unbearably long absence somewhere like Canada or South Africa, she agreed with the Queen. At least Europe was close.

The Prince of Wales would not have it. But Her Majesty would not have the colonies. As Knollys wrote to Lord Salisbury's secretary:

> Unfortunately, her views on <u>certain social</u> subjects are so strong that the Prince of Wales does not like to tell her his real reason for sending Prince Eddy away, which is intended as a <u>punishment</u>, and as a means of keeping him out of harm's way; and I am afraid that neither of those objects would be attained by his simply travelling about Europe. She is therefore giving her advice in the dark.[18]

How could Bertie explain to the Queen that Europe was full of strumpets? He did not need to; she understood exactly what he was getting at and calmly responded that there were 'as many designing pretty women in the Colonies'. Well, perhaps not in the kind of copper mine or pine forest Bertie had in mind, but... He thought about marrying the boy off to keep him out of harm's way, but there was no one except May of Teck, a nice girl, but dull; they seemed to have little in common. Sir Henry

Ponsonby, for one, thought that Eddy would groan at the suggestion. There seemed to be an impasse. Alix must decide. They spent some time together at Cowes in the first weeks of August, but still nothing was settled. He was dismally certain that his wife would choose the European option, so he watered it down with a variant of the colonial one and set off for his short annual regimen of plain living at Homburg.

Sir Francis Knollys visited Alix at Marlborough House on 19 August, the day before she left for her summer holiday in Denmark. He put to her the three alternatives that Bertie concluded were on the table.

1. The colonial expedition
2. The European cum colonial plan
3. To be married to Princess May in the spring.[19]

Quite unexpectedly, she chose that her son should be induced to marry Princess May of Teck. Alix, like most people, had her own interests at heart; and she wanted her dear son to stay at home.

Relieved that she had made her feelings plain, she set off across the Channel with her unmarried daughters. She had not been in Denmark long when rumours, current for a month in London, reached her that her husband's behaviour was once again the talk of the town. Daisy Brooke's affair with her husband threatened to attract wider publicity and, yet again, it was all because of that indiscreet letter, two years old at least, to Charles Beresford.

With her husband still at sea, Lady Beresford, having been dropped from the Marlborough House guest list for eighteen months, found her social circle so reduced that it was hardly worth being in London for the season at all. She put her house on the market and told everyone why. On that brilliant Friday in July, when the Marlborough House garden party roared with conversation and dazzled with jewels and Sybil Erskine fluttered her eyelashes at Prince Eddy, Lord Charles sat down in his cabin on the *Undaunted* and wrote a furious letter to the Prince of Wales, threatening that if his wife were not better treated he would expose everything about Bertie's behaviour. This letter he despatched to his wife, with a note instructing her to show it to Lord Salisbury. The Prime Minister, who one may aver with some certainty had other things on his mind, was supposed to spend his time settling the vindictive hysteria of these social butterflies, or immediately recall Lord Charles, so that he could publish all the ill will he felt.

When she received the letter, Lady Beresford consulted Sir Edward Clarke, that Solicitor-General who had so ably attacked the Prince of Wales in court over Tranby Croft. She then saw Lord Salisbury, wrote him a furious letter of her own, and added that her sister had written a pamphlet. Perhaps a little weary of heart, and knowing that the defamatory pamphlet was already in circulation, Lord Salisbury did not speak to the Prince of Wales but wrote to Lord Charles. Like Sir Edward Clarke, he advised calm, dignity, and a cessation of hostilities for the sake of aristocratic reputations in general. For the moment, it worked.

The Princess of Wales knew that speculation around her husband's private life had not died down since the Tranby Croft case. How could it? Light had flooded in, and the blinds could no longer be drawn over his card-playing, however many letters Bertie wrote to the Archbishop of Canterbury (and he did write, in the second week of August, a self-righteous letter about how much he abhorred gambling, no one hated it more, but of course what he did was something much less dreadful).[20] But middle-class fascination continued because

…until the supply of gossipy inventions ran low, the Press contin-ued to regale the public with these morsels. They felt that they had been given a real glimpse, more lurid than the most sumptuous imaginings of Ouida, into the private life of exalted personages, and the shock they professed to have experienced was certainly spiced by a high degree of enjoyment.[21]

And now Alix heard that people in society, who at least had always been sophisticated and discreet, were reduced to sniggering over a pamphlet about her husband's affair. She felt more threatened by Daisy Brooke than by Lillie Langtry because Daisy quite obviously saw herself as a power behind the throne; and she had had enough. She was too angry to return to Abergeldie to suffer further humiliation, and went from Denmark to join her sister Dagmar in the Crimea. There she stayed. The Prince of Wales could look forward to his fiftieth birthday in November by himself, or with whoever took his fancy: she, at any rate, could maintain her dignity.

Prince Eddy was as self-indulgent as his father about girls. He simply could not be as careful as his position demanded. He went on writing to Sybil Erskine from Ireland, and she went on keeping his letters, crest, signature and all, while being courted by a rather better bet, the son and heir of the Duke of Westmorland. It seems certain that Daisy Brooke knew about Prince Albert Victor's fondness for her young stepsister. She had pointed out to her brother Rosslyn, who had wavered before proposing marriage, the advantage of having a rich wife;[22] and it would seem in character that she should encourage Sybil to keep Eddy dangling on a line – after all, his wife would be a princess. One day he might even be looking for a mistress. She may have told the Prince of Wales about the Sybil/Eddy flirtation. There was not much he did not know.

At the end of August he somehow dispelled his gloom at the thought of Mary Adelaide of Teck waddling massively down the Sandringham corridors, and undertook to approach his son about marrying Princess May of Teck. Quite how the 'approach' was made is unknown; Prince Eddy was in Ireland. (It is possible that he was not asked by his father at all, but by his brother, who visited him there at the end of October.)

Nobody knew whether Eddy would agree, but no alternative options were presented. Knollys, who had the ear of the Prince of Wales, thought he would consent if he was told 'he *must* do it – that it is for the good of the good of the country, &c'.[23] May and her mother were in Malvern Wells, enjoying a modest holiday from the Princess's work for charity and the Prince of Teck's ill-temper (he had had a stroke in 1884 and had been crotchety ever since). The family were entirely unaware of the overwhelming changes that might soon occur.

In October, Eddy's name was announced among vice-presidents of a Royal Commission to be chaired by his father. They would meet to choose entries for the Chicago Exhibition of 1893. Prince George (who had at last been promoted to commander on 27 August) joined Eddy at the end of October, for a house party in Ireland and some Dublin Castle socialising. Around this time the Prince of Wales gave his consent; in other words, we know that Eddy had formally said he would do it. We know this because in that very week, Princess May was staying at Easton Hall in Essex, where the house party included the Prince, and Daisy Brooke wrote:

In the autumn of 1891 the Duke and Duchess of Teck, with Princess May, were our guests at Easton. I remember that among the party were Lord Sandwich, Lord Richard Nevill, Count Albert Mensdorff, the Hon Sidney Greville (my husband's brother, who was then equerry to the Prince of Wales), my sister-in-law, Lady Eva Greville, the lifelong friend and companion of Queen Mary, Lord Chesterfield, Lord and Lady Alington, Lord Chelsea, Lord and Lady Bradford, Colonel Brabazon, Lady Dorothy Nevill, Colonel Stanley Clarke, and Lady Sophia MacNamara, who was in waiting on the Duchess of Teck.

At that house party the Prince of Wales gave his consent to

the engagement of his son, Prince Eddy, Duke of Clarence and
Avondale, to Princess May. The prophecy of the Duchess of Teck
that such an alliance would be popular was more than justified...[24]

Princess Mary Adelaide of Teck – her elephantine form dominates photographs – somehow contained her delight, and waited
for the call. Nothing remained but that Queen Victoria should
inspect the potential bride. Princess May knew nothing about
it at all.

The Queen had known May since girlhood, but she needed
to be assured that there was absolutely nothing in her character
that might attract her to the kind of fast set that dear Alix, good
as she was, had never been able to resist. Princess May of Teck
was not a beauty, but she had intelligence and character. Her
mother was a wonderful woman, everybody agreed, but... you
could have too much of a good thing. Her father suffered from
the disgrace of a morganatic union only one generation back.
Both her parents were extravagant, her mother incorrigibly so.
When May was in her teens, the family had been forced to leave
England to live in cheap gentility in Florence for a couple of
years. Now they kept within their means by staying busy.

The possibility that she might marry well was pretty much
the family's only tangible asset, but hope had been fading.
Dear May was quiet, bookish, self-contained, and not a flirt;
she was not an heiress; and there was, the morganatic taint.
She was twenty-four and Prince Charming had not arrived.
She seemed destined to stay on the shelf, looking after her
father. Her brothers would marry and go away. Her mother
would grow old and die. Eventually she would be a lonely
spinster with meagre resources. And now this. This golden
opportunity.

Queen Victoria wanted a sensible girl, not bovine exactly,
strong-minded but not so witty or attractive or charming that

she would be taken up by clever, smart people. Also, she should have an international outlook; she should, preferably, have lived elsewhere in Europe. The Queen invited May, with her brother Adolphus but without their mother, for a ten-day stay at Balmoral. The diary of Louisa, Countess of Antrim, a lady-in-waiting, reveals that from 4 November onwards:

> Among the guests was Princess May of Teck, being vetted as a suitable wife for Prince Eddy of Wales. One test was for her to be driven through the mountains in the Queen's four-horse carriage, getting out now and then with Louisa to admire an icy waterfall.[25]

She seemed absolutely perfect.

Bertie was having a dreadful year. Tranby Croft; the Beresfords spreading poisonous rumours; his wife upset in a way she had never been before; his sons achieving precious little; and now, on the night of 31 October, part of Sandringham burned down. Alix was still away, with Maud and Victoria, but at least Eddy and George came back together from Ireland to celebrate his birthday on 9 November. In the great house, with its fire-damaged upper rooms, they made the best of it. A couple of days before, a deputation representing the London theatrical profession had presented him with a solid gold cigar-box enamelled with Prince of Wales feathers. It weighed 100 ounces! And Prince Eddy had agreed to stay in the Hussars for the winter. He would propose to May of Teck in January. Hélène d'Orléans would be in Spain then. And something would be done about setting Eddy up in an establishment of his own, at St James's Palace to start with, and finding him a role.

Alix did not intend to start for home until 19 November, ten days after Wales's birthday. But George, their favourite son, fell ill with what appeared to be enteric fever. The Prince of Wales took his sick son to London on Friday 16 November. Typhoid was on everyone's mind, and Dr Manby from East Rudham, who normally attended the family at Sandringham, should not be expected to deal with it alone.

Typhoid was diagnosed – caught in Ireland, they were sure.[26] The disease was unpredictable. Telegrams were sent. Alix started back from the Crimea at once. She arrived in London on 22 November, at around the time that the disease was reaching its crisis. Prince George was spared, and his parents were united once again.

At the end of the month, Prince Eddy heard a rumour that upset him. It seemed that Sybil Erskine was engaged to Lord Burghersh. On 29 November, he wrote to find out whether or not this was true. Because if it was, he added, with a touch of sad defiance:

> Don't be surprised if you hear before long that I am engaged also, for I expect it will come off soon. But it will be a very dif-ferent thing to what it might have been once… But still it can't be helped.[27]

She was engaged all right. It felt like a third rejection. Eddy, who was inclined to be dilatory about appointments and usually made other people do whatever bored him, seized the moment and took action.

There was to be a house party at Luton Hoo, the home of the Danish ambassador, Christian de Falbe, and his wife, beginning on Wednesday 2 December. If Patricia Cornwell is to be believed (and the accuracy of her account is disputed in an appendix to this book), it seems that Eddy resolved to tie up the loose ends of his bachelor existence before making an irrevocable move. According to Cornwell, he sent Lewis a gift 'in acknowledge-ment for the kindness you showed me the other day in getting me out of that trouble I was foolish enough to get into'. There had been also 'the other lady'. He had had to ask a friend to visit her 'and ask her to give up the two or three letters I had written to her... You may be certain that I shall be careful in the future not to get into any more trouble of the sort.'[28]

Princess May had seen the Waleses at various functions that year, but did not recall seeing Prince Eddy since Ascot week. She wrote in her diary for Tuesday 2 December:

> Fine day... We left for Luton. Party Eddy, Baths and Katie Thynne [the Marquis and Marchioness of Bath and their daughter], Georgie Forbes and Ida, Dudley Wards, Arthur and Clemmie Walsh, Miss Leigh, Arthur Somerset, Sir Charles Hartropp, Mrs Gregson, Mr Brownlow, Oliver Montagu etc.[29]

Arthur Somerset? Well, that is unlikely too; we will deal with the question in due course. But Luton Hoo was a grand, overheated house with a conservatory rampant with scented blooms. And on the following night, at a ball, Prince Eddy manoeuvred May into Madame de Falbe's boudoir; and he proposed.

Princess May accepted. She was so happy! Late that night she twirled around in her prettiest frock, her face radiant, and told the other girls. (She loved to twirl. The Duchess of Beaufort confided 'Princess May was very proud of her legs and ankles. As a girl she would jump onto a sofa at games, so that people could see them.')[30] May of Teck's excitement must have been wonderful to behold. Until now, her future had looked frankly dull. Of course, she had been brought up to be royal. She knew what was expected of her; she knew all the people; she knew the way they lived. The whole point of being royal was to be seen, especially to be seen doing good in the world. Yet the Tecks had lived on the edge of disappearing, socially and financially, for as long as she could remember. Only her mother's ebullient personality and perpetual round of charitable engagements had saved them from anonymity.

Now they would be secure. The Tecks would be some-body, for ever. White Lodge would be assured. She would have everything she wanted; there would be no more carping; and, best of all, she would never grow into an old spinster. She would be married. There would be children, and houses, and travel, and the royal yacht.

Eddy was tall and handsome and kind. Everybody agreed that when he smiled he was as good-looking as his mother. And she liked him. Everybody did. He had seemed wonderfully pleased when she said yes. The day after the ball, when they both knew but it was still supposed to be a secret because his parents had not yet been told, he was very good company, and in the next few days it became clear that they were temperamentally suited. He was more vulnerable than she was; he had learned a certain reserve, where she was shy. They were both interested in geneal-ogy, and the theatre – he loved musical theatre – and there was more to their rapport than that. Both of them needed to be part of a couple. Eddy had suffered humiliation as a son, had always been made to feel inadequate, and wanted to be married and less dependent upon his father's approval; yet he also wanted sup-port. May, too, had suffered humiliation. She had not forgotten the two years when her parents, herself and her three brothers had fled England and lived on scant remittances in borrowed houses, like an entire family of black sheep. She needed the psychological support of a position in the world. In any group of girls, she had never been the prettiest, the most vivacious, the belle of the ball. She too wanted to be independent – to put the Teck family behind her, in the kindest possible way, and join another, richer, more prestigious one. It was a victory for wallflowers everywhere.

On Saturday, Eddy personally informed Her Majesty at Windsor. (Coincidentally, the morning's *Times* announced the publication of *HRH The Duke of Clarence and Avondale in Southern India* by J.D. Rees.) That evening he spoke to his parents at Marlborough House, and they all went on to the opera with Victoria and Maud, Captain Holford and Major Ellis, equerry to the Prince of Wales. Shortly afterwards the announcement appeared in *The Times*; and no doubt the publisher of *HRH… in Southern India* rubbed his hands in anticipation of big sales.

Prince Eddy had done it. He had been accepted unreservedly, and he was happier than he or anyone else expected. He and Princess May spent a delightful couple of weeks in London, driving around, attending the theatre again and again, even choosing wallpaper for the apartments already prepared at St James's Palace. Wherever they went, the Christmas crowds were delighted to see them. It was cold, and only an occasional black armband on a coat, or a family in black, served to remind them of all the sickness about. The influenza epidemic had been waxing and waning all year. According to expert opinion, it had come from Bokhara, in the deserts north of Afghanistan; certainly, it was now attacking every country in Europe. But people were glad about their engagement; they were cheered in public; they were a nice-looking young couple and it was a popular match.

The only sniper was close to home. On the Teck side, Lady Geraldine Somerset, that lady-in-waiting to Princess May's grandmother who had never been able to stand Princess Mary Adelaide, seems to have been quite won over, confiding to her diary that everyone said Eddy was 'radiant and not at all shy'.[31] But Eddy's jealous aunt, Princess Christian, had hoped he would marry one of her daughters, and her nose was severely out of joint.

They would marry on 27 February and were hoping for St Paul's. The Queen wrote from Osborne to Archbishop Benson on 21 December:

My dear Archbishop,

I must thank you very much for your kind letter and congratulations on the engagement of my dear grandson Albert Victor to

Princess Victoria Mary of Teck, which promises to be a happy union. May is a charming girl, with much sense and amiability and very unfrivolous, so that I have every hope the young people will set an example of a steady, quiet life which, alas, is not the fashion in these days.[32]

Eddy spent two days at White Lodge and visited the Queen at Windsor, with May and her parents. After Christmas at Sandringham, the Tecks would come to stay with them. Everything was so cosy, so perfect, so like a fairy tale.

The politicians had to be practical. There was to be a wedding, and with any luck it would be a state occasion in St Paul's, which was what the Prince of Wales, supported by Balfour, thought most fitting; but Lord Salisbury thought they would all freeze. Everyone seemed to have either a cold or influenza this December (the Wales girls, sneezing and coughing, were isolated in their rooms at Marlborough House), and Lord Salisbury protested at the cathedral idea, joking that he was 'not anxious to antedate the demise of the crown' by choosing this venue for the marriage ceremony. The alternative would be the drawing-room at Windsor; it was up to the Queen to decide.

Then there was the much more important question of money. No one expected the Duke of Teck to provide a dowry. Had May been a foreign princess, the government would have stumped up. Lord Salisbury felt it was unfair to deprive Prince Eddy of the money, just because his bride-to-be was English; but only two years ago, the House had put its collective foot down at the time of Louise's marriage to the Duke of Fife, and a Royal Commission had made arrangements for a trust fund, which really should be adequate. It was difficult to know what to do. In the meantime, committees were being set up all over the land to contribute impressive wedding gifts, on behalf of societies and regiments, royal boroughs and masonic lodges.

Eddy, unaware of any of the strings that were being pulled, happened to be writing to his Aunt Louise and Uncle Lorne at this time:

> I wonder if you were surprised when you saw that I was engaged? I dare say you were, for I must say I made up my mind rather suddenly, which I think however was the best thing after all, and it is really time that I thought of getting married, if ever I am to be. Anyway, it is now settled at last. I think I have done well in my choice, for I feel certain that May will make an excellent wife, and you may be certain that I shall do my best to make her a good husband.[33]

The unconfined joy seems to have worn off, but at least for once he had done the right thing. It must have been worth it to see his father beaming at him. Notwithstanding another threatening letter from Charles Beresford on 17 December, the Prince had every reason to beam. Lord Wolseley, the commander-in chief- in Dublin, had made a very interesting suggestion about Eddy's future: one that seemed excellent in every way.

II

Devastation
1892

On 4 January 1892, May arrived at Sandringham with her parents. Eddy and his father had been in London for a funeral, and came back on the same day.

The men went out almost daily, and the evenings were occupied with talk and music and cards (Eddy was still an excellent whist-player). There were hundreds of letters to write and congratulations to express gratitude for, besides the wedding preparations. Princess May was almost overwhelmed. As for all the invitations, it was like a second coming of age; it was a new job. She had been her mother's secretary for years, and now she found herself organising Eddy's life as well as her own.

At one point she doubted whether she had not taken on too much. She need not have worried; Alix had operated successfully as a royal wife for nearly a quarter of a century with a fraction of the orderliness, punctuality and political understanding that

May had at her command. But this was the emotional low point of someone coming down with a heavy cold, as she was.

Unfortunately, so many people at Sandringham seemed to be ill, and shivering. Sandringham was inefficiently heated. There was no ambient temperature, but rather a series of hot and cold spots. The rooms were high and draughty and the corridors icy; the heat given off by fires in the public rooms and bedrooms was quickly dissipated through large windows and great expanses of uninsulated loft and outside wall. The high collars famously worn by both Alix and Prince Eddy had at least the virtue of warmth. In winter, men wore long woollen undergarments beneath several layers of clothing, and rode or strode about the countryside to keep warm. Women huddled around a roaring fire, constrained inside corsets and layers of petticoats from neck to ankle beneath thick dresses.

Eddy had a slight cold, which had come on after the funeral, and Princess Victoria ('Toria') was still suffering from a lingering infection which everyone now thought had been influenza. Princess Maud and George Holford had it too. The Princess of Wales had a heavy cold and Prince George was still convalescing after the typhoid.

Bertie was in good form, however, and quick to grasp the interesting suggestion from Lord Wolseley. Sir Francis Knollys wrote to Lord Salisbury's secretary, in some excitement, on Wednesday 6 January

My dear McDonnell,
The Prince of Wales thinks Lord Salisbury should see the enclosed letter from Lord Wolseley on the subject of the Duke of Clarence being appointed Viceroy of Ireland.
Please return me the letter when Lord Salisbury has done with it.[1]

(*attached*: Lord Wolseley to Duke of Cambridge)

The post of Viceroy of Ireland (and Lord Lieutenant of Dublin Castle) could be offered next year at the time of the election. It was a constitutional anomaly, and an appointment required careful thought; Lord and Lady Cadogan had been favourites for it until now, although, as one of Balfour's gossipy letters points out, they 'wanted Paris'.[2] The position was highly symbolic, as the Viceroy could theoretically exercise the Queen's power in Ireland, rather as the Pope exercised God's in the Church of Rome. No incumbent had ever actually exploited this extraordinary status, but rather treated the viceroyalty as a rallying point for the social life of Dublin Castle. As an institution representative of the Protestant ruling class, the present court was specifically a *court*, for the Anglo-Irish landowners were the biggest snobs in the world and stayed away from anything that looked at all middle-class. The present Viceroy, the Earl of Zetland, had held the post since 1889, and an observer at one of his dinners described 'a long table gradually filled with Switzer's most expensive frocks, and black coats coruscating with stars and orders'.[3]

There was a balance to maintain. The populace must defer to the might of the British Empire and civil disobedience must be contained. This disobedience took the awkward and violent form of boycotting. Typically, this meant that an entire community would refuse to trade with, for instance, a widowed smallholder who had ignored the Nationalist Plan of Campaign (which instructed withholding of rent). Because the person (it often seemed to be a frail old woman) could no longer sell goods in the market, she ended up with no money and was publicly evicted by the landlord and police. The evictions were heartrending. Then the boycotters, encouraged by their priests, grabbed and squatted in the empty property.

The penalty, under the Coercion Act of 'Bloody Balfour', for either withholding rent or conspiring to grab land was jail. Those of the Irish who did not have good jobs on Protestant estates were therefore damned if they collaborated with the occupying English and damned if they did not; they were resentful and unhappy.

So appearances in Dublin must be maintained, but not to an obscene degree – a glittering Viceroy who represented everything that was brutal and corrupt about the English aristocracy would be a disaster far beyond the Castle. All the post needed was sociability and good organisation. It had been suggested as an option for Wales, when he was newly married, and the Queen had been in favour: according to her, he would never concentrate or knuckle down until he had to, and a job like that might do him good. But Wales had never liked Ireland. Besides, over the years it became clear that he must be kept as close to home as possible.

Prince Eddy and Princess May were young, charming and genuine, besides being more biddable and less spoiled than the Waleses. Unlike his father, the young prince was too amiable to panic if crossed; he even displayed tact and sensitivity, while giving no sign that he would be so liberal in his opinions as to disturb Lord Salisbury. There was no blot on his character, publicly, at least. And of course in no time at all they would have a young family: what could be more endearing?

Lord Wolseley had been born in Dublin. His family of origin, the junior and poor branch of a distinguished clan, were minor landowners in Ireland. As the leader of outstandingly successful campaigns in India and Egypt, he had risen to his present position through strategic thinking and superb judgement. He had been commander-in-chief in Dublin for two years now; he had spent some time observing Prince Eddy, and he thought he would be right for the job.

Lord Salisbury apparently liked the idea – as he would, having spent the week before Christmas closeted with Queen Victoria in an effort to bury the Beresford scandal forever. Wales's perennial problem had been under-employment, and the son must not be allowed to slip into a life of self-indulgence like his father.

The Prince of Wales (who surely cannot have put Lord Wolseley up to it?) was delighted. What a solution! Far enough from London to satisfy him, but not so far as to make Alix unhappy, a posting at Dublin Castle even had that *piquant* element of punishment about it – Bertie had got it as an exile posting for Lord Randolph Churchill once. On 8 January, the Friday of Prince Eddy's birthday party, Knollys wrote:

My Dear McDonnell,

Many thanks for your letter on the subject of the Duke of Clarence being appointed Viceroy of Ireland.

I have shown it to the Prince of Wales, and he would very much like to see Lord Salisbury. HRH will be in London from Monday afternoon and should Lord Salisbury be coming to London on the latter day the Prince would be very glad to have a few minutes' conversation with him at Marlborough House or Arlington Street (whichever would suit Lord Salisbury the best) at 3.30.[4]

Outside, the weather was as icy as it had been in the year of Eddy's birth. The lake at Sandringham was frozen and fog lay heavy over the fens. Yesterday, Prince Eddy had insisted on going out shooting, despite his cold, and had had to return early, shivering and unwell. A large party had been invited for this, his last birthday as a bachelor. He tottered downstairs on the Friday evening to see his presents, while everyone who was well enough watched the play presented by Mr Hare's Company (who came from London and back in a special train) and celebrated his birthday without him; but he really did look very seedy and definitely had influenza. It was, as May noted in her diary, tiresome. But, in his absence, her father proposed his health anyway.

On Saturday, he still had a high temperature and pneumonia was diagnosed. Dr Laking, Physician in Ordinary to the Prince of Wales, came to assist Dr Manby and telegraphed for a specialist opinion, which arrived in the person of Dr Broadbent. On

Sunday, the invalid was getting worse, with congestion in one lung and a temperature rising above 103 degrees, and there was serious concern. By this time, Knollys had the 'flu himself, and struggled to write coherently:

> 10th January 1892
>
> My dear McDonnell,
>
> Will you inform Lord and Lady Salisbury that [owing] to the Duke of Clarence's illness he will be unable to go to Hatfield – You will see a statement.
>
> Will you at the same time tell Lord Salisbury that for the above reason he fears he shall not be able to keep his appointment with him on Tuesday.[5]

The house had been full for the birthday party, and Prince Eddy happened to be lodged in one of its smaller rooms, overlooking the lawn in front. Sandringham had undergone so many alterations over the years that its internal layout was awkward. James Pope-Hennessy, when he visited many years later, described Prince Eddy's accommodation as situated among a 'truly sinister warren' of small rooms, down a couple of steps and along a narrow corridor. The ceiling was high, and snow was now falling outside its tall bay window.

> This dim and cheerless hole is surprisingly small; opposite the door a window, to the right of the door a fireplace, then the brass bedstead, so that you could touch the mantelpiece with your hand if lying on the bed; along the other wall a cupboard and now a washbasin, taps etc.[6]

Dr Manby, from East Rudham, had been the first physician to come, and had perhaps advised keeping the invalid in this room, which was at least small enough for a fire's warmth to survive the prevailing chill. Now there were three doctors and

Sister Victoria Hallam, not all at once, but having to squeeze courteously past the Princess of Wales, dabbing at her son's forehead, or Princess May, who helped as much as she could, and the bulky Prince when he looked in.

There was not much anyone could do about influenza except provide palliative care, and perhaps quinine to lower the temperature, and let the fever take its course. The doctors were grave, and all were apprehensive.

Everything at Sandringham seemed held in suspense. Knollys and Admiral Stephenson and the others had largely recovered from their own illnesses. The Prince and Princess of Wales and the Tecks spent most of each day in and out of a small room next to the sickroom, waiting for the hopeful report which was sure to come; less than two months ago they had been worrying about George, and his typhoid had seemed a far more threatening case. Prince Eddy was young and strong; he would fight off the influenza. There had been many cases – one knew such a lot of people who had had it badly and recovered.

Decisions and events were put off until it was all over and Eddy could be pronounced well. Dr Manby, gazing from the small window, saw George and May walking outside in the grounds hand in hand. To him, it was a distinct sign that they were falling in love or were already in love. According to his daughter, Lady Willens, Manby appears to have suspected that the prince and princess were, in reality, much closer than protocol made out.[7]

Monday and Tuesday passed without much improvement. On Monday, May and George were able to speak to Eddy over the screen around his bed, but on Tuesday he was, if anything, slightly worse. Then came Tuesday night, when a second lung seemed dreadfully affected. Bulletins were posted at Marlborough House on Wednesday:

Sandringham, 9.30am
Symptoms of great gravity have supervened, and the condition of
his Royal Highness the Duke of Clarence is critical.

Crowds gathered in the Mall, waiting for the next bulletin; the
news spread by word of mouth, and there was anxiety everywhere. Sandringham was in constant contact with Osborne, and
the Lord Mayor of London and the Earl of Zetland, in Dublin,
received frequent telegrams. At one time Eddy's temperature
had fallen, but now on Wednesday it had soared to 107 degrees
– higher even than George's had been; Eddy was delirious. He
asked for Fuller, his valet. This was Charlie Fuller, who had been
with him since his babyhood. A telegram was sent and Fuller
raced to Sandringham at once.

Throughout the day, no change was reported. Everyone was
united in repeating the same heartfelt concern that this should
have happened so soon after his engagement; that he was such a
nice boy; that he was young and strong and would pull through.
The Times said comfortingly:

> It has been freely stated that the Duke of Clarence is less robust
> than his brother, Prince George, and this is practically correct: but
> the Duke has an ordinarily strong constitution, and up to five days
> ago was perfectly sound in health. Between the age of 12 and 16
> the Duke grew out of all proportion to his younger brother, and
> this may possibly have weakened him; but it is satisfactory to know
> that he does not suffer from any chronic disease.

The delirium persisted. The rooms were small and close together
and it was impossible not to hear Prince Eddy crying out. He
called the names of many people, and May perhaps was among
those who heard 'Hélène! Hélène!'[8] The crisis came in the small
hours of Thursday morning. The royal family were summoned and
the doctors avoided their eyes. Eddy suddenly spoke clearly.

'Something terrible has happened. My darling brother George is dead.'[9]

A shiver went through everyone. Did he have a premonition that he and his brother were about to be separated? The fever persisted; he lapsed into unconsciousness in the cold, silent house, with the murmuring of voices, and the gas-light from the one corridor, and at dawn he rallied.

'Who is it? Who is it?... Who is it?'

He asked the question again and again, with increasing difficulty, until the voice faded, and the doctors pronounced him dead.

The shock resounded throughout Europe. As early as Wednesday night, the prognosis of that day having been so gloomy, Prince Eddy's death had been the subject of rumours in London and Paris. Friday's black-bordered *Telegraph* said of these rumours that on the morning of Thursday 14 January

> Their falsity was manifested when the great crowd of toilers set out from the suburbs yesterday morning upon their daily round of business. In the workmen's trains, leaving the great terminal at an early hour, the number of readers was noticeably larger than it usually is, and only one topic of conversation occupied attention... [yet] to say that [the final announcement] produced a terrible shock is only feebly to express the effect.[10]

In St Paul's Cathedral, Great Tom[11] tolled through the dim morning, resounding sadly over the rooftops of the City and down to the docks, where a thousand ships groaned and creaked on mud-coloured water.

Church bells were the first signal of the tragedy in outer suburbs and small towns. Throughout the West End, traders put up narrow black mourning shutters. Trade in the City exchanges virtually ceased, and everywhere people gathered to commiserate, vicariously, with the royal family. Victoria's message to the nation, from Osborne, bordered with black, described her 'dear grandson, whom I loved as a son, and whose devotion to me was as great as that of a son'.

The shock was perfectly genuine. Somehow when a person is young, and so obviously has everything to live for, it is impossible to believe that life has been seized from them; in a more religious age, amazement was mixed with puzzlement and that sense, so much more familiar to the Victorians than it is to us, of the immanence of unknowable fate. People relived their own personal bereavements in this time of sorrow, and sympathy welled forth for the Prince and Princess of Wales and for Princess May.

Committees and lodges and societies that had gathered so gaily to discuss lads' outings and street parties and loyal toasts for the impending royal wedding now had to speak of wreaths, and messages of condolence. In cities up and down the country, where, as in Manchester, he had 'charmed everyone he met by his amiable and genial manner', court hearings were postponed, flags hung at half-mast, council meetings were cancelled and the Mayor and Corporation sent telegrams of commiseration. Most people were saddened, even in Dublin; or, in the minds of a few, especially in Dublin.

The funeral would take place at Windsor nearly a week later. Death had occurred on 14 January, that date of which the Queen stood in superstitious dread. Two days after she heard the ghastly news, she wrote to her daughter in Germany that the Prince of Wales

… is broken down, and poor dear Alix, though bearing up wonderfully, does nothing but cry, Bertie says.[12]

It was true. The Prince of Wales was dreadfully upset. He wrote to his mother:

> Gladly would I have given my life for his, as I put no value on mine… Such a tragedy has never before occurred in the annals of my family, and it is hard that poor little May should virtually become a widow before she is a wife.[13]

Prince George wrote

> It is only now that I have found out how deeply I did love him; and I remember with pain nearly every hard word and little quarrel I ever had with him and I long to ask his forgiveness but alas! It is too late now.[14]

In the words of Harold Nicolson: 'Prince George was conscious that he had lost the one companion on this earth with whom his relations had been those of absolute equality.' Despair rippled far beyond the family. Lord Selborne signed the memorial book with 'I do not think there has been a more tragic event in our time, or one which has more deeply touched the hearts of people generally.' For the entire week of that cold and foggy January, London mourned and society queued to leave condolences at Marlborough House. In less elevated circles, Thomas Newman of 4, Thorn Road, Ealing, was among many who wrote and published dreadful doggerel about the tomb, angels, lilies, roses, and soft odorous balms from 'the circling flowers that droop their head':

> …Thy Lover's gone
> Maiden fair Princess alone
> Heir to great Britannia's throne
> Now thy bridal hopes have flown.[15]

The Times was less morbid but inappropriately forward-looking, pointing out that when Alix's sister Dagmar had lost her fiancé Nicolas she had become engaged, after a suitable interval, to his younger brother.

Alix, thankfully, saw none of this. Her obsession now was to have none of the Germans at the funeral; none of the 'Osborne women'. The Waleses felt that Prince Henry of Battenberg, 'Liko', who was married to Bertie's sister Beatrice, had wormed his way into the Queen's inner circle (the old lady was too ill to leave Osborne at the moment) and that Liko and his wife did everything they could to undermine and exclude them. Also, the Waleses wanted their darling son buried at Sandringham.

But even in death, Prince Eddy must do what was expected of him. The men would take over: the masons, the soldiers. It would be a military funeral at Windsor, with no ladies. As if soldiery had been what he best loved in life!

The body lay at Sandringham for a week. Early on the cold morning of 20 January, the gun-carriage, accompanied by men of the Royal Horse Artillery, stood ready to collect it from Sandringham. Someone noticed that the coffin-board, used for Lord Napier of Magdala, was too narrow and rather short; so the horses pulled the gun-carriage to outbuildings at Sandringham, where estate carpenters removed a two-inch-high border and hurriedly hammered ends and sides of rough unplaned wood into place. The procession left half an hour after the appointed time. Prince Eddy was late for his own funeral.

Beyond the railings of Sandringham Park, near the church, crowds of black-clad villagers waited in silence on the green. Outside the church gate, the gamekeepers stood in their uniform cord breeches and green caps edged with gold lace, beside labourers in mourning wearing the white cross of St Andrew on their chests. The church bell tolled three times for the death of a man, and as the gun-carriage trundled by the men removed their hats. The princesses followed in carriages. The coffin, covered in a silk flag, was carried under the lych-gate into the church for a service of mourning.

An hour later, the crowds outside saw the coffin borne out once more to the gun-carriage. It rolled away slowly, preceded by eight mounted men of the Royal Horse Artillery and followed by the male mourners on foot. The Prince of Wales was seen to walk with a stick, with difficulty. Behind the royal party, a silent crowd followed the procession through country lanes to Wolferton Station. This is set in a natural amphitheatre; and as the gun-carriage breasted the hill, the local masons stood in a group apart from the crowds, to pay their respects as the cortège made its way towards the platform and the coffin was lifted into a carriage lined and covered with purple velvet.

At stations along the route, crowds stood silent and bareheaded in the cold. In London, the City and the West End were closed for business. Omnibus and cab drivers wore black bows on their whips. All the theatres, the Crystal Palace and Olympia Exhibition Halls were closed. Services at St Paul's and Westminster Abbey were so crowded that people stood in the aisles. There were services of remembrance at Osborne and all major towns and cities, at City churches like St Botolph's and St George's in the East, at Temple Church, at the Guards' Chapel and the Chapel Royal at St James's, at Bevis Marks and at the Great Synagogue in Aldgate, which was completely draped in black, and where the Chief Rabbi spoke movingly of Eddy's visit to Jerusalem and 'the modest, the amiable, the unassuming manner in which the lamented Prince Albert Victor discharged the public functions entrusted to him'. Guns were fired on Horse Guards Parade, and church bells tolled all over London. The following day, *The Times* would devote thirteen and a half unbroken broadsheet columns to the services and messages of 20 January, when the whole country mourned the death of a young man who had been so widely liked.

At half-past three, the funeral train approached Windsor. Every house and shop along the route through the town was hung with black crepe swags. Thousands of people gathered in the streets. Snow had fallen at Windsor that morning, but they waited quietly from late morning onwards, huddled along the icy pavements like flocks of crows. Soldiers in full dress uniform had assembled from many battalions of the British army to line the route. The railway station was decked with tall palms and smothered in white lilies and primulas.

As the coffin emerged, a minute gun was fired by a battery of the Royal Horse Artillery from the Long Walk in Windsor Great Park.

> The tolling of bells, the regular firing of guns, and the deep, muffled roll of distant drums conspired to add to the impressiveness... By degrees the music of the massed bands became more distinctly audible, and presently everyone recognised the mournful strains of Chopin's Funeral March rising and falling on the wintry air, a wailing but exquisite dirge. First of all came an outrider clad in a scarlet coat, and after him two troopers of the 2nd Life Guards, followed by an escort of the same regiment, and then the massed bands of the Guards. A party of the 10th Royal Hussars 'The Prince of Wales's Own', came next, and then, flanked on either side by officers of the 10th Royal Hussars, followed a party of the Royal Horse Artillery, with a gun carriage drawn by eight horses bearing the remains of his late Royal Highness. The coffin, which was enveloped in the Union Jack, was covered with a profusion of exquisite floral offerings, half hidden among which were the sword and busby of the deceased duke... One of the most pathetic features in the procession was the charger of the late Duke. It followed immediately behind the coffin, and was hooded and draped in black.[16]

The bands were still playing the Funeral March when the coffin reached the west entrance to St George's Chapel. It was dark in there; by now the daylight had almost gone, and only candles illuminated the solemn obsequies.

The service was almost too much for Alix to bear. She watched and wept out of sight, in Catherine of Aragon's closet. She wanted privacy in her grief, but despite her pleading the Queen (who had remained at Osborne on medical advice) had decreed that Princess Beatrice and the other ladies should attend. One was Louisa, Countess of Antrim, lady-in-waiting to the Queen, who wrote that Alix 'kissed us all – a little catch in her throat gave me such an ache'.[17] Princess May wore a black dress with white collar and cuffs.

At the end of the service, the door of the Osborne pew jammed. Princess Beatrice felt cross, suspecting that the incident had been deliberately set up so that she would lose face, and complained to Sir Henry Ponsonby, who complained to an equerry of the Prince of Wales. The following reply was received:

> The Prince of Wales desires me to say that the harem of Princesses was not locked into the further Zenana pew closet but the door got jammed; and [he] adds that they were none of them wanted at all. No ladies were to attend and the Princess of Wales especially requested privacy – and to avoid meeting her Osborne relations. So they all came.
>
> If Princess Beatrice was annoyed she must get over it – as she likes![18]

The Queen had taken over, and directed, their son's christening; the Princess could be forgiven for thinking she had done the same at his funeral. If she felt at all resentful, she was too gracious to show it.

12

Aftershock
1892 to the present

Prince George married Princess May of Teck in the Chapel Royal on 6 July 1893. Eddy's cousin, the Tsarevich Nicolas, wrote to his mother 'Poor Aunt Alix looked rather sad in church. One can quite understand why.'[1]

In 1901, Queen Victoria died and the Prince of Wales became King Edward VII. As his mother had predicted, he rose to meet the challenge, and employed his popularity across the Channel, and his extraordinary networking skills, to build an *entente cordiale* between Britain and France.

He was succeeded on his death by George and May – King George and Queen Mary. George had been in the navy for a long time by then, and had never developed his father's breadth of outlook. Nonetheless, he reigned for twenty-five years.

Charlie Fuller, the footman, corresponded with Prince George intermittently until his death in 1900. George remained friends with Canon Dalton until the clergyman's death in 1931, when he wrote to the widow 'he was my oldest and most intimate friend'. Dalton's son Hugh, the future chancellor, was at Cambridge in the twenties and found Oscar Browning still there; he was 'very kind and hospitable to me, as to so many others'.[2]

For the rest of her life, Alix, whenever she was at Sandringham, made daily visits to the room where Eddy died, often leaving fresh flowers on the bed. His uniforms and other clothes were arranged in a glass cabinet. It became a kind of shrine. She and the Prince of Wales were inconsolable at first, and Eddy's brother was grief-stricken.[3] They went away, and it was a year before they could face returning to Norfolk. They stayed first on the south coast, then in the south of France; they kept moving.

Prince Eddy was just twenty-eight when he died, and had met thousands of people and travelled around the world. Yet he had made no mark on history. He had not yet done anything remarkable or even reprehensible. He appeared to be, as one writer put it, 'spotless' when he died, and because goodness is dull, he was easily forgotten. Within ten days of his funeral, the young Earl of Rosslyn, Daisy Brooke's stepbrother, attended a shooting party where Eddy would have been a fellow-guest. The court was still in mourning, and they thought of cancelling, but agreed that 'the birds wouldn't shoot themselves', and life went on.

Princess May of Teck had been tentatively suggested as a bride for George from the first few days after the tragedy. For her at least, it was not always a happy marriage. James Pope-Hennessy interviewed the Duke of Windsor, who said that his father had a filthy temper and would humiliate his wife, attacking her verbally in front of the children. When he was not around, she was an amusing woman.[4] Pope-Hennessy visited Sandringham in 1956 and the resident *tapissier* employed to look after the vast wall-hangings in its mock-medieval halls showed him a store cupboard packed with the knick knacks and pictures which surrounded Queen Mary in her boudoir. He was surprised by the number of images of Prince Eddy.

Princess Hélène d'Orléans did not easily recover from her loss either. In the year of Eddy's death, she told Queen Victoria:

> I loved him so much. And it was probably foolish of me, but I couldn't help it. He was so good.[5]

She married the Duke of Aosta in 1895. There is a picture of her, taken around 1900, in a bowler of the type worn for riding. With her hair scraped back beneath it, she is good-looking but self-assured to the nth degree; there is no doubt in her face, none at all. They would have made a fascinating couple, but she might have overwhelmed Eddy rather. All that remained of their short-lived love affair was a wreath of everlasting flowers inscribed with 'Hélène', which remained, for many years, at Eddy's tomb.

Sybil Erskine became Countess of Westmorland in due course; she died young, in 1910.

Arthur Somerset, whose predicament so devastatingly affected Prince Eddy's reputation, settled in Hyères, at what was then the quieter end of the Côte d'Azur. The appearance of an Arthur Somerset in the guest list at Luton Hoo early in December 1891, and in a list of those paying their respects at Marlborough House a month later,[6] are explicable on careful examination of *Burke's Peerage*. The Prince of Wales had asked Lord Salisbury for permission to allow the 'unfortunate lunatic' back into England from time to time to see his parents; this would not have included invitations to meet Prince Eddy and Princess May at Luton Hoo. This house guest of the De Falbe's was the Hon. Arthur Somerset, a distant cousin of the notorious Lord Arthur Somerset. This Hon. Arthur was the second son of the second Baron Raglan. The first Baron was the youngest son of the sixth Duke of Beaufort, Lord Arthur's grandfather. Lord

Arthur Somerset died at Hyeres in May 1926. His death was not recorded by the English press.[7]

Among the other *dramatis personae*, Sam Lewis died at the end of the century, having founded a charitable trust. His wife Ada worked tirelessly for many years to provide refuges for poor women and homes for families. The Samuel Lewis Trusts were in 1998 worth £250m in property assets net of loans.

Sir George Lewis (he was knighted in 1892) had never approved of Sam. It was true that Sam's interest rates were exorbitant, but he would do anything he could to keep his clients from going broke (often by converting their loans to mortgages) and they generally ended up grateful, rather than otherwise. In a social scene where casual anti-semitism prevailed, he was genuinely popular. Sir George nonetheless believed that his co-religionists should have more care for the reputation of all Jews than to lend at high interest, and he agitated tirelessly for legislation, which finally emerged as the Moneylenders' Act of 1900. He died in 1911 and a hundred society secrets went with him to the grave.

In 1892, Alfred Fripp was among those who grieved for 'my hope of hopes and good friend'. He went on to have a distinguished medical career and a wide circle of friends. His social aspirations were fulfilled, and his medical practice assured, partly through his continuing friendship with Sir George Holford, who inherited Dorchester House and was its last owner before, in the 1920s, it was demolished to build the hotel on Park Lane.

The election of 1892 returned a Liberal government. Gladstone had been so appalled by Sir Charles Parnell's involvement with Kitty O'Shea that he had dropped Parnell and all he stood for – which meant Home Rule, for the time being. Lord Houghton (the son of the one who had been Henry Weigall's patron) became Lord Lieutenant of Ireland in 1892. He was young, unmarried, a Home Ruler, and highly effective within the limitations of the job; but essentially the post was a social one and, as his

Chief Secretary wrote, 'the most thankless office that any human being in any imaginable community could undertake'.[8] Only an individual of rare experience and extraordinary diplomatic gifts could have made the slightest difference to the worsening political situation.

When the Tories returned to power in 1895, the Cadogans occupied Dublin Castle.

The Beresford/Brooke case rumbled on until – in the spring of 1892, when the Waleses were in the south of France – Lady Beresford returned the letter. The affair between Bertie and Daisy Brooke inevitably cooled during this year of his great grief. She took up W.T. Stead, the campaigning editor, and good works; her dislike of gambling and strong drink may have had a beneficial effect on the Prince of Wales for a time. In 1901, when Bertie inherited the throne (and had already turned his amorous attentions to Mrs Keppel), Alix deputed Lord Esher (Reggie Brett) to put it to Lady Brooke, in the nicest possible way, that a mistress was not a suitable companion for a king. Her financial situation worsened and some years later she is said to have threatened blackmail, saying that her hospitality towards Wales and his friends, at Easton, had ruined her. She was dissuaded from precipitate action and lived to write an autobiography of quite beguiling innocence.

J.K. Stephen suffered an accidental blow to the head at the end of 1886. He appeared to recover, and went on to publish poetry during long periods of lucidity; but in 1891 his behaviour became increasingly eccentric, until it reached a manic phase. He was committed to the care of St Andrew's Hospital, Northampton, in November of that year. On 14 January 1892, the date of Prince Eddy's death, he refused all nourishment, and twenty days later he died from 'mania, 2 and a half months; persistent refusal of food, 20 days; exhaustion'.[9]

His father, His Honour Justice Stephen, so famous for his 1887 judgment that 'you cannot libel the dead', also sadly lost his

mind in a very public way before he died. It became apparent
to everyone during the high-profile Maybrick case of 1889 that
the judge no longer possessed that acute intelligence that had
inspired his *History of the Criminal Law.* He retired in 1891, on
medical advice, and died in 1894.

'Poor Aunt Alix looked rather sad in church. One can quite
understand why.'[10] These are not the words of a family in any way
relieved by the demise of one who would have been unworthy. It
is Arthur Newton, the solicitor to Lord Arthur Somerset, whose
later career supports, more than anything, the contention of this
book that Prince Eddy was slandered over the Cleveland Street
affair and that this has led to ever-worsening libels since.

In the late summer of 1910, the police chased Dr Crippen
and his young lover, Ethel le Neve, to Canada. Crippen had
murdered his wife Cora and fled across the Atlantic, but he was
spotted on board ship. The case was the first in which telegrams
to and from a ship at sea led to the arrest of a fugitive.

On 3 August, a reporter filed the following from Quebec,
where Crippen was in custody:

> Crippen received a telegram yesterday evening from Mr Arthur
> Newton, a London solicitor, informing him of his intention to
> defend him by the request of friends, and demanding discretion
> on the prisoner's part in the interval. Crippen has eagerly accepted
> the offer, and since its receipt appears markedly more confident
> and outwardly cheerful.[11]

The murderer was brought back to London and tried. Once
again, Arthur Newton found himself in the big league. Twenty
years after Cleveland Street, this was the era of Marshall Hall
and Travers Humphreys; people followed great barristers at the
Old Bailey as they followed favourite actors in the West End.
Crippen's trial was the sensation of the day. It sold newspapers.

Unfortunately, Newton could do precious little against overwhelming prosecution evidence. Mrs Crippen, an unsuccessful music hall artiste, had been poisoned with hyoscine and buried under the bricks of a ground floor corridor, in the genteel abode she shared with her husband. Newton appealed against conviction on his client's behalf early in November 1910, on matters of fact and law, but the appeal failed.

A picture emerged in the course of the trial of Mrs Crippen, a fat, blowsy and sociable woman with plenty of friends, and a small, sandy, bald, resentful husband, whom her friends very much suspected of having bumped her off. They had gone to the police. So who were these 'friends' of Crippen who were paying Arthur Newton? Perhaps *John Bull* and the *Daily Chronicle* knew, for they organised a petition, and Arthur Newton took all 15,000 signatures protesting the conviction to the Home Office in a taxi-cab.

The petition having failed, an 'Open Letter to Dr Crippen' appeared in Horatio Bottomley's daily *John Bull*. As far as the writer was concerned, Crippen was shielding A.N. Other.

It is a great mystery. Why don't you unravel it? Or may it be that, black as you are painted, you will go to the scaffold with lips sealed in loyalty?

Dr Crippen was in Pentonville awaiting the gallows, and did not see *John Bull*. Arthur Newton visited him there; the warders present in the room did not allow them to discuss the article or to touch or exchange anything. The following day (21 November), a letter purporting to come from Crippen appeared in *John Bull*. It was addressed to the editor.

Dear Sir,
As to making a statement which could implicate anybody else in this terrible business, that is altogether out of the question. I have

only just heard the Home Secretary's decision, and tomorrow I am expecting to see an old friend to whom I may possibly say more than I can now.

I wish however to say most emphatically that under no circumstances shall I say anything which would bring trouble to others. Mr Newton has not only been my solicitor, but especially during these past dreadful weeks has been a sincere friend to me in all my trouble...

If, when it is all over, he cares to tell you more than I can say today, I am sure you will treat the matter in the same broad and sympathetic spirit in which you have written me.[12]

This is pretty convincing evidence of a pattern. It is this author's contention that where Arthur Newton was concerned, blaming a mysterious Other had worked once and there was no reason why it would not work again – if not to save his client from hanging, at least to sell a great many newspapers.

Horatio Bottomley, who presumably paid Newton for defending Crippen, must surely have been the original of Mr Toad: a brilliant man, who successfully defended himself twice (in 1891 and 1911) against major fraud allegations and admitted that his name 'constantly cropped up in the courts' ('rarely with reverence', adds the *Dictionary of National Biography*, acidly). He would make an unsuccessful third defence against fraud charges and go down for seven years' penal servitude in 1923. He was Arthur Newton's exact contemporary, but managed to stay out of jail a little longer.

In the Crippen case, distinguished lawyers decided that the two letters were hogwash. Newton had gone too far, and should be taken to task for professional misconduct. In the summer of 1911, the Incorporated Law Society held a hearing at which Horatio Bottomley's shorthand writer testified that the alleged reply from Dr Crippen had been dictated to him, the first half by Arthur Newton and the second by Horatio Bottomley.

In his defence, Newton's barrister claimed that 'it was not professional misconduct to aid and abet an editor to humbug the public'. It was the day before King George's coronation; their lordships reserved judgment.

On 13 July, Arthur John Edward Newton was suspended from the Rolls for twelve months.

Nine decades later, a letter, recently found among Home Office papers, appeared on a Channel 4 documentary, *The Last Secret of Dr Crippen*. Purporting to have been written by Cora Crippen, it was clearly intended to back up his claim that she was not in fact dead, but had deserted him to live in America. The letter was dated 22 October 1910, the day of his conviction, and was posted in Chicago. It arrived at Pentonville prison on 25 October:

> I don't want to be responsible for your demise... but will never come forward personally as I am now happy.[13]

Although addressed to Crippen, the letter was withheld by the prison governor, who passed it on to his superiors, who sent to the Home Office to determine whether or not it was genuine. The fact that the authenticity of the letter could not be clearly established raises the crucial question as to who may have sent it and why. In light of Newton's willingness to employ falsification in defence of his clients, it would not be unreasonable for the finger of suspicion to be pointed in his direction.

During his enforced withdrawal from legal practice, Arthur Newton fell deeper into the mire. In March 1913 he appeared at Bow Street; it was claimed that in the winter of 1911/1912 he had conspired with others to swindle a rich young Hungarian out of £23,000. Newton (who was by now in his fifties), a man called Bennett (who was sometimes tempted to pose as Gordon Bennett, the American newspaper magnate) and a bankrupt

Hungarian called Count Andor Festetics were jointly accused. It was a convoluted story of dodgy syndicates and large cheques cashed in Romano's; it attracted so much publicity that the owner of a gaming house, whom he had previously defended in court, decided the time was right to recover some of the money he had entrusted to Arthur Newton at the time of his own trial. His attempt failed, but Newton and the others were found guilty of obtaining money by false pretences in the conspiracy case. Newton got three years' penal servitude and was struck off. Count Festetics had hopped onto the Channel ferry, but acting as watching brief on his behalf was none other than Harry Wilson, Prince Eddy's old friend. 'Before too long I have no doubt we shall see you a prominent attorney...'.

Newton was released on 29 September 1915. He wrote about 'The Mystery Murder of Camden Town' of 1907, and other experiences, in the *Sunday Express* of 3 February 1924, but prison had done nothing to remove his magnetic attraction towards trouble. Even the 'Mystery Murder' story brought a libel suit from an indignant reader, who thought it identified him as the murderer.[14]

On 17 October 1928, Lord Alfred Douglas, once the passion of Oscar Wilde's life, but now fifty-seven and living in married bliss at 26, Brunswick Square, Hove, brought a libel action against Harrods for selling a book by Frank Harris, which purported to be the 'confessions' of Oscar Wilde and which contained material he considered defamatory. The book had been bought at Harrod's Book Department on Lord Alfred's behalf by Mr Arthur John Newton, of The Confidential Agency, Oxford Street.[15]

In 1934, Lord Sholto Douglas sued for regular remittances outstanding from a Mrs Beresford. This lady was Dutch, and had come to England in 1918. In her life there had been four husbands (if you count a marriage contracted with a son of the Sultan of Turkey and annulled in Vienna). Her husband in the early 1920s had been Lord Sholto. He proved, she told the court, to be a leech who spent all his time with undesirable friends, to whom she objected. Among these friends was Arthur Newton, the ex-solicitor, who had been struck off in 1913 and now ran the Confidential Agency. When she demanded a divorce, Arthur Newton drew up an agreement. In return for providing evidence of adultery, his friend Lord Sholto Douglas expected a considerable annual income. She signed the paper and got evidence of an illicit stay at a hotel, and a separation order, in return. She paid the money for a while, until she read about a similar case where an order had been overturned; then she decided to stop…[16]

Wherever Arthur Newton intervened, trouble followed. With hindsight, his character is common to sociopaths through the ages. He identified what people most wanted and made them pay for it. They had only themselves to blame for what followed. Lady Douglas had wanted her freedom, and found that she was expected to shell out indefinitely. The young Hungarian was greedy, and lost his fortune. Horatio Bottomley (who was himself notorious) sold a lot of newspapers, but later felt constrained to bring a libel suit against a writer who accused him of forging the Crippen letter.

And Lord Arthur Somerset? Looking back at the events of 1889, it is possible to identify almost to the day the point where Arthur Newton decided to throw up the smokescreen of Eddy's name. Algernon Allies was taken into police custody in mid-August, but Newton had been unable to lay hands upon the incriminating evidence written by Somerset: his managing clerk, Augustus de Gallo, had left Sudbury empty-handed, and very probably Allies's parents had been unable to tell him whether or not any letters had been burned, or taken to London by PC Hanks. Therefore, Newton could not be sure whether or not the police had seized proof of an infatuation which, if it came out in open court, would ruin his client for life and probably result in a prison sentence to boot.

Only at committal, which took place on 12 September, would the prosecution's case have been clear to him. They held incriminating letters and postal orders. It followed that his client must be found guilty, and the case lost. With it would go his big opportunity to make his name.

Three days later, on 15 September, Cuffe had heard of the threat to Eddy. At first, the story was confined to lawyers, like himself, who were sceptical. But Arthur Newton was smarter than his client, and knew how to plant the seed of suspicion.

Lord Arthur Somerset had the strongest of motives for deflecting attention onto someone else. He was undergoing the most mortifying experience that a man of his standing could possibly suffer at the time. Social disgrace would be anguish. Yet just the merest hint that Arthur Somerset, third son of the Duke of Beaufort, was not running away from justice, but nobly remaining tight-lipped in order to defend an esteemed superior, and he would gain sympathy, even admiration. He would not be shunned at all; people would understand. The Prince of Wales would no longer speak harshly of him; he would be impressed, indeed deeply grateful to a friend who had sacrificed his own career in order to conceal the peccadilloes of another.

Arthur Somerset was a fighting man; he had survived Tel El Kebir. He had learned lessons, and one was to aim for the Achilles heel. Prince Eddy's name had come as a surprise... but he was certainly the weakest link in the edifice of privilege. A person Somerset barely knew. Wales rather despised him already. Golden, hopeless – and due to inherit the lot. No third son he.

Lord Arthur Somerset seized upon this story: it soothed him; it transmuted shame into noble sacrifice. He liked confiding what he had heard to people who supported him. Nothing would happen to the young prince, of course. He would be completely immune. The case against both of them would just be dropped.

Thus did Lord Arthur, who was desperate to retain his honour, repeat Arthur Newton's lie. History may judge him a lesser man for doing so.

After 1889, there was not the remotest hint in any English newspaper or book that Prince Eddy had been even tangentially involved with Cleveland Street; that he had been a dunderhead; that his heterosexual adventures were notorious; that he had fathered an illegitimate child; that he had been unprincipled; that he had entered into a masonic conspiracy; or that he had ever known, or indeed heard of, the famous painter of the Camden Town school, Walter Sickert.

All these allegations were made later. The young man whose death resulted in such a theatrical national display of grief is vaguely recalled today, if he is recalled at all, as a suspect in the Ripper case. To find out how this came about, it is necessary to trace the gradual blackening of his character.

It began with a single fault: laziness. Some of his contemporaries did say that he didn't exert himself much, unless an activity really interested him. Dalton was not the only one to notice 'apathy' in Eddy as a child. Lady Georgina Somerset, who was lady-in-waiting to the Duchess of Cambridge, never had much time for the Wales family or the Tecks, and her journal described Princess Louise (Eddy's younger sister) as having 'the same inert, apathetic nature' as Prince Eddy. The Grand Duchess Xenia, a cousin of the Wales children interviewed in old age, said Eddy never *minded* anything.[17] The Duke of Cambridge said he was 'charming' and 'as nice a youth as could be', but 'an inveterate and incurable dawdler, never ready, never there'.[18]

The official biography of Prince Eddy by J.E.Vincent appeared in 1893. Harry Wilson was a particularly generous contributor of his time and correspondence, and Vincent paints a picture of a good and faithful friend who, it had to be admitted, could be lazy.

In 1910, the self-styled wizard Aleister Crowley published a book called *The World's Tragedy*, in which he claimed to possess compromising letters written by Prince Eddy to a boy called Morgan, whose mother ran a shop in Cleveland Street. Aleister Crowley was well known as a histrionic fantasist even in 1910, and the book seems to have sunk without trace. The letters were never produced.

In 1930, Sir Lionel Cust described, in his memoir, how he assisted with the move from Marlborough House to Buckingham Palace when the Prince of Wales became king.

> I arranged for the King in his bedroom or dressing room por-
> traits of his mother, his sister, the Empress Frederick, and his elder
> son, the Duke of Clarence, to all of which the King gave special
> attention.[19]

Prince Eddy's memory was 'obviously was very dear to him'. There are worse faults than laziness, and it had been Bertie's own failing, in his parents' eyes, as a young man.

In 1941, John Gore wrote the first official biography[20] of King George, who had died five years before. He wrote that when the brothers were small, George was his father's favourite,

> …while Prince Eddy, more delicate and diffident, with a particu-
> larly sweet nature, had perhaps in childhood the larger share of his
> mother's sympathy. There was in him an apathy which his father
> tried – sometimes rather roughly – to combat.

Not until 1952 was this 'apathy' ratcheted up a notch. Harold Nicolson, the second distinguished biographer of King George V, wrote about how the brothers were brought up together. He referred to Prince Eddy's 'backwardness' and 'constitutional lethargy'. These were his words, and he drew his conclusions from Mr Dalton's determination that the boys should not be separated, either before they went aboard the *Britannia* or, later, when the *Bacchante* cruise was in the offing. Mr Dalton had written that the navy would help Eddy to develop 'those habits of promptitude and method, of manliness and self-reliance, in which he is now somewhat deficient'. Eddy was at the time thirteen, and if he lacked those qualities at that age he was not necessarily suffering from backwardness or constitutional lethargy. His brother performed no better. But Harold Nicolson was writing a biography of a king; and any hint that the wrong king had come to the throne, or that the hero of the book had failed to stand out as the obvious candidate for kingship throughout his life, would not have served his purpose.

In 1959, James Pope-Hennessy published his biography of Queen Mary. Such a writer would avoid any impression that the first fiancé had been a great loss, and that the second was second-best. He undertook pretty exhaustive research in the royal archives, and does not paint a picture of a stupid or idle young man; rather, he claims that both princes were sadly under-educated, and that Prince Eddy was romantically susceptible and decidedly lovable. Like May, he did not share the family passion for practical jokes, but took an interest in history and genealogy.

In 1972, Michael Harrison wrote an account called *Clarence*, which put Eddy right at the centre of gay London in the 1880s, frequenting pubs in the Charing Cross Road and louche clubs. He named no source for any of it. Prince Ernest of Hesse was gay, and about the same age; just possibly, an earlier writer had confused them. Whatever the facts, Harrison's book is typical of its time. With the repeal of the Blackmailers' Charter in 1967, the love that dared not speak its name had been released to shout it from the rooftops; and homosexuality fascinated the reading public. Harrison seems to have been deeply suspicious of men like J.K. Stephen and Oscar Browning. In his account, gay men are morally contagious, and any young man who frequently found himself in their company could be tainted. Given the evidence of crushes on princesses and so on, he was, however, driven to conclude that Eddy was 'panerotic' – from which he segued into a thumping hint that Sarah Bernhardt had given birth to Prince Eddy's baby. (Her only son, Maurice, was born to an unnamed father when Eddy was six.)

In 1973, a BBC producer was put in touch with Joseph Sickert (born Joseph Gorman in London in 1925). Sickert told the programme's researcher that his mother had been the illegitimate daughter of an Annie Crook, tobacconist's assistant of Cleveland Street, and Prince Eddy. The story, briefly, was that Alix thought Prince Eddy was over-protected at court, so she hired Walter Sickert (the artist, then young and making his name) to show him the seamier side of life. As a result, Eddy married Annie (a Catholic) in secret, the baby was sent to an orphanage and, via a masonic conspiracy too tedious to relate, Prince Eddy and Sir William Gull set out to murder Annie Crook's friends in Whitechapel because they knew the truth. All the Ripper murders were committed to this end.

Joseph Sickert said he knew all this because he was the illegitimate son of Walter Sickert, who had told him. The BBC produced a programme about it, and a book by Stephen Knight – *Jack the Ripper: the Final Solution* – was a best-seller. The case appeared to be solved (unless you knew that Joseph Sickert was born Joseph Gorman, that Alix was shocked when Eddy and George were allowed to read *The Three Musketeers*, and that Walter Sickert was completely unknown to the Wales family, who would have found his paintings incomprehensible. And that Stephen Knight was fascinated by all things Masonic; his next book would be *The Brotherhood*.)

In 1976, discounting the murder theory but giving the impression that Prince Eddy had been a boor, Theodore Aronson wrote

A Family of Kings about the Danish royal family – Alix and her relations. Of Eddy, he wrote

> Even in infancy, this eldest son of Princess Alexandra had shown signs of being subnormal. He was not exactly an imbecile; merely slow-witted. As a boy he had been listless, slow to react and utterly unable to concentrate his attention on anything for long.[21]

'Not exactly an imbecile' is quite outrageously wide of the mark. Nor was Eddy slow-witted, as his handling of the Hélène affair showed.

In 1976, Joseph Sickert repudiated the best-selling story he had told, first to the BBC and later to Stephen Knight – except for the bit about being a grandson of Prince Eddy.

In 1991, Stephen Knight having passed away, Sickert collaborated with another author, Melvyn Fairclough. He resumed his earlier version of events, claiming he had repudiated it in 1976 because of a falling-out with Knight. Fairclough's book, *The Ripper and the Royals*, was even odder than *The Final Solution*: Prince John had been swapped for Alice Crook's son Charles; Prince Eddy never died but was locked up at Glamis Castle until his death in 1933. Abberline had apparently kept a diary which proved that some of this material was true, and just as the book was published Joseph Sickert was putting it in the hands of Scotland Yard. Readers held their breath… Maybe it got lost in the post. Scotland Yard has waited since 1988 and 'we believe the diary to be a forgery, if it in fact exists'.[22]

In 1984, Anne Edwards's biography of Queen Mary, *Matriarch*, picked up the 'ambivalent house of assignation' allegation from Jullian and ran with it, declaring that; 'during that [1889 Cleveland Street] raid it was alleged that Prince Eddy's close friend, Lord Arthur Somerset, had been found with a young man'. Lord Arthur Somerset was not Prince Eddy's close friend; they barely knew each other. Nor had Lord Arthur Somerset been found with a young man in the course of any 'raid'; the police broke into 19, Cleveland Street that sunny Saturday in an attempt to catch Hammond, and found it empty. She further states that:

> From infancy the Prince had been blighted with poor health. As he matured, his lack of character and his inordinate slowness were causes for greater concern. From birth he bore a hearing deficiency, a problem which accounted for his learning disability…[23]

According to Anne Edwards, Alix was kept in ignorance of his alleged deafness because she suffered from the same thing and was sensitive about it. In fact, Alix fell prey to otosclerosis several years after Eddy was born, and the single contemporary reference to Eddy in this regard (and that a mere suspicion that he might be deaf) came from Sir Henry Ponsonby, when Eddy was nineteen. One struggles to imagine Alix not being told, for twenty-eight years, that her eldest son could not hear. As for a learning disability, there is no evidence that Eddy's (or George's) poor academic performance was due to anything other than low aspiration and uninspired teaching.

At least there is one reference to deafness, and several to idleness, in the documents. For the following there is none:

> Prince Eddy was inclined to dark moods and though his manners were correct, he was aloof and awkward, suffered a nervous tic and possessed a piercing, unpleasant, high-pitched voice.[24]

There is no attribution for any of this. She goes on:

> In childhood, he had bullied her [Mary] and she had thought him dull-witted, and had far preferred the company of his younger brother Georgie.[25]

No source is given, and the adjective 'boorish' is applied to Prince Eddy. Perhaps Ms Edwards was looking for dramatic coherence – a happy ending. What a narrow escape her heroine has had! Prince George is 'eminently more attractive'. But of course. She claims that during the voyage on HMS *Bacchante*:

> ...while Prince George learned the duties of a sailor, his elder brother absorbed little except (according to Mr Dalton) things 'of a dissolute nature', referring to the young man's liking for alcohol and his penchant for escaping Mr Dalton's careful guard while in port to frequent seaside dives with young ruffians of poor reputation.[26]

So far as this writer knows, there is no evidence that Dalton thought Eddy was absorbing 'dissolute' things; if he had been, Dalton would have been recalled in disgrace. The Princes were supervised, and reports of their conduct sent back to their father, at least until their early twenties.

And then we have Prince Eddy as homosexual, emotionally dependent on and willingly succumbing to the advances of an older man. Edwards's account of J.K. Stephen appears inaccurate and heavy with innuendo. Stephen was Eddy's tutor at Cambridge, she writes. A Mr Prior was actually his tutor there. And Stephen was not twelve years older than Eddy, but five.

With no real attempt to get at the truth of the matter, Edwards veers in one short sentence from what she calls 'homosexual indiscretions' to an account of his penchant for falling in love with 'unsuitable' ladies. But they would not fall in love with him because had not yet grown a beard (p.24), and besides 'his neck and arms were freakishly long and out of proportion to the rest of his body'. What a monster! The thing was, he wore big collars and cuffs to hide this, as well as a deerstalker hat – and *so did Jack the Ripper*. 'The accusation was never proved, but the Duke of

Clarence's name remained linked with the horrendous crimes.' And so on, and on.

In 1994, Theodore Aronson gleefully re-hashed much of the unattributed material from Michael Harrison's book in *Prince Eddy and the Homosexual Underworld*.

In 2002, Patricia Cornwell dismissed the Jack the Ripper allegation with justifiable scorn, but took up Walter Sickert as the culprit.

All one can say is that Freud has a lot to answer for. Sickert, an intensely sociable and original artist, had been born with a fistula (that is, a hole in the penis); it was fixed by a distinguished English surgeon when he was five years old – the family moved to England partly so that this could take place. He married, never had any children, was unfaithful to his wife and went on to have several long-term relationships with women. He always had women friends. And yet out of this fistula, Cornwell somehow extrapolates a deeply insecure man, the most notorious serial killer of all time. She believes it, too.

Arthur Newton set off the suspicion about Prince Eddy. Lord Arthur Somerset took it up, and the Beresfords, and anti-royalist newspapers – and, sixty years later, a long line of biographers. Every one of these people had a different personal reason for wanting to believe that Prince Eddy was a royal black sheep: career advancement, vindication, spite, political point-scoring, plot enhancement, or sensation-mongering. Suspicions about Prince Eddy linger still. None seems to have any foundation in fact. But you cannot libel the dead.

Appendix I

Patricia Cornwell claims to have two letters to George Lewis in her possession. They are dated 1890 and 1891; in *Jack the Ripper: Case Closed*, published by Time Warner in 2003, the date '1891' is confirmed in two places. I have seen Eddy's letters and he usually writes the date thus: month and date/year, with the oblique, e.g. April 1st/89. There is confusion over dates, though. Cornwell says (on p.112) that the first letter dates from November 1890 and the second from 'two months later' (I quote her) in '(November crossed out) December, 1891'.

This second letter is from the 'Cavelry [*sic*] Barracks'. There are thirteen months between November 1890 and December 1891. Is this merely sloppy editing? Or is the second letter a forgery? Eddy spelled 'cavalry' (and almost every other word) correctly in previous correspondence.[1] Furthermore, 2 December 1891 is the date of his engagement to Princess May and, as far as we know, he did not return to the cavalry barracks at York after the proposal. The likeliest interpretation is that at the end of November 1891 he was at the cavalry barracks at York, and that on 1 December, the day before his departure for Luton

Hoo, he wrote to George Lewis. This would account for the crossing-out of 'November'.

Unfortunately for this neat theory, on 1 December he was in London celebrating his mother's birthday.[2] At the opening of the Victorian Exhibition that day, he saw the new portrait of himself by Mr Sant.

Or does Cornwell mean that the first letter is dated at the beginning of November and the second at the end of December, 1890? That would make sense of her 'two months later...'. In that case, the year is twice misprinted. Until Ms Cornwell decides to elucidate her information in the interests of historical accuracy, it is impossible to say. She has not so far responded to my attempts to contact her.

Appendix II

During the production of the Channel 4 documentary *Prince Eddy*, prominent graphologist Elaine Quigley was asked to analyse Eddy's handwriting. She was shown a variety of letters written by Eddy between 1885 and 1892 and from these was able to draw a conclusion regarding aspects of his character.

The following examples, set at three-year intervals, provide a valuable insight into the development of Eddy's personality as observed by Elaine Quigley:

> The writing style changes over the years, from copybook style to more personal garland style, where the letters m, n and h are made as cups, rather than humps. Eddy was a warm and sensory young man, who liked people, needed their presence and the diversions that they provided, but who was also generous and ready to listen and support, even though he could be selfish at times in wanting his own way. That's all part of the dependency culture. Being a prince, he didn't need to defer to others and the closeness of the words and lines show his immersion in the current scene/activities and also how he absorbed the energy generated by companions.

This could have made him demanding, but it was more from a friendly wish to be involved than for conscious using of people.

The garland style of writing started to kick in on the 1885 letter, which also contains the former angle and arcades styles. This is likely to have come about as he experienced the social freedom of university, compared with the stifling control and limitations of his home life.

By 1888 the garland style dominates, though the other styles are still there, but this shows his burgeoning warmth and confidence in his personal influence. He was certainly more interested in people and being part of their lives, as time went by.

Throughout all the letters there is variation in the flow; but the pen is likely to have had a lot to do with this. The spontaneity that was part of his style would have also encouraged his varying pressure. He just was not the solid, procedure type.

Tuesday, January 13th, 1885. More mature and a calmer and more clearly laid out script. He is likely to have matured considerably. The light pressure does not indicate a lot of energy, but social skills are more fluent. Still a bit anxious to avoid criticism, the impression is of a young man who rushes through what has to be said and done; rather than a languid sophisticate.

October 7th, 1888. This is now becoming more independent, flowing and consistent. The pressure varies, but it is difficult to decide whether it is the pen or tension. The greatest area of ink-flooding is in the upper zone, where it is all to do with anxiety as to image and achieving what people expect of him, rather than the fulfilling of sexual appetites as would be relevant if he was a Ripper personality. Social warmth and belonging have increased by this letter; though his sense of security has not improved in the lower zone. However, he is more in control of his performance at this stage.

January 5th, 1892. This letter actually looks more tense than the other letters in the sense that it is more independent in appearance, the size of script is more extended and it looks more dominant altogether. It was a strong and flowing stroke from a man just nine days away from death. The lower zone, the energy area, varies. There are some strong loops and some of the old-style evasive curves, some with pressure and some not.

A very interesting item has caught my eye and I've been through all the samples and it is nowhere else but on the word 'May'. The shape of the lower zone of the 'Y' is the only instance of this 'mother' feature. It is nowhere else to been seen!

Does it mean that he's marrying May because his mother wishes it (after all May's mother was his mother's close friend), or does he see May as a mother figure? She was younger than him but also, it seems, a strong character, and we know that he required strong people around him, even though he grew in strength and personality over the course of these letters.

The thing was that his personality grew socially more effortless and it would have stood him in good stead had he been able to rule, but he also had a personality that needed bonding and belonging.

Throughout all the letters his lines are level or slope up, even when the difficult times must have made him feel despairing, so it shows that he had an upbeat personality and was resilient. This last letter showed the greatest degree of resilience. Maybe he had psyched himself up to do his duty and he was approaching it with manly determination – we shall never know.

Abbreviations Used in Notes and Bibliography

CCAC   Churchill College Archive Cambridge
DPP   Director of Public Prosecutions
GARF   Gosudarstvennyi arkhiv Rossiiskoi Federatsii
         (National Archives of the Russian Federation)
HO   Home Office
NAPRO National Archives Public Record Office (Kew)
RA   Royal Archives (Windsor)

Notes

1 Scandal 1889

1 On 1 and 4 July *Le Courrier de Londres* described the visit for its French readers

2 Public Record Office dossier DPP 1/95/1-7. Further information from Home Office files HO 144/477/X24427 and X244277. Correspondence indicative of Lord Arthur Somerset's whereabouts and of his friends' support for him is in James Lees-Milne, *The Enigmatic Edwardian*, Sidgwick & Jackson 1986

3 Horatia Durant, *The Somerset Sequence*, Newman Neame 1951, p.59

4 *The Cleveland Street Scandal*, p.48

5 *The Cleveland Street Affair*, p.48 *et seq.*

6 *The Enigmatic Edwardian*, p.78

7 *The Cleveland Street Affair*, p.42

8 *The Cleveland Street Affair*, p.46

9 Roland Pearsall, *The Worm in the Bud*, Weidenfeld & Nicholson 1969, p.21

10 *The Cleveland Street Affair*, p.69

11 *The Cleveland Street Affair*, pp.71-73

12 *The Cleveland Street Affair*, p.74

13 According to Philippe Jullian in *Edouard VII*, Hachette 1962, his true role was to provide intelligence

2 Great Expectations 1864–71

1 J.E. Vincent, *HRH The Duke of Clarence and Avondale*, John Murray 1893, p.42

2 *Letters of Queen Victoria,* 2nd Series, ed. George Earl Buckle, I.64 (14 January 1864)

3 Georgina Battiscombe, *Queen Alexandra*, Constable 1969, p.63

4 Battiscombe, *ibid*

5 Theo Aronson, *A Family of Kings*, Cassell 1976, p.11ff

6 Battiscombe, *ibid*

7 Letter of 7 July 1865 to King Leopold, quoted by John Gore, *King George V, a personal memoir*, John Murray 1941, p.1

8 The Disraeli story is recounted in Battiscombe, p.50

9 Aronson, *ibid*

10 John Martin Robinson, *Royal Residences*, Macdonald 1982

11 Vincent, p.44ff

12 Vincent, *ibid*

13 Vincent, *ibid*

14 A letter to King Leopold of 8 June
    1865, quoted by John Gore, p.1, *ibid*
15 For instance RA/A/15/2852
16 RA/Add/A/3/131
17 E.F. Benson, *As We Were*, Longmans,
    Green & Co 1930, p.55
18 Vincent, p.47
19 Lady Macclesfield's correspondence
    from the Macclesfield Papers quoted
    in Battiscombe, p.83
20 Photograph (1866) from the Royal
    Library, Windsor
21 De Rothschild letters quoted in
    John Gore, pp.13-14
22 Gore, *ibid*
23 From Esher's *Journals and Letters*,
    Nicholson & Watson 1934, Vol.1
    p.345, in a letter to his son dated 28
    July 1902
24 Vincent, p.48
25 Kronberg Letters, 11 December
    1867, cited in Elizabeth Longford,
    Victoria RI, Weidenfeld & Nicholson
    1964
26 RA, Add. MSS. A. 3/117
27 Michael Harrison, *Clarence*, W.H.
    Allen 1972, p.29
28 Philip Magnus, *Gladstone*, John
    Murray 1954, p.207
29 Philip Magnus, *Gladstone*, John
    Murray 1954, p.212
30 RA.Add.MSS.A.3/125 Letter from
    Egypt of 26 February 1969
31 RA.Add.MSS.A.3/151 letter of 24
    October 1869
32 The Mordaunt case is summarised
    in Philippe Jullian, *Edouard VII*,
    Hachette 1962, and elsewhere
33 Translated from Jullian, *ibid*
34 Battiscombe, *ibid*, p.108

3: Britannia 1871–79

1   Hugh Dalton, *Call Back Yesterday:
    Memoirs 1887-1931*, Frederick Muller
    Ltd 1953, p.20ff
2   Dalton, *ibid*
3   Dalton, *ibid*
4   Letter quoted in Dalton, *ibid*
5   Lord de Ros to Sir Henry Ponsonby,
    30 December 1871, cited in John
    Gore, *King George V, a personal
    memoir*, John Murray 1941, p.40

6   RA/Add/U/32, 17 March 1872
7   Gore, *ibid*, p.15
8   Their timetable is outlined in
    Harold Nicolson, *King George V*,
    Constable 1952, p.7. Nicolson used
    papers from the Royal Archive,
    George's diaries and letters, but
    the (fully indexed) book has no
    footnotes
9   Nicolson, *ibid*
10 This information from Lillie Langtry,
    The Days I Knew, Hutchinson 1924,
    and Richard Ellman, *Oscar Wilde*,
    Hamish Hamilton 1987
11 Quoted 'from one intimate with
    King George in later years' by John
    Gore, *ibid*, pp.19-20
12 Nicolson, *ibid*
13 Kenneth Rose, *Superior Person: A
    portrait of Curzon and his circle in late
    Victorian England*, Weidenfeld &
    Nicholson 1969, p.69
14 Macclesfield Papers cited by
    Georgina Battiscombe, *Queen
    Alexandra*, Constable 1969
15 Roy Jenkins, *Sir Charles Dilke*,
    Collins 1965, p.72
16 RA/A/17/512
17 RA /Z 453/9 letter of 6 April 1879
18 Dalton, *ibid*
19 Frances Evelyn Warwick, *Life's Ebb
    & Flow*, Hutchinson 1929, p.41ff
20 Gore, *ibid*, p.12
21 RA/Dalton Papers, 21 September
    1877
22 RA/AA/28/47 and RA/AA/29/26
23 Interviewed in 1958. James Pope-
    Hennessy, *A Lonely Business*, ed.
    Peter Quennell, Weidenfeld &
    Nicholson 1964, p.97
24 *Letters from India During the Prince of
    Wales' Visit 1875-76, from William S
    Potter to his Sister*, privately printed in
    London, 1876
25 Battiscombe, *ibid*, p.134
26 E.F. Benson, *As We Were*, Longmans,
    Green & Co 1930, p.3ff
27 Quoted in Hugh Kingsmill, *After
    Puritanism*, Duckworth London
    1929, p.111ff
28 Nicolson, *ibid*
29 Nicolson, *ibid*
30 Victoria Wester Wemyss, *The Life and*

Letters of Lord Wester Wemyss, GCB CMG MVO Admiral of the Fleet, Eyre and Spottiswoode 1935, p.26

31 RA/Add/A/17/882

32 Vincent, *ibid*

33 Wester Wemyss, *ibid*

34 From G.W. Hillyard's essay in *Lawn Tennis at Home and Abroad,* ed. A. Wallis Myers

35 Transcript of BBC broadcast reproduced by Nicolson, *ibid,* and Gore, *ibid* pp.30-31

36 Quoted by Gore, *ibid,* pp.32-33

37 Kenneth Rose, *Kings, Queens and Courtiers,* Weidenfeld and Nicholson 1985, p.62

38 Letter to the Queen of 14 November 1877, cited by Gore, *ibid*

39 This, like subsequent quotations, is from *Sermons to Naval Cadets by J N Dalton aboard the Britannia 1877-79,* Kegan Paul 1879

4 *Bacchante 1879–82*

1 Quoted in Kenneth Rose, *King George V,* Weidenfeld & Nicholson 1983, p.8

2 Victoria Wester Wemyss, *The Life and Letters of Lord Wester Wemyss, GCB CMG MVO Admiral of the Fleet,* Eyre and Spottiswoode 1935, pp.27-28

3 Lillie Langtry, *The Days I Knew,* Hutchinson 1924, p.51ff

4 Langtry, *ibid*

5 Michael Harrison, *Clarence,* W.H. Allen 1972, p.39

6 Letter to General Dillon quoted in Harold Nicolson, *King George V,* Constable 1952, p.22

7 Nicolson, *ibid*

8 Sarah Toohey, *The Life of Queen Alexandra,* Hodder & Stoughton 1902, p.44

9 Rose, *ibid*

10 J.E.Vincent, *HRH the Duke of Clarence and Avondale,* John Murray 1893, takes his account from Dalton

11 Lady Waterford quoted in Toohey, *ibid*

12 Letter of 22 May 1880 cited by

Harrison, *ibid,* p.59

13 RA.Z 473/34

14 Harrison, *ibid*

15 Isaac M. Marks, MD, *Living with Fear,* McGraw-Hill 1978, p.29

16 Frances Evelyn Warwick, *Life's Ebb and Flow,* Hutchinson 1929, p.46

17 Information variously from Noel B. Gerson, *Lillie Langtry,* Robert Hale 1972; Ernest Dudley, *The Gilded Lily,* Odhams 1958; and Langtry, *ibid*

18 Accounts of the princes' voyage are to be found in *The Cruise of the Bacchante,* 1886, and more entertainingly in the notes kept by Prince Louis during his service on the *Inconstant,* which are extensively quoted in Admiral Mark Kerr, *Prince Louis of Battenberg,* Admiral of the Fleet, Longmans, Green & Co. 1934

19 Nicolson, *ibid*

20 Nicolson, *ibid*

21 Prince Louis's *Recollections* quoted in Richard Hough, *Louis and Victoria,* Hutchinson & Co. 1974, p.100

22 Account attributed to the princes in *The English Illustrated Magazine,* March 1885, extracted from later (1886) publication *The Cruise of the Bacchante*

23 *The English Illustrated Magazine, ibid*

24 *The South Australian Advertiser,* 15 June 1881

25 *The South Australian Advertiser, ibid*

26 *The Argus,* Melbourne, Tuesday 5 July 1881

27 *The Argus,* Melbourne, Thursday 7 July 1881

28 The *Brisbane Courier,* 18 August 1881

29 Wester Wemyss, *ibid*

30 Diary entry quoted in Herbert Sullivan & Newman Flower, *Sir Arthur Sullivan,* Cassell & Co. 1927

5 *Student Prince 1882-–85*

1 The would-be assassin was said to be a madman by the name of Robert Maclean

2 This story appears in Roy Jenkins, *Sir Charles Dilke,* Collins 1965, p.144

3 S. Gwynn and M. Tuckwell, *Life of*

Sir Charles Dilke, Vol.1, quoted in
Philip Magnus, *Edward VII*, John
Murray 1964, p.329

4   Quoted in Jenkins, *ibid*
5   Henry Broadhurst MP, *From a
    Stonemason's Bench to the Treasury
    Bench*, Hutchinson 1901, p.147
6   Broadhurst, *ibid*
7   Broadhurst, *ibid*
8   Broadhurst, *ibid*
9   Jenkins, *ibid*
10 Ponsonby Papers cited by Georgina
    Battiscombe, *Queen Alexandra*,
    Constable 1969, p.163
11 RA.Z/162/7
12 Harold Nicolson, *King George V*,
    Constable 1952, p.35ff
13 J.E. Vincent, *HRH The Duke of
    Clarence and Avondale*, John Murray
    1893, p.139ff
14 Vincent, *ibid*
15 Letter from J.K. Stephen quoted in
    Vincent, *ibid*
16 Gwen Raverat, *A Cambridge
    Childhood*, Faber & Faber 1952, p.24
17 RA.Z 474/63
18 Vincent, *ibid*
19 Vincent, *ibid*
20 Vincent, *ibid*
21 Cecil E.M. Roberts, *Alfred Fripp*,
    Hutchinson 1932, p.121
22 Raverat, *ibid*
23 Hugh Dalton, *Call Back Yesterday:
    Memoirs 1887-1931*, Frederick Muller
    Ltd 1953, p.56
24 Raverat, *ibid*
25 E.F. Benson, *As We Were*, Longmans,
    Green & Co. 1930, p.128ff
26 Raverat, *ibid*.
27 Sir Lionel Cust, *King Edward VII and
    his Court*, John Murray 1930, p.33
28 Frances Evelyn Warwick, *Life's Ebb
    & Flow*, Hutchinson 1929, p.74ff
29 Quoted by John Gore, *King George
    V, A Personal Memoir*, John Murray
    1941, p.2ff
30 According to Magnus, *ibid*, p.140
31 Michael Harrison, *Rosa – Rosa Lewis
    of the Cavendish*, Peter Davies 1962,
    p.45
32 *Pall Mall Gazette,* 13 August 1884
33 Southampton University Archive,
    MB1/T77/f2

34 A full account is to be found
    in David Duff, *The Shy Princess
    – Princess Beatrice,* Evans Bros 1958
35 As reported by *The Times*, 3 February
    1885
36 Southampton University Archive,
    MB1/T77/f2
37 Richard Hough, *Louis and Victoria*,
    Hutchinson 1974, and Frances
    Evelyn Warwick, *Life's Ebb & Flow*,
    Hutchinson 1929, p.79
38 *The Times*, Saturday 21 March 1885,
    p.7 col.b
39 *Cork Examiner,* 10 April 1887
40 *Cork Examiner,* 10 April 1887
41 Reprinted in the *Cork Examiner,* 10
    April 1887
42 *Cork Examiner,* 14 April 1887
43 *Cork Examiner,* 13 April 1887
44 *Dublin Weekly News,* 11 June 1887
45 Quoted anonymously in J.E.
    Vincent, *HRH The Duke of Clarence
    and Avondale,* John Murray 1893,
    p.164

6 Privacy in Public Life 1885–88

1   Leader in the *Pall Mall Gazette,* 1
    April 1884
2   Robert Fuller, *Recollections of a
    Detective*, John Long 1910, p.67
3   M Harrison, *Clarence*, W.H. Allen
    1972, p.92
4   *Ibid*, p.90
5   Letter quoted in Vincent, *ibid*
6   Theo Aronson, *Prince Eddy*, John
    Murray 1994, p.74
7   John Gore, *King George V, a personal
    memoir*, John Murray 1941, p.2ff
8   Letter cited in J.E. Vincent, *HRH
    The Duke of Clarence and Avondale,*
    John Murray, p.190–192
9   RA.T.9/59
10 *Ibid*
11 Gladstone quoted in Roland Pearsall,
    The Worm in the Bud, Weidenfeld &
    Nicholson 1969, p.74
12 Letter cited in Vincent, *ibid*
13 Philip Magnus, *King Edward VII*,
    John Murray 1964, p.246
14 Frank Harris, *My Life and Loves,* Vol.
    2, Obelisk Press 1945, p.101

15 Roy Jenkins, *Sir Charles Dilke,* Collins 1965, p.215ff

16 E.F. Benson, *As We Were,* Longmans, Green & Co. 1930, p.27ff

17 Gwen Raverat, *A Cambridge Childhood,* Faber & Faber 1952, p.98ff

18 Ponsonby Papers quoted in Georgina Battiscombe, *Queen Alexandra,* Constable 1969, p.186

19 Letter of 27 December 1886 quoted by Harold Nicolson, *King George V,* Constable 1952, p.38

20 John Gore, *King George V, a personal memoir,* John Murray 1941, p.2ff

21 From *Kings, Courts and Society* by 'a Veteran', Jarrold & Co 1930, p.89

22 Roland Pearsall, *The Worm in the Bud,* Weidenfeld & Nicholson 1969, p.99

23 J.K. Stephen in *Granta,* June 1891

24 Quoted by Pearsall, *ibid*

25 Julian Osgood Field, *Uncensored Recollections,* Eveleigh Nash & Grayson 1924, p.94

26 RA Geo V AA 36 20

27 Cecil E.M. Roberts, *Alfred Fripp,* Hutchinson 1932, p.121

28 Kenneth Rose, *King George V,* Weidenfeld & Nicholson 1983, p.20: the source is James Lees-Milne's *Harold Nicolson,* Chatto & Windus, Vol.II, p.230

29 Guy Deghy, *Romano's,* The Richards Press 1958, p.56

30 Gerry Black, *Lender to the Lords, Giver to the Poor,* Valentine Mitchell 1992, p.122

31 *Kings, Courts and Society,* by 'a Veteran', Jarrold 1930, p.45

32 Deghy, *ibid*

33 Extract from the Queen's Journal in *Letters of Queen Victoria 1886-1901,* Series 3 Vol.I, edited by George Earl Buckle, John Murray 1930

34 From the Queen's Journal, *ibid*

35 Vincent, *ibid*

36 *The Times,* 3 November 1888

37 Southampton University Archive, MB1/T77/f2

38 Broadlands Archive, letter to Victoria, Marchioness of Milford Haven (Prince Louis's wife) of 2 March 1887

39 Denys Sutton, *Walter Sickert: A Biography,* Michael Joseph 1976, p.112

40 Extracted from the Queen's Journal, 17 November 1888

41 *Letters of Queen Victoria, 1886-1901,* Series 3 Vol.I, edited by George Earl Buckle

7 Cleveland Street 1889

1 *Letters of Queen Victoria, 1886-1901,* ibid

2 *The Times,* 14 May 1889

3 *The Times,* ibid

4 *The Times,* 21 May 1889

5 'Il est simplement curieux de noter qu'en giflant une celebrité on attire plus l'attention du public qu'en produisant n'importe quelle oeuvre d'art.' Quoted in Guy Deghy, *Romano's,* Richards Press 1958

6 *New York Times,* 30 June 1889

7 Sir Edward was chairman of the Metropolitan and District Railway (the London underground railway) and achieved its relentless advance as far as Amersham, before retiring in 1894

8 *Le Courrier de Londres,* 4 August 1889

9 Hammond's correspondence appeared in the *North London Press,* 21 December 1889 and 11 January 1890

10 For dates and general background to this chapter see note 2 above

11 James Lees-Milne, *The Enigmatic Edwardian – the life of Reginald 2nd Viscount Esher,* Sidgwick & Jackson 1986, p.78

12 Southampton University archive MB/T77/f2

13 There are accounts of this affair in (among others) Philip Magnus, *King Edward VII,* John Murray 1964, and Gerry Black, *Lender to the Lords, Giver to the Poor,* Valentine Mitchell 1992

14 The charges are listed in detail in *The Cleveland Street Affair,* p.75

15 Esher Papers, CCAC, ESHR 12/3. The letters of Hammond were

reprinted in 1890 in the *North London Press*

16 Chester, Leitch & Simpson, *The Cleveland Street Scandal*, pp.41–42

17 Amount stated in Lees-Milne

18 *The Cleveland Street Affair*, p.74

19 The story is to be found in (among other places) E.F. Benson, *As We Were*, Longmans, Green & Co. 1930, p.89

20 *The Cleveland Street Affair*, p.92

21 *The Cleveland Street Affair*, pp.78–79

22 *The Cleveland Street Affair*, p.80

23 *The Cleveland Street Affair*, p.83

24 *The Cleveland Street Affair*, pp.93–94, *The Cleveland Street Scandal*, pp.76–77

25 *The Cleveland Street Affair*, p.104

26 *The Cleveland Street Affair*, p.104

27 *The Cleveland Street Affair*, p.106

28 *The Cleveland Street Affair*, pp.110–111

29 The phrase is used in *The Cleveland Street Affair*, p.112

30 *The Cleveland Street Affair*, p.114

31 Southampton University archive MB1/T77/f2

32 Kronberg Letters, 7 May 1889, quoted in Elizabeth Longford, *Victoria RI*, Weidenfeld & Nicholson 1964, p.512

33 Philip Magnus, *King Edward VII*, John Murray 1964, p.273

8 Under the Carpet 1889–90

1 *Hansard's Parliamentary Debates*, 3rd Series Vol.341 cols 1618–19

2 *The Cleveland Street Scandal*, p.95

3 Quoted in *The Cleveland Street Affair*, pp.117–118

4 *Dictionary of National Biography*

5 J.D. Rees, *HRH The Duke of Clarence and Avondale in Southern India*, Kegan Paul 1891, p.12

6 Her correspondence quoted by Rees, *ibid*

7 Rees, *ibid*

8 Rees, *ibid*

9 *The Cleveland Street Affair*, p.118

10 Letter to Reggie Brett quoted in *The Cleveland Street Scandal*, p.118

11 *New York Times*, 10 November 1889

12 *The Enigmatic Edwardian*, p.80

13 *The Cleveland Street Scandal*, p.59

14 Letter quoted in *The Enigmatic Edwardian*, p.80

15 Quoted in *The Cleveland Street Scandal*, p.126

16 *New York Herald*, 22 December 1889

17 *North London Press*, 16 November 1889

18 Quoted in *The Cleveland Street Scandal*, p.128

19 Kathleen Fitzpatrick, *Lady Henry Somerset*, Jonathan Cape 1923, p.112

20 Salisbury Papers, cited by Magnus, *ibid*

21 As witnessed by Winifred Sturt, daughter of Lord Alington, who was also a visitor; *viz.* her scandalised letter of 23 January 1890 to her fiancé Charles Hardinge (Hardinge Papers, cited in Magnus)

22 *The Times*, 21 December 1889

23 *The Enigmatic Edwardian*, pp.80–81

24 *The Times*, 24 January 1890, p.14 col.a

25 *The Times*, *ibid*

26 Quotations in this paragraph are from Rees, *ibid*

27 Rees, *ibid*

28 Holford's diary quoted by J.E. Vincent, pp.216

29 Vincent, *ibid*

30 Vincent, *ibid*

31 Vincent, *ibid*

32 Vincent, *ibid*

33 *Truth*, 14 November 1889

34 *The Enigmatic Edwardian*, p.82

35 *Hansard's Parliamentary Debates*, 3rd Series Vol.341 cols 1534–1611

36 *Hansard's Parliamentary Debates*, 3rd Series Vol.341 cols 1618–19

37 Vincent, *ibid*

38 R.A., A.M. A/8 396

39 Crown Princess Sophie of Greece, Duchess of Sparta, to Empress Frederick, 25 April 1890, quoted in J. Pope-Hennessy, *Queen Mary*, George Allen & Unwin 1959, p.190

40 *The Times*, 17 May 1890

9 Indisposed 1890

1 RA Geo V AA 39 62

2 '…une jeune fille grande, belle,

sportive, originale, dotee d'une personnalité bouillannante et d'énormément de panache', *La Diversité des Destins*

3 Kronberg Letters, 7 May 1889, quoted by Robert K. Massie, *Nicholas and Alexandra,* Victor Gollancz 1968

4 R.A.Z.475/3

5 Letter of 6 February 1891 from Prince George on HMS *Thrush* to Queen Victoria (RA, quoted by Harold Nicolson in *King George V,* p.43)

6 Julian Osgood Field, *Uncensored Recollections,* Eveleigh Nash & Grayson 1924, p.78

7 Michael Harrison, *Rosa, the Biography of Rosa Lewis,* Peter Davies, 1962, p.112

8 Kenneth Rose, *King George V,* Weidenfeld and Nicolson 1983, p.20

9 Cecil E.M. Roberts, *Alfred Fripp,* Hutchinson 1932, p.89

10 Theo Aronson, *Prince Eddy,* John Murray 1994, p.192ff

11 Frank Harris, *My Life and Loves,* Vol. 4, Obelisk Press Paris 1945, p.89

12 Roberts, *ibid*

13 Roberts, *ibid*

14 *Salisbury-Balfour Correspondence,* edited by Robin Harcourt Williams. Hertfordshire Record Publications Vol.4, Hertfordshire Record Society 1988

15 *Salisbury-Balfour Correspondence, ibid*

16 *Salisbury-Balfour Correspondence, ibid*

17 *Salisbury-Balfour Correspondence, ibid*

18 *Salisbury-Balfour Correspondence, ibid*

19 *Salisbury-Balfour Correspondence, ibid*

20 *Salisbury-Balfour Correspondence, ibid*

21 Roberts, *ibid*

22 *Salisbury-Balfour Correspondence, ibid*

23 Letter quoted by Probyn to Fripp, in Roberts, *ibid*

24 Roberts, *ibid*

25 Zachary Cope MD, *The Versatile Victorian,* Harvey and Blythe 1951, p.98

26 Correspondence quoted in Cope, *ibid*

27 Frank Harris, *ibid,* Vol.2. Lord Randolph Churchill died of what

was then called general paralysis of the insane

28 Kenneth Rose, *Arthur James Balfour,* Bell & Sons 1963, p.105

29 Roberts, *ibid*

30 Cope, *ibid*

31 Cope, *ibid*

32 Cope, *ibid*

33 RA Geo V, 39 63

34 RA, *ibid*

35 Patricia Cornwell, *Portrait of a Killer: Jack the Ripper, Case Closed,* Time Warner 2003, p.135ff

36 Memo submitted to the Queen on the proposed Orléans marriage, 9/9/1890, HH/F2 (Hertfordshire Record Publications, *ibid*)

10 Resolution 1890–91

1 Cecil E.M. Roberts, *Alfred Fripp,* Hutchinson 1932, p.77

2 The Earl of Rosslyn, *My Gamble with Life,* Cassell 1928, p.34

3 Rosslyn, *ibid*

4 As witnessed by Winifred Sturt, daughter of Lord Alington, who was also a visitor; *viz.* her scandalised letter of 23 January 1890 to her fiancé Charles Hardinge (Hardinge Papers, cited in Magnus)

5 Rosslyn, *ibid*

6 James Pope-Hennessy, *Queen Mary,* George Allen and Unwin 1959, p.67

7 Frank Pope Humphrey, *The Queen at Balmoral,* T. Fisher Unwin 1893, p.12

8 J.E.Vincent, *HRH The Duke of Clarence and Avondale,* John Murray 1893; *The Times,* 5 May 1891, p.10

9 R.A.AM/A12 1879

10 R.A.AA/31/17

11 Quoted by Roland Pearsall, *The Worm in the Bud,* Weidenfeld & Nicolson 1969, p.77

12 Westmorland Papers, letters of Duke of Clarence to Lady S. St Clair Erskine

13 *Ibid*

14 See list of guests reported in *The Times,* 9 August 1891

15 R.A.Z. 475 244

16 R.A.Z. 475/18

17   RA.Z /475/17

18   Salisbury Papers cited by Philip
      Magnus, *Edward VII*, John Murray
      1964, p.98

19   RA, AM: A/12 1797

20   E.F. Benson, *As We Were*, Longmans,
      Green & Co 1930, p.206ff

21   Benson, *ibid*

22   Rosslyn, *ibid*

23   RA Add.MSS A.12/1797 letter from
      Knollys to Ponsonby on 19 August
      1891

24   Frances Evelyn Warwick, *Life's Ebb
      and Flow*, Hutchinson 1929, p.66

25   Elizabeth Longford, *Louisa Lady in
      Waiting*, Jonathan Cape Ltd 1979,
      p.89

26   This Irish bacillus theory appeared
      in *The Times*, and is said to have
      come from royal sources. George
      had been in Dublin a couple of
      weeks before. Laymen, at least, were
      only hazily aware of the incubation
      period

27   Westmorland Papers, Prince Albert
      Victor to Lady Sybil, 29 November
      1891

28   Appendix

29   Pope-Hennessy, p.209

30   James Pope-Hennessy, *A Lonely
      Business*, ed. Peter Quennell,
      Weidenfeld & Nicolson 1964, p.232ff

31   Pope-Hennessy in *Queen Mary, ibid*,
      quoting from the journal of Lady
      Geraldine Somerset, 8 December
      1891 (RA), p.79

32   E.F. Benson, *As We Were*, Longmans,
      Green & Co. 1930, p.220ff

33   RA.A17/843

5   Hatfield, *ibid*

6   James Pope-Hennessy, *A Lonely
      Business*, Weidenfeld & Nicholson
      1964, p.230

7   Lady Willens, the wife of Sir
      Frederick Willens, was interviewed
      by James Pope-Hennessy in 1958.
      Her account was included in *A
      Lonely Business*, p.226

8   Anne Edwards in *Matriarch*, Hodder
      & Stoughton 1984, attributes this
      story to a letter (unattributed) from
      Alix to Hélène's parents; it does not
      seem to be from the account Alix
      wrote to her own parents cited in
      Battiscombe

9   From the account written by the
      Princess of Wales to her parents
      and held in the Rigsarkivet in
      Copenhagen – cited by Georgina
      Battiscombe, *Queen Alexandra*,
      Constable 1969, p.145

10   *Daily Telegraph*, 15 January 1892

11   The church bell Great Tom dates
      from 1883

12   *Letters of Queen Victoria*

13   RA.Z95/5

14   Harold Nicolson, *King George V*,
      Constable 1952, p.45

15   *Biographical Tracts 1891–95* in the
      British Library

16   *The Times*, 21 January 1892

17   Quoted in Elizabeth Longford,
      Louisa Lady in Waiting, Jonathan
      Cape Ltd 1979, p.78

18   Arthur Ponsonby, Henry Ponsonby,
      1942 cited in David Duff, *The Shy
      Princess – Princess Beatrice*, Evans Bros
      1958, p.56

11 Devastation 1892

1   *Salisbury-Balfour Correspondence*,
      edited by Robin Harcourt Williams,
      Hertfordshire Record Publications
      Vol.4, Hertfordshire Record Society
      1988

2   *Salisbury-Balfour Correspondence, ibid*

3   P. Fitzgerald, *Champagne and Silver
      Buckles: Recollections of Dublin Castle
      and Dublin Society*

4   Hatfield House, Knollys 1875–1892

12 Aftershock 1892 to the present

1   Letters of Tsar Nicolas and Empress
      Marie, ed. Edward J. Bing, Ivor
      Nicholson and Watson 1937; original
      correspodence is held by GARF in
      Moscow

2   Hugh Dalton, *Call Back Yesterday*,
      Memoirs 1887–1931, Frederick Muller
      Ltd 1953, p.67

3   James Pope-Hennessy, *A Lonely
      Business*, Weidenfeld & Nicolson

1964, p.231

4 James Pope-Hennessy, p.214, *ibid*

5 'Je l'aimais tant – et j'ai peut-être été imprudente, mais je n'ai pas pu faire autrement, je l'aimais tant – il était si bon.' From James Pope-Hennessy, *Queen Mary*, George Allen & Unwin 1959. Battiscombe says the conversation took place in November 1892

6 James Pope-Hennessy, *Queen Mary*, George Allen & Unwin 1959, p.209

7 Lord Arthur Somerset (Henry Arthur George Somerset), third son of the 8th Duke of Beaufort was born in Dublin on 17 November 1851 and died at Hyeres, France on 26 May 1926 (Entry No. 102, Register of Deaths, Vice Consul at Hyeres, France). The 8th Duke had four sons all named Henry (Henry Adelbert Wellington; Henry Richard Charles; Henry Arthur George; Henry Edward Brudenell). Arthur Charles Edward Somerset was born on 11 December 1859 (Entry No. 11, Register of Births in the Registration District of Westminster, Sub-District of St Margaret in the county of Middlesex), and died 24 March 1948 (Entry No. 261, Register of Deaths in the Registration District of Chelsea in the Metropolitan Borough of Chelsea)

8 John Morley (Viscount Morley) Recollections, Vol. 1, 1917, p.77

9 Entry No. 198, Register of Deaths in the Registration District of Northampton in the Sub-District of Saint Giles in the Country of Northamptonshire, 3 February 1892

10 Letters of Tsar Nicolas and Empress Marie, Ivor Nicholson and Watson, 1937 and GARF, Moscow

11 *The Times*, 3 August 1910

12 November's letter in *John Bull* reprinted in *The Times*, 21 June 1911

13 *The Last Secret of Dr Crippen*, a Justabout Production for Channel 4 in association with A&E Television Networks, TX 17 July 2004, 8.00 p.m.

14 *The Times*, 28 April 1925, p.5

15 *The Times*, 17 October 1928, p.6

16 *The Times*, 27 and 30 October 1934

17 Cited in James Pope-Hennessy, *A Lonely Business*, Weidenfeld & Nicolson 1964, p.255ff

18 Cited in Kenneth Rose, *King George V*, Weidenfeld & Nicholson 1983, p.45

19 Sir Lionel Cust, *King Edward VII and his Court*, John Murray 1930, p.98

20 John Gore, *King George V, A Personal Memoir*, John Murray 1941, p.56

21 Theo Aronson, *A Family of Kings*, Cassell 1976, p.56

22 Letter to the author, 16 October 2003, from John Ross, curator, the Crime Museum, New Scotland Yard

23 Anne Edwards, *Matriarch, Queen Mary and the House of Windsor*, Hodder & Stoughton 1984, p.21-23

24 Edwards, *ibid*

25 Edwards, *ibid*

26 Edwards, *ibid*

Appendix I

1 See for instance 6 September 1889 to Prince Louis; 25 May 1886 to Harry Wilson; and many other letters

2 See *The Times*, 2 December 1891

Bibliography

Theo Aronson, *Prince Eddy and the Homosexual Underworld* (John Murray, 1994)
—, *A Family of Kings* (Cassell, 1976)
Georgina Battiscombe, *Queen Alexandra* (Constable, 1969)
E.F. Benson, *As We Were* (Longmans, Green & Co., 1930)
Gerry Black, *Lender to the Lords, Giver to the Poor* (Valentine Mitchell, 1992)
Henry Broadhurst MP, *From a Stonemason's Bench to the Treasury Bench* (Hutchinson, 1901)
George Earl Buckle (ed.), *Letters of Queen Victoria*, 2nd Series (London, 1864)
Lewis Chester, David Leitch and Colin Simpson, *The Cleveland Street Affair* (Weidenfeld
    & Nicolson, 1977)
Patricia Cornwell, *Portrait of a Killer* (Time Warner, 2003)
Zachary Cope, *The Versatile Victorian* (Harvey & Blythe, 1951)
Aleister Crowley, *The World's Tragedy* (Falcon Press, 1985)
Tom Cullen, *The Empress Brown* (Houghton Mifflin Company, 1969)
Sir Lionel Cust, *King Edward VII and his Court* (John Murray, 1930)
J.N. Dalton, *Sermons to Naval Cadets* (Kegan Paul, 1879)
Hugh Dalton, *Call Back Yesterday* (Frederick Muller Ltd, 1953)
Mark Daniel, *Jack the Ripper* (Penguin, 1988)
Guy Deghy, *Romano's* (Richards Press, 1958)
David Dickinson, *Goodnight Sweet Prince* (Constable, 2002)
Ernest Dudley, *Gilded Lily* (Odhams, 1958)
David Duff, *The Shy Princess – Princess Beatrice* (Evan Brothers, 1958)
Horatia Durant, *The Somerset Sequence* (Newman Neame, 1951)
Anne Edwards, *Matriarch* (William Morrow & Co, 1984)
Melvin Fairclough, *The Ripper & The Royals* (Duckworth 1991 & 2002)
Julian Osgood Field, *Uncensored Recollections* (Eveleigh Nash & Grayson, 1924)
Kathleen Fitzpatrick, *Lady Henry Somerset* (Jonathan Cape, 1923)
Robert Fuller, *Recollections of a Detective* (John Long, 1910)

Martin Gilbert, *Rumbold, Portrait of a Diplomat* (Heinemann, 1873)

John Gore, *King George V* (John Murray, 1941)

Noel Gerson, *Lily Langtry* (Hale, 1972)

Frank Harris, *My Life and Loves*, Vol. 2 (Obelisk Press, 1945)

Michael Harrison, *Rosa – Rosa Lewis of the Cavendish* (Peter Davies, 1962)

—, *Clarence* (W H Allen, 1972)

Richard Hough, *Louis and Victoria* (Hutchinson, & Co, 1974)

Frank Humphrey, *The Queen at Balmoral* (Fisher Unwin, 1893)

Roy Jenkins, *Sir Charles Dilke* (Collins, 1965)

Elwyn Jones & John Lloyd, *The Ripper File* (Futura, 1975)

Philippe Julian, *Edouard VII* (Hachette, 1962)

Mark Kerr, *Prince Louis of Battenburg* (Longmans, Green & Co, 1934)

Hugh Kingsmill, *After Puritanism* (Duckworth, 1929)

Stephen Knight, *Jack the Ripper, The Final Solution* (Harrap, 1976)

Raymond Lamont-Brown, *John Brown* (Sutton, 2000)

Lillie Langtry, *The Days I Knew* (Hutchinson, 1924)

James Lees-Milne, *The Enigmatic Victorian* (Sidgwick & Jackson, 1986)

Elizabeth Longford, *Victoria RI* (Weidenfeld & Nicolson, 1964)

—, *Louisa Lady in Waiting* (Jonathan Cape, 1979)

Philip Magnus, *King Edward VII* (John Murray, 1964)

Isaac Marks, *Living With Fear* (McGraw-Hill, 1978)

H. Montgomery Hyde, *The Cleveland Street Scandal* (W H Allen, 1976)

Harold Nicolson, *King George V* (Constable, 1952)

James Pope Hennessy, *A Lonely Business* (Weidenfeld & Nicolson, 1964)

Roland Pearsall, *The Worm in the Bud* (Weidenfeld & Nicolson, 1969)

Gwen Raverat, *A Cambridge Childhood* (Faber & Faber, 1952)

J.D. Rees, *The Duke of Clarence in Southern India* (Kegan Paul, Trench, Trubner & Co, 1891)

Andrew Roberts, *Salisbury, Victorian Titan* (Weidenfeld & Nicolson, 1999)

Cecil Roberts, *Alfred Fripp* (Hutchinson, 1932)

John Martin Robinson, *Royal Residences* (Macdonald, 1982)

Kenneth Rose, *Arthur James Balfour* (Bell & Sons, 1963)

—, *Kings, Queens and Courtiers* (Weidenfeld & Nicolson, 1985)

—, *King George V* (Weidenfeld & Nicolson, 1983)

—, *Superior Person: A Portrait of Curzon and His Circle* (Weidenfeld & Nicolson, 1969)

The Earl of Rosslyn, *My Gamble with Life* (Cassell, 1928)

Donald Rumbelow, *The Complete Jack the Ripper* (W H Allen, 1975)

Herbert Sullivan and Newtown, *Sir Arthur Sullivan and Newton Flower* (Cassell, 1927)

Denys Sutton, *Walter Sickert: A Biography* (Michael Joseph, 1976)

Sarah Toohey, *The Life of Queen Alexandra* (Hodder & Stoughton, 1952)

James Vincent, *HRH Duke of Clarence & Avondale* (John Murray, 1893)

Frances Evelyn Warwick, *Life's Ebb & Flow* (Hutchinson, 1929)

Victoria Wester Wemyss, *The Life and Letters of Lord Wester Wemyss* (Eyre & Spottiswoode, 1935)

List of Illustrations

1   The Prince and Princess of Wales (Eddy is at his father's feet), 1866. Author's Collection.
2   The Prince and Princess of Wales with Princes Eddy and George and Princess Louise, 1868. Author's Collection.
3   The Prince and Princess of Wales with Princes Eddy and George and Princesses Louise, Maud and Victoria, 1870. Author's Collection.
4   Prince Eddy, 1871. Author's Collection.
5   Prince Eddy, 1875. Author's Collection.
6   Prince Eddy, 1875. Author's Collection.
7   Prince Eddy and Princess Maud, 1875. Author's Collection.
8   The Princess of Wales with Princes Eddy and George, 1877. Author's Collection. 9 Prince Eddy, 1876. Author's Collection.
10 The Princess of Wales with her children George, Eddy, Louise, Victoria and Maud, 1876. Author's Collection.
11 Princes Eddy and George as naval cadets, 1880. Author's Collection.
12 Prince Eddy in naval cadet's uniform, 1880. Author's Collection.
13 The Princess of Wales with Princes Eddy and George and Princesses Louise, Victoria and Maud, 1880. Author's Collection.
14 The Princess of Wales with Princes Eddy and George, 1880. Author's Collection.
15 The Prince and Princess of Wales and their family on board the royal yacht *Osborne*, Cowes Week, 1884. Author's Collection.
16 Princes Eddy and George in respective army and naval officer's uniforms, 1885. Author's Collection.
17 The Princess of Wales with Prince Eddy, who is in naval cadet's uniform. Author's Collection.
18 Inspector Frederick Abberline, 1889. *Illustrated Police News.*
19 Marlborough House. Westminster City Archive.
20 Prince Eddy in Hussar's uniform, 1888. Author's Collection.
21 Prince Eddy in Hussar's uniform, 1888. Author's Collection.

22   The Hon. Arthur Somerset. Courtesy of James Lonsdale.
23   Lord Arthur Somerset. *Illustrated Police News.*
24   Somerset's solicitor, Arthur Newton. Author's Collection.
25   Eddy as Duke of Clarence and Avondale, 1890. Author's Collection.
26   Eddy as Duke of Clarence and Avondale, 1890. Author's Collection.
27   Princess May of Teck among guests of the de Falbe's at Luton Hoo (the Bishop of
     St Albans is in the centre). The Thurston Collection, Luton Museum.
28   The Wales family, 1890. Author's Collection.
29   Eddy as Duke of Clarence, 1891. Author's Collection.
30   Eddy and Princess May the day after their engagement at Luton Hoo, 4 December
     1891. The Thurston Collection, Luton Museum.
31   Lady Sybil St Clair-Erskine. Victoria and Albert Museum.
32   Photograph claimed to be the Duke of Clarence in 1910. Author's Collection.
33   Effigy of the Duke of Clarence, Memorial Chapel, Windsor. Dean and Canons of
     Windsor.
34   'The last moments of the Duke of Clarence', January 1892. *Daily Graphic.*

Index

Abberline, Inspector Frederick 166:
Cleveland Street inquiry 15–18, 20–1,
24, 154–5, 176–7, 180, 203; Jack the
Ripper case 9, 144, 293
Aden 93, 191
Alexandra (Alix), Princess: birth of children
35, 36, 38, 39, 43; children's upbringing
38–40, 42, 53, 80, 109–10, 129; deafness
38–9, 73, 294; with family 161, 163, 164,
165, 168; marriage 30–1, 38–9, 43, 44,
59–60, 62–3, 73, 74, 251–2; Schleswig-
Holstein dispute 32–3; visits Denmark
35–6, 58
Alexandra of Hesse (Alicky) 119–20, 142,
157–9, 183–5, 216
Allies, Algernon 22–3, 155, 156–7, 175–6, 177,
203, 287
Ames, Bertie 20, 172, 175, 178
army 119–25, 135, 165, 166, 247–50
Aronson, Theodore 222, 292–3, 296
Australia 84–92
Aylesford, Lord ('Sporting Joe') 58, 59, 137
Bacchante, HMSS: Dalton's book 77–8, 86–7,
102, 110; princes join ship 70–2, 74–5;
princes rated midshipman 79; round
the world voyage 82–94, 295; storm
damage 85–6, 87; voyage to West Indies
74, 75–80
Balfour, A.J. 136, 225–9, 260, 264

Balmoral 98, 101, 141, 157, 228, 232, 233–4,
242, 255
Barbados 78, 79
Beatrice, Princess 77, 82, 113, 119, 273, 276
Beaufort, Duke of 12, 18–19, 137, 147, 174–5
Benson, E.F. 37–8, 107–8, 174
Beresford, Lady Charles 159–60, 201–2,
250–1, 281
Beresford, Lord Charles 58, 94, 108, 137,
150–1, 160, 183, 201–2, 250–1
Beresford, Lord Marcus 180, 183, 195
Bertie, Prince of Wales: becomes king 277;
behaviour/reputation 23–4, 36, 38, 42–3,
54–5, 110, 130, 136–7, 251; children's
upbringing 37, 41, 53, 80, 109; Cleveland
Street scandal 187–8, 190–1, 198, 201–2,
208, 209; Daisy Brooke 159–60, 202,
250, 281; with family 161, 165, 168;
financial problems 186; gambling scandal
239–41, 244; India 57–9; Ireland 115,
126; Lady Mordaunt relationship 43–4;
Lillie Langtry 63, 73, 74, 76, 81, 82,
83; marriage 30–1; marriage problems
38–9, 43, 44, 59–60, 62–3, 251–2; politics
96–9, 109, 122, 126–7, 135; relationship
with Eddy 74–5, 290; social scene 54–5;
Somerset as Equerry 12, 13; Suez Canal
94; typhoid fever 51–2
Blackburn, Mrs Mary (nurse) 34–6, 41

Bottomley, Horatio 283, 284–5
Brett, Reggie (Viscount Esher): Alix 40;
 letter from Blanche Waterford 200;
 letters from Somerset 22, 179, 180, 181–
 2, 189, 196–7, 199–200; moneylenders
 137; support for Somerset 23, 153, 156,
 171, 176–7, 202–3, 209
Britannia, training ship 62, 63–9
Brooke, Lady Daisy 151, 159–60, 183, 201,
 239–41, 246, 250, 252–3, 281
Browning, Oscar 60, 106–8, 278, 291
Cambridge 98, 101–10, 115, 118–19
Churchill, Lord Randolph 9, 59, 213, 217,
 231
Clayton, Sir Oscar 228–31, 234–5
Cleveland Street scandal: brothel discovery
 14, 16; committal proceedings 23–5, 160,
 171, 173, 208, 214; Eddy's involvement
 rumours 25–6, 172–4, 182–3, 188, 195–8,
 287–9, 293–4; investigation 17–23,
 152–7, 171, 176–7, 210–11; Somerset
 arrest warrant 195–6, 210–11; Somerset
 prosecution question 171–83, 188–9,
 195–6
Cornwell, Patricia 235–6, 256, 296–8
Cuffe, Hon. Hamilton 23–5, 172–3, 176,
 178–9, 181, 288
Curzon, George 51, 60
Cust, Charles 64, 108
Cust, Sir Lionel 108, 109, 290
Dagmar, Princess 35, 54, 56, 252, 273
Dalton, Rev. John Neale: appointed tutor
 46–9, 52–3, 61–2, 123; HMSS *Bacchante*
 71–2, 76–8, 80, 85–7, 89, 291, 295; book
 77–8, 86–7, 102, 110; *Britannia* 63, 66–9,
 291; death 278; engagement/marriage
 66, 71–2, 95, 110; Lausanne 95–6; St
 George's Chapel 110, 239; Trinity
 College 101–6, 108
Denmark 30–3, 35, 58, 183, 187, 250
Dilke, Sir Charles 50, 97–8, 100, 127–9
Disraeli, Benjamin (Lord Beaconsfield) 31,
 55, 71, 97
du Puy, Maud 102–3, 106, 107
Eddy, Prince (Albert Victor Christian
 Edward, Duke of Clarence): appearance
 74–5, 87, 295; army career 119–25, 135,
 165, 166, 247–50, 255; baptism 27–8;
 birth 29–30; career prospects 247–50,
 253, 255, 261, 263–6; character 52, 56,
 61, 75, 80–1, 101, 109, 115, 289–95;
 299–301; childhood 33–40, 42, 161,
 162, 163; Cleveland Street scandal

7–8, 25–6, 172–4, 182–3, 187–8, 190–1,
 195–200, 202, 208–10, 293–4; death/
 funeral 7, 10, 170, 270–6, 293; diaries
 77–8, 86–7; education 41–2, 47–9,
 52–3, 55–7, 60–2, 66, 96, 101–4, 123;
 engagement to May 252–5, 257–61;
 fashion 130, 132–3, 295; final illness 170,
 266–70; handwriting 299–301; health 29,
 34–5, 40–1, 62, 81, 101, 213–14, 220–3,
 229–35, 237, 294; Heidelberg University
 110–11; homosexuality rumours 25, 174,
 291–2, 295; honorary degrees 135, 140;
 illegitimate children rumours 292; India
 150, 175, 191–4, 202, 204–8, 211–12; Jack
 the Ripper suspect 7–10, 289, 292–6,
 297–8; Lausanne 95–6, 98; made Duke
 of Clarence and Avondale 167, 168, 170,
 219–20; marriage prospects 17, 142, 150,
 157–9, 183–5, 212–13, 215–17, 223–9,
 231–2, 236–7, 242–4; naval cadetship
 62, 63–9, 164, 165; Order of the Garter
 98, 101; private life 131–5, 139; public
 duties begin 88–92, 113–14, 119, 125;
 public engagements 135, 140, 149–50,
 243; relationship with father 74–5,
 109; relationship with George 56, 75,
 130–1; relationship with mother 109;
 relationships with women 106, 108,
 134, 142, 157–9, 183–6, 220, 235–6, 242,
 244–6; Trinity College 98, 101–10, 115,
 118–19
Egypt 93–4, 190, 191, 212, 213
Erskine, Lady Sybil St Claire 169, 241–2,
 245–6, 252, 256–7, 279
Eton College 60, 96, 106
Euston, Lord 16, 20, 177, 188, 198–9, 202,
 204
Fairclough, Melvyn 8, 9–10, 293
Falklands Islands 83, 84
French refugees 135, 148–9
Fripp, Alfred 105–6, 108, 134, 220–3, 228–33,
 235–9, 245, 280
Fuller, Charles 33, 72, 101, 269, 277
Gallo, Augustus de 23, 149, 176, 203, 287
gambling 134, 137–8, 146–7, 239–41, 244
George, King of Greece 31–2, 56, 94
George, Prince: birth 36; character 61, 75,
 291; childhood 38, 39–40, 42, 161, 163;
 confirmation 95; diaries 77–8, 86–7;
 Eddy's death 272; education 47–9, 53–7,
 60–2, 66, 96; health 68, 255–6; Ireland
 visit 135–6; Lausanne 95–6, 98; marriage
 to May 268, 277; naval cadetship 62, 63–

9, 164; naval career 96, 98, 101, 109–10, 129, 130, 165, 247, 253; relationship with Eddy 56, 125, 130–1; relationships with women 134, 217

Gibraltar 75, 152

Gill, Charles 179, 199, 203

Gladstone, William 42, 97, 103, 124–6, 213, 240, 280

Gordon-Cumming, Sir William 239–41, 244

Gore, John 57, 66, 67, 125, 131, 290

Greece 31–2, 56, 94, 188, 190

Greville, Captain the Hon. A.H. Fulke 121, 131, 140, 141, 191, 193

Gull, Dr William Withey 8, 62, 147, 292

Halsbury, Lord (Lord Chancellor) 155, 176, 178, 179, 181

Hammond, Mr: blackmail threats 200; Cleveland Street brothel 14–18; committed for trial 160, 177; emigration plans 178, 203, 209; extradition 19–21, 171, 178; flees France 172, 175; police investigation 21, 23, 151, 152–5, 196, 198

Hanks, PO Constable Luke 13–17, 22, 154, 176, 179, 287

Harris, Frank 60, 128, 222, 231, 286

Harrison, Michael 291–2, 296

Heidelberg University 110–11

Hélène, Princess of Orléans 215–17, 223–5, 235–7, 242–3, 279

Henry of Battenberg 113, 119, 242, 273

Hewett, Frank 16, 20, 204

Hillyard, George 64–5, 72, 76

Holford, Captain George 141, 191, 193, 196, 204–7, 213, 231, 233, 235, 263, 280

homosexuality: Cleveland Street brothel 14–18, 160; Eddy rumours 25, 174, 291–2, 295; Eton College 60; legislation 15, 208–9; navy 89

Hua, Monsieur 66, 96, 102

Hussars 119–25, 135, 165, 166, 247–8, 255, 275

Inconstant, HMSS 82–5, 89–91, 93, 94

India: Bertie visits 57–9; British interests 55, 91, 97, 152; Eddy visits 150, 175, 191–4, 202, 204–8, 211–12

Ireland: Hussars stationed in 248; royal visits 116–18, 135–6, 253; troubles 96–7, 115, 125–6, 147, 280–1; Viceroy proposition 263–6

Jack the Ripper murders 8–10, 143–4, 146, 155, 289, 292–8

Jenner, Sir William 40, 50, 51, 62

Jervois, Colonel 16, 20, 177

Jullian, Philippe 9, 293

Knight, Stephen 8, 292, 293

Knightsbridge Barracks 20–1, 24, 49, 152

Knollys, Sir Francis 71, 180–2, 187–8, 199–200, 210–11, 249–50, 253, 263, 266–7

Labouchère, Henry 97, 138, 150, 186, 208–10

Langtry, Lillie 49, 63, 73–4, 76, 81–3, 96–7, 103, 138

Lausanne 95–6, 98

Le Courrier de Londres 17, 148, 151–2

Lewis, George 83, 147–9, 153, 159–60, 181, 188, 202, 235–6, 280, 297–8

Lewis, Sam 137–8, 147, 280

Louis of Battenberg, Prince: Indian visit 58; letters from Eddy 81–5, 89–94, 111–15, 141–2, 157–9, 183–5; Lillie Langtry affair 82–3

Louise, Princess (Duchess of Fife) 16–17, 38, 150–1, 157, 161, 163, 164, 165, 212–13, 244, 260

Luton Hoo 168, 256, 257, 279

Macclesfield, Lady 28, 29–30, 39, 51

Margaret of Prussia 'Mossy' 212, 241

Marlborough Club 22, 24, 137, 180, 188

Marlborough House 29, 31, 33–4, 38–9, 49, 54, 166, 250–1

Mary Adelaide, Princess (Duchess of Teck) 57, 130, 212, 226, 252–4, 257

Matthews (Home Secretary) 19–21, 23, 25, 144, 155, 157, 172–4

Maud, Princess 39, 43, 161, 162, 163, 164, 165, 255, 259, 263

May of Teck, Princess (Queen Mary) 168: biographies 291, 293; considered as bride 212–13, 226, 249–50; engagement to Eddy 252–5, 257–63, 279; marriage to George 268, 277, 278

Monro, Commissioner James 15, 17, 19, 144, 172, 178, 181

Montagu, Oliver 94, 155, 179, 180, 189, 199–201

navy: *Britannia* cadetship 62, 63–9; George's career 96, 98, 101, 109–10, 129, 130, 165, 247, 253

New York Herald 198, 202, 208

New York Times 150, 195

Newlove, Henry 14–18, 20, 23, 25–6, 153–4, 160, 171, 173, 209

Newton, Arthur (solicitor) 167: Cleveland Street case 18, 23–5, 153–7, 171–3, 176–8; early career 147–8, 149; later career 283–7; police charges 202–4, 208, 214; responsibility for rumours 172–4, 182,